The Genealogy of Violence

The Genealogy of Violence

Reflections on Creation, Freedom, and Evil

Charles K. Bellinger

UNIVERSITY PRESS

2001

OXFORD

UNIVERSITY PRESS

Oxford New York
Athens Auckland Bangkok Bogotá Bombay Buenos Aires
Calcutta Cape Town Dar es Salaam Delhi Florence Hong Kong
Istanbul Karachi Kuala Lumpur Madras Madrid Melbourne Mexico City Nairobi
Paris São Paulo Shanghai Singapore Taipei Tokyo Toronto Warsaw

and associated companies in
Berlin Ibadan

Published by Oxford University Press, Inc.
198 Madison Avenue, New York, New York 10016

Oxford is a registered trademark of Oxford University Press.

Library of Congress Cataloging-in-Publication Data
Bellinger, Charles K., 1962-
The genealogy of violence: reflections on creation, freedom, and evil / Charles K. Bellinger.
p. cm.
Includes bibliographical references and index.
ISBN 0-19-513498-2
1. Kierkegaard, Søren, 1813–1855. 2. Girard, René, 1923– 3. Violence—Religious
aspects—Christianity. 1. Title.
B4378.V56   2000
179.7—dc21   99-086200

9 8 7 6 5 4 3 2 1

Printed in the United States of America
on acid-free paper

ACKNOWLEDGMENTS

This book was fifteen years in the making. Along the way, many friends and professors contributed to my intellectual journey. Special thanks go to Doug Frank, John Linton, Sam Alvord, and Jim Titus at the Oregon Extension, whose contribution to this book is as deep as it is subtle. I hope that those familiar with the "OE theology" will be able to see the influence. These professors had me read Ernest Becker, which started this long train of thought. Thanks go to my many friends in Charlottesville, Virginia, during the 1990s; to the members of my dissertation committee, Jamie Ferreira, James Hunter, Robert Scharlemann, and Daniel Westberg; and to members of the Kierkegaard and Girard societies who were always warm and helpful. This work is dedicated with great love to my parents, Frank and Josi Bellinger.

When God began to create the heavens and the earth,

the earth was without form and void,

and darkness was upon the face of the deep;

and the Spirit of God was moving over the

face of the waters.

Genesis 1:1–2

CONTENTS

ABBREVIATIONS

These abbreviations are used for Søren Kierkegaard's works. See the bibliography for full citations.

CA *The Concept of Anxiety: A Simple Psychologically Orienting Deliberation on the Dogmatic Issue of Hereditary Sin*

CD *Christian Discourses*

COR *The Corsair Affair*

EUD *Eighteen Upbuilding Discourses*

FSE and JFY *For Self-Examination* and *Judge for Yourself!*

JP *Søren Kierkegaard's Journals and Papers, I-VII*

LD *Letters and Documents*

PC *Practice in Christianity*

PV *The Point of View*

SUD *The Sickness unto Death: A Christian Psychological Exposition for Upbuilding and Awakening*

TA *Two Ages: A Literary Review*

TM   *The Moment and Late Writings*

UDVS   *Upbuilding Discourses in Various Spirits*

WA   *Without Authority*

WL   *Works of Love*

The Genealogy of Violence

INTRODUCTION

Through my writings I hope to achieve the following: to leave
behind me so accurate a characterization of Christianity and its
relationships in the world that an enthusiastic, noble-minded young
person will be able to find in it a map of relationships as accurate as
any topographical map from the most famous institutes. I have not
had the help of such an author. The old Church Fathers lacked one
aspect, they did not know the world.

Søren Kierkegaard, JP, 6: 6283 (1848)

The past century has been very violent. The Nazis formulated and carried out a plan to kill as many Jews as they possibly could. Stalin's
regime brought about the deaths of millions of Soviet citizens. The Khmer Rouge
executed or starved to death approximately two million people in Cambodia during the late 1970s. The Hutus in Rwanda slaughtered Tutsis by the hundreds of
thousands more recently, despite the "success" of Christian missions there, which
has led to the majority of both tribal groups identifying themselves as Christian.
Many other similar historical examples could be cited, but the issue has been suf-
ficiently brought forward. From time to time throughout human history large-
scale eruptions of violence have resulted in the deaths of thousands, hundreds of
thousands, and millions. In this study, I ask one basic question: Why?

Why are human beings violent? How can we best understand the root motivations for large-scale political violence, such as the Holocaust and Stalin's purges?
In these situations, it is clear that the violence is not coordinated with any rational, sane perception of reality by individuals who are stable and morally mature.
We are considering extreme cases of psychological and social pathology, where
human action has completely fallen off its hinges and become demonic. In other
words, the task is to understand morally disordered human action from a vantage
point that will see through the insanity. But where is this vantage point?

Authors addressing this issue have reflected on the roots of violence and come
forward with a variety of theoretical models for violent behavior. Alice Miller, for
instance, argues that the violent actions of adults can always be traced to violence
they suffered as children. Ervin Staub describes how "difficult life conditions" lead
social groups to attempt to improve their situation through acts of scapegoating.
William Brustein argues that the Nazis gained power because they offered to the

German people the promise of economic improvement; to support the Nazis was not an act of irrational primitivism but rather of rational self-interest. Irving Louis Horowitz focuses on the power of the state and attempts to distinguish between the degrees of murderousness that inhabit the various state bureaucracies of the world in the twentieth century. Russell Hardin comments on situations such as Bosnia and Rwanda, arguing that the notion of "ancient ethnic hatreds" has no scientific validity; these hatreds have been aroused by ethnic leaders who believe that "preemptive" strikes must be launched against other ethnic groups in order to gain an advantage in political maneuvering. Zygmunt Bauman forcefully argues that the Holocaust should not be seen as a form of primitivism, but as the logical outcome of the Enlightenment idea of social engineering and progress. Carl Jung analyzes the "shadow" side of the human psyche, which is projected onto the alien other and attacked. Ernest Becker argues that the mainspring of human behavior is the fear of death, which leads us to attempt to overcome our mortality by killing a scapegoat that symbolically represents death. René Girard believes that violence functions to create social unanimity at a time of crisis, when the society is on the verge of chaos as a result of the transformation of acquisitive mimesis into conflictual mimesis. These nine authors, out of many more who could be mentioned, give us a feeling for the great variety, or should we call it the great *confusion*, present in the twentieth-century attempt to understand violence.[1] It is clear that no one theory has won the field in social science and historiography by convincingly clarifying the motivations that underlie human violence.

This point has been made very effectively by Ron Rosenbaum in his survey of the many attempts to comprehend the personality of Adolf Hitler.[2] Rosenbaum

---

1. Obviously, these one-sentence summaries do not do justice to these authors' works. See Alice Miller, *For Your Own Good: Hidden Cruelty in Child-Rearing and the Roots of Violence*, trans. Hildegarde and Hunter Hannum (New York: Farrar, Straus, Giroux, 1984); Ervin Staub, *The Roots of Evil: The Origins of Genocide and Other Group Violence* (Cambridge: Cambridge University Press, 1989); William Brustein, *The Logic of Evil: The Social Origins of the Nazi Party, 1925–1933* (New Haven: Yale University Press, 1996); Irving Louis Horowitz, *Taking Lives: Genocide and State Power* (New Brunswick: Transaction, 1997); Russell Hardin, *One for All: The Logic of Group Conflict* (Princeton: Princeton University Press, 1995); Zygmunt Bauman, *Modernity and the Holocaust* (Ithaca: Cornell University Press, 1989); Carl Jung, *Aion: Researches into the Phenomenology of the Self*, trans. R. F. C. Hull (New York: Pantheon, 1959); Jung's concept of shadow projection is developed by Erich Neumann in *Depth Psychology and a New Ethic*, trans. Eugene Rolfe (New York: Harper & Row, 1973); Ernest Becker, *The Denial of Death* (New York: The Free Press, 1973), *Escape from Evil* (New York: The Free Press, 1975); René Girard, *Things Hidden since the Foundation of the World*, trans. Stephen Bann and Michael Metteer (Stanford: Stanford University Press, 1987).

2. "Explaining Hitler," *The New Yorker*, May 1, 1995, 50–70. Rosenbaum has expanded this article into a major book: *Explaining Hitler: The Search for the Origins of His Evil* (New York: Random House, 1998).

notes that despite the extensive efforts invested in Hitler research, there is yet a pervasive "feeling of something still missing, something still inexplicable." Hitler's character remains "elusive," "a frightening mystery," in short, an enigma. Rosenbaum's research led him to this conclusion:

> No finite number of explanatory facts—psychological traumas, patterns of bad parenting, political deformations, personal dysfunctions—can add up to the magnitude of evil that Hitler came to embody and enact. No explanation or concatenation of explanations can bridge the gap, explain the transformation from baby picture to baby killer, to murderer of a million babies. It is not just a gap . . . it is an *abyss*. . . .
>
> What one discovers from an immersion in the postwar Hitler literature and from conversations with leading Hitler interpreters is that Hitler explanations often tell us as much about the explainers as they do about Hitler. That, in a sense, when we talk about Hitler we are talking about who we are—and who we are not. We project upon the inky Rorschach of the evidence an image of our anti-self. Hitler theories are cultural self-portraits in the negative—ways of distancing ourselves from him. And ways of protecting ourselves.[3]

Rosenbaum's summary of the Hitler literature is perceptive and troubling. In a sense, his basic conclusion is that human beings have failed in their attempt to understand themselves. And if we have not made any progress in understanding ourselves, then what will prevent a repetition of the Hitler era?

This lack of consensus among "scientific" authors, coupled with my own familiarity with the writings of Kierkegaard, prompted me to ask whether Kierkegaard's thought could provide us with a perspective from which violence could be understood. In this work I attempt to show that this is a viable possibility. It may seem at first an odd enterprise, given that the idea that Kierkegaard was concerned with violence will strike many readers as strange. He spoke about religious inwardness, "angst before the good," becoming a "self," and so forth, but did he ever say anything about violence? Actually, he did. In his journals, for example, Kierkegaard asks; "How did it happen that Christ was put to death?" He suggests that the answer is found in the nature of the demand that Christ placed upon his contemporaries: to *become spirit*, which involves "dying to the world." He called on his hearers to open themselves to the possibility of growth into spiritual maturity. But his hearers, the "natural men," did not want to heed this message; they wished to remain immature spiritually. Christ's challenging message disturbed them profoundly. In fact, Kierkegaard suggests, they were so disturbed that they became enraged and *rushed upon Christ to slay him*, so that his message would be silenced (JP, 4: 4360 [1854]).

---

3. "Explaining Hitler," 50–52.

This journal entry is just one of many passages in Kierkegaard in which he reflects on the crucifixion of Christ and on other examples of violence in human history. I have gathered together many of these texts in the pages that follow, and they establish that violence was in fact an important concern for Kierkegaard. I demonstrate that the reflections on violence that are scattered throughout his published and unpublished writings can be collected and coordinated with the psychological themes in his authorship, to produce a well-developed theoretical understanding of the roots of violence. The primary goal of this book is to articulate the philosophical anthropology that underlies these passages in Kierkegaard's writings. I hope to show that Kierkegaard's writings, far from being apolitical, as some have claimed, are actually a rich resource for reflections on violence.

Chapter 1 surveys and assesses four of the approaches to understanding violence I have referred to briefly in the discussion above: Alice Miller, Ervin Staub, Carl Jung, and Ernest Becker. I hope that the widely disparate nature of these efforts to comprehend violence will convince the reader of the deeply enigmatic character of the problem at hand. While these efforts are all thought-provoking, I attempt to indicate why I find them to be unsatisfying in various ways. They raise questions that they are not able to answer, or they seem to omit important concerns. (One particularly troubling issue they have difficulty addressing is moral responsibility for violent actions.)

In chapter 2 I lay the groundwork for the development of a Kierkegaardian understanding of political violence by presenting an overview of the doctrine of creation in Kierkegaard's thought, stressing the theme of creation as an *ongoing process*. I draw primarily on his signed works and journals here, but the pseudonymous *Philosophical Fragments* and *The Concept of Anxiety* also address this theme. I argue that the concept of continuing creation forms the foundation of *The Concept of Anxiety*, as seen in the idea that angst is a uniquely human emotion. Human beings experience angst because they are coming into existence as spiritual creatures. This theme is brought out through a contrast with David Hume's *Natural History of Religion*. Where Hume depicts human beings as animals with a highly developed self-consciousness, who are motivated by their fear of death, Kierkegaard suggests that human beings are significantly different from the lower animals. We can experience an emotion that the animals cannot—angst— which arises not in response to external threats to our well-being but out of the mysterious depths of our spiritual nature; we are beings who exist *physically*, yet we are always in the process of coming into existence *psychologically*. *The Concept of Anxiety* suggests that the origin of sin is found in the illegitimate way human beings try to control or reduce their feelings of angst. Such attempts to manage angst reveal our lack of openness to the divinely directed process of creation.

Chapter 3 consists of an interpretation of *The Sickness unto Death*. This work provides an anthropological vision that leads us further toward a theological understanding of violence. While *The Concept of Anxiety* focuses primarily on the

question of the *origin* of sin, *The Sickness unto Death* develops a more detailed picture of sin as an *ongoing state*. More specifically, this work defines sin as a position
that the individual takes in defiance of the divine call to selfhood. Sin is not a negation, such as ignorance, but an active attempt to avoid "becoming oneself before God." *The Sickness unto Death* can be read, then, as a commentary on the psychological state of those persons whom Kierkegaard has in mind when he reflects
on the crucifixion of Christ. The key expression that summarizes *The Sickness unto
Death* is "ego-protection." The individual who seeks to avoid the process of spiritual maturation construes the divine demand to grow as a threat to the ego. The
ego becomes a hardened shell, which believes that it must protect itself from the
possibility of its "death," that is, its spiritual death, which would lead to a more
mature form of selfhood. It fears this possibility more than anything else. Yet this
possibility arises out of the self itself, which leads to a situation of entangled, conflicted selfhood.

Chapter 4 explicitly presents the theoretical understanding of the roots of political violence that can be developed out of Kierkegaard's writings. The basic definition, "God is love," is crucial to Kierkegaard's theological interpretation of the
human condition. God's ongoing work of creation is a work of love. Insofar as
human beings reject this work of creation and attempt to hide from God, they are
turning their souls away from love and toward hate. Kierkegaard notices this
ubiquitous phenomenon of human existence and expresses it in the repeated
phrase: "in this world love is hated." Humanity's hatred and distrust toward God
expressed itself in the crucifixion of Christ. Christ is at the same time the *exemplar*
of the authentic selfhood and love of neighbor to which all persons are called, and
the *communicator* of the call of God, which is so disturbing to the hardened ego.
Thus the execution of Christ is the central revelation within human history of the
nature of sin. In Kierkegaard's thought, this revelation at the heart of the New
Testament comes to philosophical articulation, as he shows that conflict between
persons in the external world is a dramatic playing out of the internal conflict of
the self's resistance to its own potential selfhood. In other words, *persons become
violent because they are seeking to avoid becoming more mature spiritually*. They are
seeking to avoid becoming authentic human beings before their Creator. The basic
motive at work here can be described as *the self not wanting to become an other to
itself*. The self needs to seek out and attack scapegoats, *others*, as a means of avoid-
ing the possibility of spiritual collapse and regeneration, which would result in the
coming into existence of a "new" self.

In chapter 5 I compare Kierkegaard's thought with René Girard's theory of
mimetic desire and scapegoating. I propose that despite their differing emphases,
Kierkegaard and Girard are highly compatible contributors to a distinctively Christian understanding of social pathologies. The points of convergence between the
two can be seen in a consideration of such themes as mimetic desire, the "crowd"
that is "untruth," and the phenomenon of scandal or offense.

Chapter 6 considers a question that arises from an ambiguity in Girard's thought. Does his message fit within the confines of the methodological atheism of mainstream social science, or is it intrinsically theological in nature, since he uses the Bible as his main source of anthropological knowledge? I argue that the latter is closer to the truth, which is as it should be. Christian theology should not just speak to the spiritual and moral situation of the believer; it should also expand out into a fully developed *social science,* which can compete with secular interpretations of human behavior in the marketplace of ideas. I argue, in fact, that secular approaches to social understanding are self-crippling; they can never comprehend the human condition adequately. This is the conclusion toward which the writings of Girard and John Milbank point.

At this point the basic theoretical elements of a Christian understanding of violence will be in plain view. Chapter 7 will turn this theoretical perspective to the task of interpreting the history of Christianity itself. I argue that when Christians went on crusades, burned heretics at the stake, killed Jews, and so on, they were acting in complete opposition to the central theological and ethical insights of the New Testament. They were acting in a sinful manner, as the psychological and sociological ramifications of sin are analyzed by Kierkegaard and Girard. Thus, the Anabaptist idea that Christianity underwent a "fall" in the course of its history is confirmed and further elucidated. I note that both Kierkegaard and Girard see themselves as attempting to "reintroduce Christianity into Christendom" in the wake of this "fall."

Chapter 8 applies the insights of Kierkegaard and Girard to the problem of understanding Naziism and Stalinism. I argue here that the Kierkegaardian idea of the aesthetic and ethical spheres of existence is very helpful as a mode of social understanding. The Nazis embodied one possible form of the aesthetic sphere. The Stalinists embodied one possible form of the ethical sphere. Both are examples of willful evasion of the ongoing process of creation. The need for scapegoats makes this evasion manifest as the external drama of internal angst. I show that Kierkegaard was remarkably prescient with regard to these events, which occurred a century after his time.

The concluding chapter points toward the doctrine of the Atonement. It would require another book to treat fully the questions this involves, but some general comments on the meaning of redemption serve to round out this work.

In this book I work with the assumption that the enterprise of developing a Kierkegaardian understanding of violence is possible, valid, and worthwhile. I point this out to stress the fact that I do not agree with those commentators who believe that Kierkegaard's thought is so "radically individualistic" that no valid insights into society and politics can be gained from him. Such commentators have suggested that the most one may possibly gain from Kierkegaard is a better understanding of the individual's existence before God. They hold that he viewed social relations in an entirely negative light: society is a "temptation" or a "ruin" to be avoided at all costs so that one may gain one's own radically individualistic salvation.[4]

There is another trend in Kierkegaard interpretation, however, that I consider to be a much more accurate approach to understanding the authorship. This more positive and constructive model has been articulated by several different scholars who have contributed in various ways to the general project of clarifying the ethical, social, and political aspects of Kierkegaard's writings.[5] According to this approach, Kierkegaard's critique of "the crowd" should not be simplistically written off as an example of "individualism." Rather, it needs to be recognized that he was criticizing social phenomena because he had a positive vision for the spiritual development of individuals *and* the communities they comprise. He placed great stress on the existence of the individual before God, precisely because he realized that it is out of this relationship that genuine love of the neighbor can grow. If his authorship seems to be out of balance in the direction of critique, that reflects how far the society of his day had deviated from understanding and practicing love of the neighbor. He was, in his own words, a *corrective* for his time.

Concerning the question of moral responsibility for violent actions, I suggest that Kierkegaard provides an understanding of the roots of immoral behavior that does not relieve those who are being understood of culpability. Such a relief of responsibility is the unfortunate tendency of most of the "scientific" pathways to understanding violent behavior referred to earlier. For Kierkegaard, the root of violence is spiritual evasion, and this evasion is a (non-necessary) sin of which the person is guilty. Thus Kierkegaard's thought establishes a solid bridge between social theory and ethics. He not only interprets the human condition but also calls human beings to a life of responsible and loving relations with the neighbor. This call to responsibility is not tacked on as an afterthought but grows directly out of the heart of the anthropological vision.

I must note with disappointment that theologians in the twentieth century did not as a general rule take advantage of the opportunity to address the question of the roots of political violence. They seem to have left this question to the secular

---

4. See, for example, Martin Buber, "The Question to the Single One," in *Between Man and Man*, trans. Ronald Gregor Smith (New York: Macmillan, 1965), and Louis Mackey, "The Loss of the World in Kierkegaard's Ethics," in Josiah Thompson, ed., *Kierkegaard: A Collection of Critical Essays* (Garden City: Anchor Books, 1972).

5. In the bibliography see Beabout, Cauchy, Connell and Evans, Davis, Eller, Elrod, Gouwens, Kirmmse, Malantschuk, Stanley Moore, Plekon, Viallaneix, and Westphal. Also of note here are the Kierkegaard-influenced contributions of political philosopher Glenn Tinder. Sociologist Harvie Ferguson describes his book on Kierkegaard as "a book which seeks to explain why sociologists, and anyone else interested in the character of modern life, should read Kierkegaard" (ix). In conversation with me, Ferguson described Kierkegaard as "unequaled" as a psychologist of modernity.

theorists. It would be appropriate for the problem of the psychological roots of violence and war to be treated as part of the doctrine of sin and as an adjunct to a consideration of the problem of moral evil. But this possibility has rarely if ever been explored. Unfortunately, most religious thinkers seem to have been content to simply view violence as a form of sin or "the demonic" and leave it at that. "People are violent because they are sinful" is a true statement, but it is also inadequate as a stopping point for thought. It provides an answer at the precise point where one should be asking further questions. I attempt to demonstrate in the following chapters that the question concerning the roots of violence can and ought to be addressed as an explicitly theological question.

René Girard has in recent years begun to turn the attention of theologians to the problem of understanding violence. He is thus the main dialogue partner for Kierkegaard in these pages. His thought can be understood as the most sophisticated development to date of Kierkegaard's dictum, "The crowd is untruth." His analysis of the "horizontal" dimension of human existence is extremely thought-provoking and challenging. I argue that his understanding of mimetic desire and the scapegoat mechanism can be effectively coordinated with Kierkegaard's vision of the "vertical" dimension of existence in relationship with God, to produce an explicitly theological theory of the roots of violence.

While Kierkegaard and Girard are the two key thinkers considered, two others play important supporting roles: Karl Barth and Eric Voegelin. In one sense, Barth is an example of the aforementioned tendency of theologians to avoid reflection on violence. He even asserts directly, "The pathology of the man of sin is not part of the true subject-matter of dogmatics"(*Church Dogmatics*, IV/3.1, 469). On the other hand, he read Kierkegaard and was deeply influenced by him. This means that Kierkegaard's understanding of human pathology is woven deeply into the texture of Barth's thought, and it surfaces from time to time. I include quotations from Barth to demonstrate this point and to further strengthen my overall project of showing how the Christian intellectual tradition has significant resources for interpreting human pathology and violence. Eric Voegelin is another author who is working within the same intellectual ken as Kierkegaard, Barth, and Girard. I would describe this shared mode of thought as focusing on philosophically interpreting and criticizing modernity from a point of view rooted in the tradition of biblical theology. These thinkers see the Enlightenment as a mixed blessing, which freed human beings from certain slaveries and immaturities—only to introduce new ones. One demon is exorcised and seven others come in. What is needed, from the "neo-orthodox" point of view, is not a simplistic rejection of the wisdom of the past but a refined comprehension of that wisdom, which is gained through an existential openness to the divine source of all life.

I have noticed in my research that major thinkers and their followers tend to operate in unjustifiable isolation from one another. Barth makes comments on Kierkegaard that reveal, at times, a lack of careful reading and interpretation;

he most likely never read anything by Voegelin. Voegelin rarely ever mentions Kierkegaard or Barth and most likely never read anything by Girard. Girard rarely ever mentions Kierkegaard or Barth and most likely has never read anything by Voegelin. I find this situation frustrating and disappointing, a *failure of erudition* at certain key points where the greatest potential for dialogue and cross-fertilization exists. Overcoming this unjustifiable isolation, and bringing these thinkers into conversation with each other, is a major goal for me.

I want to make clear at this point what this work is not. First, it is not a treatise on the problem of moral evil, although I believe that an understanding of the roots of violence ought to be a part of a consideration of moral evil (which it usually is not). Second, this is not a treatise on the doctrine of sin in general, although it is focused on the sin of murder. Third, this is not a comprehensive historical or sociological study of Naziism and Stalinism or any other event of large-scale political violence. I am not trying to compete directly against detailed empirical studies, such as Raul Hilberg's *The Destruction of the European Jews,* Robert Conquest's *The Great Terror,* or Hannah Arendt's *The Origins of Totalitarianism,* which attempt to explain the Holocaust and Stalin's Purges in terms of their historical timing and logistical mechanisms. I point to these situations, however, as key instances of the phenomenon I am attempting to interpret. Instead of focusing on individual occurrences of murder, I try to theoretically comprehend situations in which murder becomes a social or political principle of action. Naziism and Stalinism are particularly clear and horrific examples of such a phenomenon. And fourth, this is not a treatise on the *ethics* of war, revolution, pacifism, and so on. This work contributes to ethics not in the narrow sense of addressing arguments concerning correct and incorrect actions, but in the more diffuse sense of presenting a vision of the psychological roots of immoral behavior. In other words, a reader of this book would be incorrect to assume that I am either a pacifist or a nonpacifist in the realm of ethical convictions and argue for or against what I am saying on that basis. I hope that future considerations of the ethics of violence will be connected with, rather than disconnected from, the kind of anthropological and psychological enquiry I am here undertaking.

Positively stated, this book is a work of theodicy (in a general sense, rather than as a narrowly defined philosophical argument concerning the problem of evil). I attempt to suggest a certain way of theologically interpreting (rather than empirically explaining) human evil, in relation to human free will and the creative activity of God. I work in the genre of narrative theology, seeking to make sense of violence in human history.

This work is and is not original. It is original, or at least, I hope, thought-provoking, in suggesting a certain way of reading Kierkegaard which is out of the ordinary. I aim to show that the body of Kierkegaardian texts speaks to the problem of understanding (and thus struggling against) violence. In Voegelinian terms, I attempt to show that Kierkegaard was deeply engaged in the same *resistance to untruth* that characterized those twentieth-century thinkers who opposed the ascendancy of the ideologies of murder. This work is not original, however, in that many authors have contributed to the development of the ideas expressed here. These contributions will be clearly acknowledged either in the text or in the notes. In other words, I do not feel that I am climbing out on a weak limb in the following pages. The argument of this book has the character of an accumulation and coordination of insights, as I attempt to build on the contributions of others.

1

CONTEMPORARY PERSPECTIVES
ON THE ROOTS OF VIOLENCE

The more I pursue the matter, the more I see that the confusion is
not only in Denmark, not only in Protestantism, and not only in
Christendom, but the confusion is in the nature of man.

JP, 3: 2333 (1854)

Whenever we ask an important question, it is a good idea to think
carefully about the question itself before rushing to an answer.
The question with which we are concerned in this book, "Why violence?" has been
asked by several authors in the twentieth century. By surveying their answers,
we will gain a more rounded grasp of the question itself and how it presents itself
to the human mind. Through considering these answers and questioning them
in turn, we will develop a deeper respect for the problem at hand. As we notice
the widely disparate character of the possible approaches to answering this question, the profoundly enigmatic nature of violence will come into clear view. Why
is it that these intellectuals cannot even begin to forge some kind of consensus? Is
there something wrong with them, some fundamental flaw in their assumptions
that could be identified? Or is it simply that the reality of evil overwhelms human
efforts to comprehend it? As you read this chapter, I encourage you to ask such
questions about the question, along with any others that occur to you.

Alice Miller

In *For Your Own Good: Hidden Cruelty in Child-Rearing and the Roots of Violence*,
German psychologist Alice Miller explains the roots of violence by focusing on
childhood traumas. Her ambition is to provide a perspective on the actions of Adolf
Hitler and his followers, as we can see in her introductory remarks:

> Since the end of World War II, I have been haunted by the question of what
> could make a person conceive the plan of gassing millions of human beings to
> death and of how it could then be possible for millions of others to acclaim him
> and assist in carrying out this plan. The solution to this enigma, which I found
> only a short while ago, is what I have tried to present in this book. . . . It can

hardly be considered an idle academic exercise when somebody attempts to expose the roots of an unbounded and insatiable hatred like Hitler's; an investigation of this sort is a matter of life and death for all of us, since it is easier today than ever before for us to fall victim to such hatred. (*For Your Own Good*, vii–viii)

Miller believes that a psychologically informed commentary on twentieth-century political events can produce important insights into the motivations that underlie eruptions of violence such as the Holocaust.

Miller's explanation of violence focuses on the circumstances in which children are raised. She argues, in a nutshell, that people become violent in later life if they are beaten as children. In her words, "Every act of cruelty, no matter how brutal and shocking, has traceable antecedents in its perpetrator's past" (*For Your Own Good*, ix). She builds on this idea by examining the childhood of Adolf Hitler, and of other German children of the same era. What she finds there confirms her thesis. She surveys the child-rearing practices that were common in Europe in general and in Germany in particular from the eighteenth century up to the twentieth. She labels these practices "Poisonous Pedagogy" and summarizes them in this way:

1. Adults are the masters (not the servants!) of the dependent child.
2. They determine in godlike fashion what is right and what is wrong.
3. The child is held responsible for their anger.
4. The parents must always be shielded.
5. The child's life-affirming feelings pose a threat to the autocratic adult.
6. The child's will must be "broken" as soon as possible.
7. All this must happen at a very early age, so the child "won't notice" and will therefore not be able to expose the adults.

The methods that can be used to suppress vital spontaneity in the child are: laying traps, lying, duplicity, subterfuge, manipulation, "scare" tactics, withdrawal of love, isolation, distrust, humiliating and disgracing the child, scorn, ridicule, and coercion even to the point of torture. (*For Your Own Good*, 59)

Miller finds that this approach to child-rearing was pervasive throughout German culture at the time of Hitler's birth. Thus his character and the character of his followers can be interpreted as a result of "poisonous pedagogy."

Miller recounts that Hitler's father was born as the illegitimate son of a poor servant girl. It is possible that she was impregnated by the son of the Jewish man for whom she was working, but this cannot be determined with certainty. In any case, Adolf Hitler's father Alois grew up without a father, and Alois was given up for adoption at the age of five. Later on in life he became a successful civil servant and officially changed his last name from Schicklgruber, his mother's name, to Hitler, the name of his foster father. He was very proud of his position in life and enjoyed dressing up in an official uniform "aglitter with buttons."

There is much evidence that Alois Hitler beat his son often and harshly. This is confirmed by Adolf's sister Paula:

> It was my brother Adolf who especially provoked my father to extreme harshness and who got his due measure of beatings every day. He was rather a nasty little fellow, and all his father's attempts to beat the impudence out of him and make him choose the career of a civil servant were in vain. (*For Your Own Good*, 153)

Miller theorizes that Alois Hitler beat his son Adolf in an attempt to overcome the disgrace that he felt concerning his own childhood. Adolf, in turn, redirected his hatred of his father toward the Jews. The idea that child abuse is a repeating cycle is central to Miller's argument. When a child is beaten by a physically superior adult, rage builds up that will be released at some point in the future when the grown-up child has power over someone else. A dictator has power over an entire region. In Miller's words:

> The way Hitler unconsciously took on his father's behavior and displayed it on the stage of world history is indicative of how the child must really have seen his father: the snappy, uniformed, somewhat ridiculous dictator, as Charlie Chaplin portrayed him in his film and as Hitler's enemies saw him, is the way Alois appeared in the eyes of his critical son. The heroic Führer, loved and admired by the German people, was the other Alois, the husband loved and admired by his subservient wife, Klara, whose awe and admiration Adolf no doubt shared when he was still very little. (*For Your Own Good*, 160)

Miller's argument is rounded out with the idea that Hitler's experience of childhood beatings was not unusual but common at that time. "The fact that Hitler had so many enthusiastic followers proves that they had a personality structure similar to his, i.e., that they had had a similar upbringing" (*For Your Own Good*, 170). This point has been established through her historical sketch of "Poisonous Pedagogy."

Ervin Staub

Psychologist Ervin Staub's *The Roots of Evil: The Origins of Genocide and Other Group Violence* surveys social scientific efforts since World War II to understand the behavior of perpetrators of political violence. Staub, who has read Alice Miller and many other authors, attempts his own theoretical analysis of the roots of mass killing. He describes his overall project in these words:

> Certain characteristics of a culture and the structure of a society, combined with great difficulties or hardships of life and social disorganization, are the start-

ing point for genocide or mass killing. The resulting material and psychological needs lead the society to turn against a subgroup in it. Gradually increas-
ing mistreatment of this subgroup ends in genocide or mass killing. (*The Roots
of Evil*, 4)

His historical examples include the Holocaust, the Turkish genocide of the Arme-
nians, the Killing Fields of Cambodia, and mass killings in Argentina.

When he speaks of cultural and social characteristics, Staub has in mind the
following phenomena. A culture's self-concept may posit its superiority over
others. If this superiority is brought into question by historical events, the resulting sense of self-doubt may awaken a strong need for psychological self-defense.
"When a sense of superiority combines with an underlying (and often unacknowledged) self-doubt, their contribution to the potential for genocide and mass killing
can be especially high" (*The Roots of Evil*, 19). Other cultural characteristics may
include nationalism, "us"-"them" differentiation, strong respect for authority, and
inclination to obedience. Some cultures tend to be monolithic rather than plural-
istic, which increases the likelihood of violence against a subgroup they exclude.

The concept of "difficult life conditions" is central to Staub's theory, that is,
negative economic conditions, internal or external political instability, widespread
criminal violence, and rapid social and technological change. Such difficulties can
create mental instability, which in turn leads people to seek solutions to their problems. In some cases the solutions involve violent actions against a subgroup in
order to satisfy the psychological needs created by the social disorganization. In
other words, the preconditions for mass killing may lay dormant in a society for
many years, until they are triggered by changing historical circumstances.

Staub claims that underlying violent actions we can find motives that seem to
be good, or at least understandable, given "difficult life conditions." Economic
problems can threaten physical well-being. Social change can undermine psychological stability. Political change can lead to incomprehension, fear, and angst.
In response to these conditions, individuals become motivated to defend themselves physically and psychologically (*The Roots of Evil*, 15). They seek to make right
what they perceive is wrong with the world; they seek to regain a sense of self-
worth; they seek to attain a renewed sense of control over the circumstances of
their life. In themselves, such motivations seem to be morally good—they certainly
are in the eyes of those who are inspired by them.

When a subgroup within a society becomes marginalized and turned into a
scapegoat for the problems facing the society, a progression of more and more
violent actions are taken against them. At first, verbal insults may be directed at
the out-group by members of the in-group. Then beatings and random killings may
take place. Businesses are "legally" confiscated. Discrimination in employment and
education become the law of the land. Then the "aliens" are rounded up and moved
into ghettos and camps. They begin to be systematically killed. This process, which

takes place over a period of years, constitutes a "continuum of destruction" that gradually habituates the members of the in-group to killing without remorse or question. People change as a result of watching the actions of others, and they learn by participation. In Staub's words: "Perpetrators change and become more able and willing to act against victims. In the end people develop a powerful commitment to genocide or to an ideology that supports it" (*The Roots of Evil*, 18).

Carl Jung and Erich Neumann

Psychiatrist Carl Jung has made an important contribution to reflection on the problem of violence, through the concept of the "shadow." He and his collaborator Erich Neumann explain this concept in the following way.

The human psyche has two primary divisions: the conscious and the unconscious. The conscious mind consists of the ego and the persona. The ego is the individual's intellectual perception of reality and of self, the "I" that forms the continuing sense of personal identity through time. The persona is the presentation of the self to the world as a "mask." It represents the way in which the individual plays certain social roles and engages in various behaviors in order to fit in and be successful in his surroundings.[1]

The unconscious mind consists of two parts, the personal unconscious and the collective unconscious. The personal unconscious holds memories relating to the individual's life history and her personal dreams. The collective unconscious is the individual's point of connection with the human race as a whole and its history. The "shadow" consists of the negative traits, inadequacies, guilt feelings, and so on, which the individual seeks to hide from himself. In Neumann's words:

> The shadow is the other side. It is the expression of our own imperfection and earthliness, the negative which is incompatible with the absolute values; it is our inferior corporeality in contradistinction to the absoluteness and eternity of a soul which "does not belong to this world." But it can also appear in the opposite capacity as "spirit," for instance when the conscious mind only recognizes the material values of this life. The shadow represents the uniqueness and transitoriness of our nature; it is our own state of limitation and subjection to the conditions of space and time. (*Depth Psychology and a New Ethic*, 40)

If the shadow remains unacknowledged and unintegrated into the conscious personality, then it can become a very dangerous and destabilizing force, leading the individual into various kinds of distorted behavior that result from ego-inflation:

---

1. See Erich Neumann, *Depth Psychology and a New Ethic* (New York: Harper & Row, 1973), 37–38.

Ego-inflation invariably implies a condition in which the ego is overwhelmed by a content which is greater, stronger and more highly charged with energy than consciousness, and which therefore causes a kind of state of possession in the conscious mind. What makes this state of possession so dangerous— irrespective of the nature of the content which lies behind it—is that it prevents the ego and the conscious mind from achieving a genuine orientation to reality. (*Depth Psychology and a New Ethic*, 42)

The Jungian understanding of the roots of violence builds on the idea of the "projection of the shadow." Since the shadow is that part of the personality which contains repressed feelings of inferiority and guilt, the ego attempts to reinforce its positive self-image by projecting the shadow onto other human beings. Political entities express this by seeing evil in some other group which must be struggled against to the death. Human beings do not want to face honestly their own moral failings and inadequacies, so they see tyranny, oppression, treachery, and other negatives in the "enemy." This process of projecting the shadow outward onto others makes it impossible for the people who are projecting to see reality clearly. They live in a fog of illusions created by their own minds, changing "the world into the replica of one's own unknown face." In Jung's words, "All hysterical people are compelled to torment others, because they are unwilling to hurt themselves by admitting their own inferiority. But since nobody can jump out of his skin and be rid of himself, they stand in their own way everywhere as their own evil spirit—and this is what we call a hysterical neurosis."[2] Erich Neumann expresses this idea in a particularly succinct way:

The shadow, which is in conflict with the acknowledged values, cannot be accepted as a negative part of one's own psyche and is therefore projected— that is, it is tranferred to the outside world and experienced as an outside object. It is combated, punished, and exterminated as "the alien out there" instead of being dealt with as "one's own inner problem." (*Depth Psychology and a New Ethic*, 50)

The scapegoat is the person or group onto whom the shadow is projected. Human beings seem to have a universal tendency to create such scapegoats, and this poses a great danger to the future of the human race, given that the technological means of violence become more powerful as history continues. Wars and revolutions are "eruptions" of the "unconscious forces which have accumulated in the collective." In such cases dark and primitive behaviors that have been long repressed spill out onto the historical stage, revealing the psychological immaturity of the human race:

---

2. Carl Jung, *Civilization in Transition*, trans. R. F. C. Hull (New York: Pantheon Books, 1964), 203, 299, and *Aion*, trans. R. F. C. Hull (New York: Pantheon, 1959), 9.

For primitive man—and the mass man in every nation reacts, as we know, like a primitive man—evil cannot be acknowledged as "his own evil" at all, since consciousness is still too weakly developed to be able to deal with the resulting conflict. It is for this reason that evil is invariably experienced by mass man as something alien, and the victims of shadow projection are therefore, always and everywhere, the aliens.

Inside a nation, the aliens who provide the objects for this projection are the minorities; if these are of a different racial or ethnological complexion or, better still, of a different color, their suitability for this purpose is particularly obvious. (*Depth Psychology and a New Ethic*, 52)

Neumann's book was written in 1949, as a reflection on the catastrophe of World War II. He attempts to understand the Holocaust and Stalin's deadly regime, which at that time was still in power. Thus he claims that "the Fascist plays the same part in a Communist society as the Communist in a Fascist society." Both political camps engage in the projection of the shadow.

Ernest Becker

The last two books of cultural anthropologist Ernest Becker, *The Denial of Death* and *Escape from Evil*, attempt to understand the roots of human behavior. His theory centers on one key idea, that fear of death is the driving force behind the formation of human character and culture. He states his thesis at the beginning of *The Denial of Death*:

The prospect of death, Dr. Johnson said, wonderfully concentrates the mind. The main thesis of this book is that it does much more than that: the idea of death, the fear of it, haunts the human animal like nothing else; it is a mainspring of human activity—activity designed largely to avoid the fatality of death, to overcome it by denying in some way that it is the final destiny for man. . . .

In these pages I try to show that the fear of death is a universal that unites data from several disciplines of the human sciences, and makes wonderfully clear and intelligible human actions that we have buried under mountains of fact, and obscured with endless back-and-forth arguments about the "true" human motives. (*The Denial of Death*, ix)

Becker believes that human beings desire above all else to perpetuate their physical existence. Their lives thus become continuous attempts to evade, or transcend, the ultimate evil from the perspective of self-conscious protoplasm: death. Here lies the root of all narcissism. But human narcissism takes on a character different from that of other forms of protoplasm because our minds enable us to live in a world of symbols and dreams. Our sense of self-worth and organismic success can be built up symbolically, thus freeing our drive for immortality from the nar-row instinctual limitations of the other animals. Our ingenious and imaginative minds give us the ability to create cultural systems that transform the personal, organismic quest for immortality into an ongoing societal project. "The fact is that this is what society is and always has been: a symbolic action system, a structure of statuses and roles, customs and rules for behavior, designed to serve as a ve-hicle for earthly heroism" (*The Denial of Death*, 4). Each cultural hero-system is somewhat different from the next, but they all share the same underlying dynamic: society is a stage on which people perform heroic deeds that lift them into a posi-tion of "cosmic specialness" and "symbolic immortality." Every society has at its root the religious yearning for "eternity," regardless of whether or not the society portrays itself as "secular."

Of course, human beings cannot in reality avoid death. If, then, our character is organized around the idea that death can be avoided or transcended in some way, we are basing our life on a falsehood. This is precisely Becker's view of "normal" human character, which leads him to entitle one of his key chapters "Human Char-acter as a Vital Lie." He sees psychoanalysis as having uncovered this lie for the first time in history, which accounts for our subtle or overt hostility toward it:

> We called one's life style a vital lie, and now we can understand better why we said it was vital: it is a *necessary* and basic dishonesty about oneself and one's whole situation. This revelation is what the Freudian revolution in thought really ends up in and is the basic reason why we still strain against Freud. We don't want to admit that we are fundamentally dishonest about reality, that we do not really control our own lives. We don't want to admit that we do not stand alone, that we always rely on something that transcends us, some sys-tem of ideas and powers in which we are embedded and which support us. . . .
>
> The defenses that form a person's character support a grand illusion, and when we grasp this we can understand the full drivenness of man. He is driven away from himself, from self-knowledge, self-reflection. He is driven toward those things that support the lie of his character, his automatic equanimity. (*The Denial of Death*, 55–56)

Becker rejects what he calls "easy environmentalism"—the attempt to explain mental illness simply on the basis of the ineptitude of the parents in raising chil-dren, which is said to distort and damage their developing psyches (*The Denial of Death*, 62). For Becker, the essential optimism of this position is untenable, because he sees reality as terrifying and overwhelming. (Alice Miller, as we have seen, puts forward an environmental explanation of the roots of violence.) According to Becker, human beings want above all else to endure and prosper, to achieve some sort of immortality. But this project can only be successful if knowledge of one's mortality is *denied* and *repressed*. "It is repression, then, that great discovery of psychoanalysis, that explains how well men can hide their basic motivations even from themselves" (*Escape from Evil*, 92). Human beings repress awareness of the simple fact that they are mortal animals. With this basic psychological situation as a given, the way is prepared for politicians to step in and identify for the people an individual or a group that they can turn into a scapegoat through the psychological mechanism of *projection*. The repressed awareness of mortality is projected onto the scapegoat, who becomes the embodiment of animality and death. In killing the scapegoat, one separates oneself from death and identifies oneself with power, control, and immortality.

Becker brings the Jungian concept of the "shadow" into his argument at this point. "To speak of the shadow is another way of referring to the individual's sense of creature inferiority, the thing he wants most to deny" (*Escape from Evil*, 94). The shadow is that awareness of mortality that the conscious mind wants to banish from its precincts, it is the "other side" that is incompatible with the individual's project of self-immortalization. The person can manage the problem of mortality on an ongoing basis by actively splitting self-consciousness into two parts: the person identifies himself with life, goodness, light, etc. and looks for everything dark, inferior, and culpable in *others*.[3]

> And so . . . we have the dynamics for the classic and age-old expedient for discharging the negative forces of the psyche and guilt: scapegoating. It is precisely the split-off sense of inferiority and animality which is projected onto the scapegoat and then destroyed symbolically with him. When all the explanations are compared on the slaughter of the Jews, Gypsies, Poles, and so many others by the Nazis, and all the many reasons are adduced, there is one reason that goes right into the heart and mind of each person, and that is the projection of the shadow. No wonder Jung could observe—even more damningly than Rank or Reich—that "the principal and indeed only thing wrong with the world is man."[4]

For Becker, all societies, regardless of their ostensible ideology, are in fact built on lies, because they are all hero systems that promise victory over evil and death (*Escape from Evil*, 124).

Critical Response

In my view, Miller's book *For Your Own Good* should be required reading for parents because it so effectively sensitizes the reader to the various ways in which parents can psychologically harm their children. It holds up a mirror to adults,

---

3. See Jung, *Civilization in Transition*, 203.

4. Becker, *Escape from Evil* (New york: Free Press, 1975), 95, referring to *Civilization in Transition*, 216.

forcing them to reflect on how they were raised. This process of reflection can break cycles of harm that have been passed down for generations. Breaking these cycles can genuinely liberate parents to raise their children in a way that more fully embodies the love they have for them. As a general theory seeking to explain the roots of all violence, however, Miller's theory invites very troubling questions. The most obvious one concerns her apparent reductionism. Is she not reducing all violence to one narrowly conceived cause? It is difficult to see how this can be established. There is no doubt that severe child abuse causes great psychological harm, which in some cases leads to violent behavior in adults. But in many other cases violent acts are committed by individuals who were not severely abused as children. How does Miller's theory help us to understand these cases? Could she prove that every terrorist who ever committed a violent act did so because he was beaten as a child? In many situations, it would seem that another explanation, perhaps focusing on ideology as an inspiration to action, would be more plausible as a theoretical understanding.[5] Could Miller actually establish that all of the people who committed atrocities in Rwanda did so solely because they were abused as children? It seems more plausible to maintain that other factors need to be considered, some of them social and historical considerations that transcend the details of any particular individual's life. What Miller says is not invalid; but when she claims to put forward *the* one correct understanding of the roots of violence, she is claiming too much.

Another difficulty with Miller's commentary on Hitler is the lack of proportionality between cause and effect. We can understand that Hitler hated his father, and that rage had built up inside him because he was beaten. It would make a certain amount of sense if Hitler, as a grown man, had seen a man who resembled his father and had flown into a fit of rage and killed the look-alike. But to kill *six million* Jews because one hated one's father? The lack of proportion here is so drastic that a more nuanced understanding is clearly needed. Hitler did not kill all of those people by himself. He received the active or passive cooperation of most of the German people. Thus, a more adequate understanding of the roots of violence will consider the social dynamics of scapegoating. At this level, it is not adequate

---

5. Commenting on Hitler, Ervin Staub writes: "The predisposition to fanaticism does have roots in childhood and personality, but once a person makes a fanatic commitment to an ideology, knowledge of the ideology, and not his childhood and personality, is the best guide to understanding his behavior" (*The Roots of Evil*, 98). Zygmunt Bauman also criticizes the approach represented by Miller: "Most conclusions flowing from Milgram's experiments may be seen as variations on one central theme: cruelty correlates with certain patterns of social interaction much more closely than it does with personality features or other individual idiosyncrasies of the perpetrators. Cruelty is social in its origin much more than it is characterological." See *Modernity and the Holocaust* (Ithaca: Cornell University Press, 1989), 166.

to simply point to the child-rearing traditions of a culture. Reductionism at the social level is not any more convincing than reductionism at the individual level.

A further difficulty with Miller's book is the way it diverts moral responsibility away from the murderers and places it on their parents or on society in general. Violent people are understood by her to be *victims* of psychological oppression so great that they cannot really be held responsible for their actions:

> Readers who interpret my treatment of Hitler's early childhood as sentimental or even as an attempt to excuse his deeds naturally have every right to con- strue what they have read as they see fit. People who, for example, had to learn at an early age "to keep a stiff upper lip" identify with their parents to the ex- tent that they consider any form of empathy with a child as emotionalism or sentimentality. As for the question of guilt, I chose Hitler for the very reason that I know of no other criminal who is responsible for the death of so many human beings. But nothing is gained by using the word *guilt*. We of course have the right and the duty to lock up murderers who threaten our life. For the time being, we do not know of any better solution. But this does not alter the fact that the need to commit murder is the outcome of a tragic childhood and that imprisonment is the tragic sequel to this fate. (*For Your Own Good*, 195)

Notice that her argument must hinge on terms such as "tragic" and "fate" because she does not want to use the word "guilt." Thus we are to learn from her that six million Jews were killed by the Nazis, yet no one is guilty, no one is responsible. Is it necessary for me to criticize this position?

Ironically, Miller's argument ends up supporting the Nazi cause, in the sense that such an obliteration of responsibility for personal actions was one of the chief means used by the Nazis in organizing their machinery of death. Zygmunt Bauman has spoken to this point eloquently in his book on the Holocaust:

> We may surmise that the overall effect of such a continuous and ubiquitous responsibility shifting would be a *free-floating responsibility*, a situation in which each and every member of the organization is convinced, and would say so if asked, that he has been at someone else's beck and call, but the mem- bers pointed to by others as the bearers of responsibility would pass the buck to someone else again. One can say that *the organization as a whole is an instru- ment to obliterate responsibility*. (*Modernity and the Holocaust*, 163)

In Kierkegaard's language, we could describe Naziism as an organization designed to make it impossible for persons to live according to their conscience.[6] Miller does

---

6. Michael Plekon confirms this idea: "Contrary to the tendencies of contemporary social scientific and political assumptions about human nature's inherent innocence, Kierkegaard refuses to absolve the human self of ethical responsibility by viewing that self

not call persons to develop a conscience, a sense of personal moral responsibility for one's actions, because her interpretation of evil does not find the perpetrators of it guilty in any real sense. Her argument seems to be just another way of excusing oneself from responsibility by blaming one's actions on one's parents.

Staub's understanding of the roots of evil is broader than Miller's. Instead of narrowly focusing on one idea, such as childhood trauma, Staub paints a canvas involving many elements. He is presenting a general *gestalt* of violence, rather than a penetrating *theory* of violence. Some readers may find this broad approach appealing because it is highly inclusive of many factors and perspectives. But other readers, myself included, may find it to be philosophically weak because of its generality and journalistic character.

At times, Staub simply states the obvious, but in such a way that he thinks that he is providing his reader with important "scientific" insights. For example, he informs us that "studies show that SS members were authoritarian and followed orders without concern about their moral implications or the victims' fate" (*The Roots of Evil*, 132). Do we really need "studies" to show us that? He also explains to his readers: "Recent research in psychology has shown that human beings have a tendency to divide the world into 'us' and 'them'" (58). He sometimes makes tautological statements such as, "a feeling of responsibility for other people's welfare greatly increases the likelihood of helping during an accident or sudden illness" (xi). And further:

> A person's values determine his or her orientation to others' welfare. In extreme cases, harming others can become a value in itself. We can call this an antisocial value orientation, the devaluation of human beings and the desire to harm them, whether conscious or unconscious. It makes empathy with victims unlikely. (71)

In a book such as the one you are reading now, which deals with violence and evil, this is the best I can do in the way of comic relief. If "science" can only arrive at conclusions that are utterly obvious to any intelligent person, then it has no real power to improve our understanding. And if this is the case, then what is the point of presenting the "findings" of "modern science" concerning genocide?

Staub does not seem to realize that his "conclusions" should be the starting point of thought, not its end. He does not seem to be aware that he is begging the question. We should be asking *why* people divide the world into "us" and "them." We should be asking *what scapegoating reveals about the structure of human societies*, rather than being content to list "scapegoating" as one psychological response

---

as ultimately determined by its various environments. Rather, Kierkegaard asserts the intentionality of the self and thus its potential for good and evil." See "Anthropological Contemplation," *Thought* 55 (1980): 368.

to "difficult life conditions." We should be asking *how violence arises out of the depths of the individual human psyche*, rather than simply gesturing toward "cultural characteristics," "social disorganization," "hardships of life," and other impersonal concepts as an explanation of the roots of violence. In other words, Staub seems to lack a basic anthropological theory. He makes comments and observations that are accurate and to a certain extent helpful, but he does not challenge us with a philosophically penetrating vision of the human condition.

Judging from their popularity, the writings of Carl Jung and his followers strike many people as having a deep ring of truth. I concur with this intuition, particularly with regard to the concept of the projection of the shadow. This idea strikes a chord as a very fruitful approach to understanding violent behavior. That many cases of violence arise out of a condition of immaturity and a lack of psychological integration seems to be obviously true. But when a fruitful approach is taken in regard to such a crucially important question, it becomes very important to make sure that the insight is developed fully and accurately, within the broadest possible philosophical horizon. I am not entirely convinced that this is true of Jung.

I raise the following questions concerning Jung's thought. In speaking of the "archetypes" that inhabit the "collective unconscious," has Jung invented entities that relieve human beings of moral responsibility for the conduct of their lives? His essay on "Wotan," published in 1936, is very striking in this regard. There he argues that the behavior of the Germans can be understood as the reawakening of the god Wotan after his long slumber during the cultural dominance of Christianity. Jung describes Wotan as an "*Ergreifer* [seizer, possessor] of men," who has turned the average German into an *Ergriffener* (one who is possessed). "The impressive thing about the German phenomenon is that one man, who is obviously 'possessed,' has infected a whole nation to such an extent that everything is set in motion and has started rolling on its course towards perdition" (*Civilization in Transition*, 185). Jung recognizes the dark and violent aspects of National Socialism, but he attributes these to the influence of the god, rather than calling the German people to ethical responsibility. Thus he writes, "As an autonomous psychic factor, Wotan produces effects in the collective life of a people and thereby reveals his own nature" (187). And even more clearly, "We who stand outside judge the Germans far too much as if they were responsible agents, but perhaps it would be nearer the truth to regard them also as *victims*" (192). If external forces are causing human beings to do evil, then we are not genuinely responsible for our actions. We can say, "The devil made me do it" and be speaking the truth. But is this the way to respond to Naziism, by "understanding" it as the eruption of an "archetype"?

Following the war, Jung wrote another essay on Germany, entitled "After the Catastrophe." There he speaks very harshly of the Germans as a nation of hysterical murderers:

> The phenomenon we have witnessed in Germany was nothing less than the first outbreak of epidemic insanity, an irruption of the unconscious into what seemed to be a tolerably well-ordered world. A whole nation, as well as countless millions belonging to other nations, were swept into the blood-drenched madness of a war of extermination. No one knew what was happening to him, least of all the Germans, who allowed themselves to be driven to the slaughterhouse by their leading psychopaths like hypnotized sheep. (*Civilization in Transition*, 212)

Jung speaks of the collective guilt of the Germans, which has spread to become the collective guilt of Europeans in general. In this essay he does not speak as often of the idea of "Wotan" as an explanatory hypothesis. He blames the Germans for the crimes that they committed in their state of psychological derangement. Yet I am not certain that Jung has fully reckoned with the problem of moral accountability, since he bases his comments on the idea that Germany as a nation is like an inmate in an insane asylum. "To my mind, the history of the last twelve years is the case-chart of a hysterical patient" (209). In response to Jung, we can ask whether it is possible to put forward an understanding of the psychological roots of violence that holds the subjects responsible for their actions. Or will any "understanding" exonerate the "patients" in some fundamental way?

Becker's theory of violence appears to improve on the theories of Miller, Staub, and Jung in two important aspects. First, it grows out of a deeper reflection on the existential core of the human condition. Becker's interpretation paints a penetrating picture of the human condition in general, rather than falling into some form of reductionism regarding child-rearing, difficult historical circumstances, or mythical archetypes. Becker's vision seems to represent philosophical anthropology on a grand scale, in that he leads us to ask fundamental questions about our motivations. Second, Becker does not relieve human beings of moral responsibility for their actions. He maintains that violence arises out of our insistence upon lying to ourselves about our mortality. He implies that if we were more "honest" existentially, we would not be so prone to create scapegoats. This aspect of his thought lends Becker's message a prophetic aura. He is calling people to abandon idolatry and delusionary thinking.

Further reflection, however, raises certain questions regarding the adequacy of his explanation of violence. In the spring of 1999, two boys walked into their school in Colorado, shot dead thirteen people, and then killed themselves. If the fear of physical death is the mainspring of human behavior, then how is this act explained? Note that Becker does not seriously address suicide in *The Denial of Death* and *Escape from Evil*, which points to a major flaw in his theory. The teenage boys in Colorado were obviously psychologically disturbed. Does Becker's theory actually help us to understand the nature of this disturbance? I submit that it does not do that very effectively—it simply makes no sense to say that persons who commit suicide are motivated by a fear of death. Here the theory breaks down, and a breakdown at this point is too crucial to be ignored. On a larger scale, we can ask about the mass suicide at Jonestown. And we can ask why soldiers throughout history have been so willing to turn themselves into cannon fodder. Becker's explanation is that dying in the service of a state (or a religion) is a form of self-sacrifice that leads to a kind of immortality. But is this explanation really convincing? If "fear of death" is the answer to the question of why people are giving up their lives, then the problem has been transposed onto a level of paradoxicality that short-circuits the theory.

Clearly, a more effective understanding of violence should explain the mad gunmen in terms more specific to their situation; generalities about the human condition and mortality do not help us here. Yet we do not want to lose sight of Becker's penetrating anthropological vision. I suggest that the key concept Becker is missing is the possibility of psychological growth into greater human maturity. His theory can be described as working within a nonteleological, synchronic framework; he analyzes the person in a static relationship with mortality and asks about the person's honesty. But human beings do not exist in a static moment in time; human beings exist diachronically. We are moving through time and we have the potential to develop psychologically as we are drawn toward a greater fullness of life and understanding. Time is not simply an external environment in which we live; time is a reality within us as we develop spiritually. The roots of violence, then, can be sought in the dynamics of personal growth, rather than in a static aspect of the finitude of the human condition. This is the key insight that Becker lacks.

Each of the authors just surveyed focuses on an aspect of human relationality. For Miller, the key relationship is that between parent and child. Staub stresses the person's relation to his society at a particular time, his "age." Jung evokes the interrelations of the parts of the self. Becker paints a picture of human beings existing before Death, the transcendent limit of the ego. But none of these authors, from Kierkegaard's point of view, has discovered the most important relationship, the one thing needful: the relationship between the individual and God.

2

CREATION AND ANGST
IN KIERKEGAARD

That God could create beings free over against himself is the cross
which philosophy could not bear but upon which it has remained
hanging.

JP, 1: 1237 (1838)

The principal goal of this book is to show how Kierkegaard's writings
can be used to form the basis for an understanding of the psychological roots of human violence. I work toward this goal in three steps. First, I focus
on the concept of creation. What does it mean to say that human beings are creatures of God? Does this idea only refer to the past, or does it have significance for
our present and future as existing beings? The second step concentrates on the
concept of sin. How can we develop a deep, rather than a superficial, understanding of sin as a fracture in the relationship between human beings and God?
The third step gathers together the elements discussed in the first two steps and
crafts them into an articulation of the "theory" of violence, which is present in
Kierkegaard's thought. I surround "theory" with quotation marks because we are
dealing not with a strict parallel to the arguments of Alice Miller and others but
rather with an interpretation of Kierkegaard that is imaginative and constructive
while still remaining faithful, I hope, to his central concerns and beliefs.

Continuing Creation

There are various options for thought concerning the relationship between God
and the event of creation. Of course, one can subscribe to an atheistic position
which holds that the universe does not have a Creator. There is no design to nature, and life has come into existence by chance. Or, one could take a deistic approach that views God as a kind of "watchmaker" who created the world at the
beginning of time and then stepped back from it. Since then, the universe has been
running according to the laws built into it by God, while God remains aloof and
distant. Or, one could take a pantheistic view of creation, which understands the
being of God as immanent within the world. God continues to develop as the universe changes and develops. Or, one could think of creation as an event that oc-

curred entirely in the past. God created for a period of time, and then he stopped creating. Since then, God has worked miracles from time to time, but his creative activity is in the past. Or, one could understand creation as an ongoing event throughout time. On this view, God's work of creation was not completed in the past but continues in the present; the Genesis account of creation should be interpreted as revealing a God who *began* to create in the past and *continues* to create in the present.[1] I show in this chapter that Kierkegaard opts for this last possibility. He understands creation as an ongoing process, energized and guided by God, who transcends the universe while maintaining an intimate relationship with it.

The idea that creation is ongoing has been articulated by several Christian thinkers. Luther, for instance, clearly articulates this view of creation in his sermons on the Gospel of John:

> The fact that I grow and develop is God's work alone; without Him I would have died many years ago. If the Creator, who continues to work forever and ever, and His Co-worker were to interrupt Their work, all would go to wrack and ruin in a twinkling. . . .
>
> It is not true, as several heretics and other vulgar persons allege, that God created everything in the beginning, and then let nature take its own independent course, so that all things now spring into being of their own power; thereby they put God on a level with a shoemaker or a tailor. This not only contradicts Scripture, but it also runs counter to experience. In the doctrine of creation it is of primary importance that we know and believe that God has not withdrawn His sustaining hand from His handiwork. (Sermons on the Gospel of St. John, 28–29)

Emil Brunner argues that while God creates the lower animals in a finished state, human beings are always being created: "God retains *man* within His workshop, within His hands. He does not simply make him and finish him; human nature, indeed, consists in the fact that we may and must remain in the hands of God" (*Man in Revolt*, 97). Dorothy Sayers compares God with a human author who is continually writing:

> We consider God as a living author, whose span of activity extends infinitely beyond our racial memory in both directions. We never see His great work finished. Here and there we seem to recognize something which looks like the end of a chapter or the last page of a volume; or an episode presents itself to us as having a kind of completeness and unity in itself. There is, indeed, a school of thought which imagines that God, having created His universe, has now

---

1. Jon Levenson echoes other biblical scholars in suggesting that Genesis 1:1 should be translated "When God began to create the heavens and the earth." See *Creation and the Persistence of Evil* (Princeton: Princeton University Press, 1994), 121.

screwed the cap on His pen, put up His feet on the mantelpiece and left the work
to get on with itself. This, however, rather comes into St. Augustine's category
of figures of speech or enigmatic sayings framed from things which do not exist
at all. We simply do not know of any creation which goes on creating itself in
variety when the creator has withdrawn from it. (*The Mind of the Maker*, 58)

Ted Peters has recently argued that we should think of creation as occurring "in
the present tense":

> Should we speak of creation in the past tense? Are we tied down to thinking of
> the creative event as having happened only once at a single point of time in
> the past? Might God still be at work making things? In fact, this is what I will
> argue in this chapter: God creates continually and will not finish this creative
> work until the creation is consummated in the eschaton. The destiny of all
> things determines what they are. . . . God creates from the future, not the past.
> (*God—the World's Future*, 122, 134)

With this approach, the Genesis account teaches us that God *is* the Creator, not
that God *was* the Creator; creation *is* what God *does*.[2]

The basic common sense of the Judeo-Christian tradition of thought confirms the
validity of the idea of continuing creation. When a couple has a child, they say a
prayer of thanksgiving to God for the gift of this child. They do not pray to the Great
World Machine. They pray to God, the Creator, who has worked in the mother's
womb to "knit together" this baby (Ps. 139:13). To say that God is not the Creator of
this child is clearly not an option within the grammar of Christian thought. Thus,
the idea that God's work of creation only took place in the past is untenable.

Kierkegaard's authorship is complex, consisting of a tangled web of journals,
pseudonymous works, and signed works. It can be shown, however, that Kierkegaard's writings in all three of these venues express the view that creation is an
ongoing event. This idea forms the foundation of his interpretation of
human existence. In the journals, for example, he makes these comments on the
Incarnation:

> Here one rightly sees the subjectivity in Christianity. Generally the poet, the
> artist, etc. is criticized for introducing himself into his work. But this is precisely
> what God does; this he does in Christ. And precisely this is Christianity. Cre-
> ation is really fulfilled only when God has included himself in it. Before Christ
> God was included, of course, in the creation but as an invisible mark, some-
> thing like a water-mark in paper. But in the Incarnation creation is fulfilled by
> God's including himself in it. (JP, 2: 1391 [1849])

---

2. John Milbank also affirms the doctrine of continuing creation; see *Theology and Social Theory* (Cambridge: Basil Blackwell, 1991), 305 and 423–427.

Since Christ is the Word through whom all things have come into existence, his entry into human history renders the idea of the watchmaker God completely impossible for Christian theology. When Christ forgives sins, heals the sick, and commands his followers to love their neighbor, human beings are addressed by the Word of the Creator. In Christ, God may be *incognito*, but he can never be described as *aloof*. In Christ, the Creator enters into human history to fulfill his work of creation by suffering within himself the consequences of human sin.

In the signed works, which Kierkegaard published as "upbuilding discourses" in a series that paralleled his pseudonymous works, we find the theme of ongoing creation expressed very clearly. Here the focus lies on the Word of creation, the divine speech that brings human beings into existence. Human beings have the ability to hear the voice of creation and respond to it. Thus, in one of his early discourses, Kierkegaard quotes James 1:19: "Therefore let every man be quick to hear." What is the person supposed to hear? Is it the "discourses of doubt," or the "opinions of men," or "his own heart"? No, it is the "divine Word" that sounds when "the crowd is dispersed and gone" (EUD, 137–138). The individual who listens to this Word allows himself to be drawn forward into authentic existence as a human being.

It is in a discourse such as this that the true heart of Kierkegaard's thought is found. Unfortunately, Kierkegaard has very often been misconstrued as articulating a "philosophy" of radical self-creation. He is described in many encyclopedia entries, articles, and books as if he were a disciple of Jean-Paul Sartre. But this is clearly not an accurate approach to understanding Kierkegaard, when we consider the whole authorship and focus on that which was most important to him. A particularly obvious example of the way Kierkegaard has been misconstrued is found in the work of Alasdair MacIntyre. In *After Virtue*, for example, he describes Kierkegaard as destroying "the whole tradition of a rational moral culture" by forcing his reader to make a "radical choice" between the aesthetic and the ethical modes of life.[3] MacIntyre is strangely blinded to the deep-rootedness of Kierkegaard's thought in the Christian theological tradition. MacIntyre has labored strenuously to articulate and champion this tradition in the academic world, and he should see Kierkegaard as an ally in this effort, but he does not. Far from basing his message on a philosophy of radical choice, Kierkegaard is most accurately described as a biblical theologian who is urging his reader to find the true meaning of existence in a relationship with God the Creator. Kierkegaard is first and foremost a devout reader of the Bible who is seeking to allow the words

---

3. *After Virtue* (Notre Dame: University of Notre Dame Press, 1984), 41. For a more extensive critique of MacIntyre, see my essay, "Kierkegaard's *Either/Or* and the Parable of the Prodigal Son," in *International Kierkegaard Commentary: Either/Or*, Part II, ed. Robert L. Perkins (Macon: Mercer University Press, 1995), 59–82.

of the scriptures, the "divine Word," to resonate through his writings in such a way that they reach out and connect with the reader, finding him "where he is" and calling him forward into greater spiritual maturity (PV, 27).

At the same time Kierkegaard published *The Concept of Anxiety* and the *Philosophical Fragments*, he also published a set of three upbuilding discourses, the first of which is entitled, "Think about Your Creator in the Days of Your Youth."[4] Whereas the works of the pseudonyms Haufniensis and Climacus reflect on creation as a philosophical idea, as will be made clear in the following discussion, here the reader is directly addressed and challenged to appropriate what has been said. Thus the text of the Preacher is described as communicating a "concerned" rather than an "unconcerned" truth. A concerned truth is not "indifferent to the single individual's particular condition," but rather it is a truth "for him" (EUD, 233). The truth being conveyed here is that all human beings, regardless of whether they are rich or poor, are all children of the same Creator, and all have equal access to God. This relationship with God is the most central core of human personality. The youth, the child, has a natural openness to this relationship that may be lost in the older adult who is weighed down with the cares and distractions of the world. In this discourse, the reader is addressed by the author, S. Kierkegaard, yet in such a way that the author recedes into the background. The voice that the reader is led to hear is the voice of God:

> For the youth, God lives close by. In the midst of his joy and his sorrow, he hears God's voice calling; if he does not hear it, he misses it immediately, has not learned subterfuges, does not know how to conceal himself—until he hears it again. When one grows older, it is a long way to heaven, and the noise on earth makes it difficult to hear the voice; and if one does not hear it, the noise on earth makes it easy not to miss it. (EUD, 242–243)

For Kierkegaard, theological anthropology is the most important point at which the doctrine of continuing creation comes into play. An "objective" study of the relationship between God and nature can be a disinterested enterprise carried on by those who feel called to do so. But the "subjectively" existing human being is personally caught up in the event of creation. Creation is happening within her soul, or it has the potential to happen within her soul. Therefore the doctrine of continuing creation is a matter of *concerned* knowledge, not disinterested knowledge. Theological anthropology, in the last analysis, must take the form of self-knowledge. One cannot understand the human condition in the abstract without understanding one's own condition.

---

4. Kierkegaard's signed discourses were consciously designed to respond to the ideas articulated by his pseudonyms. See Nelly Viallaneix, *Ecoute, Kierkegaard* (Paris: Cerf, 1979), I: 24–25.

We can see, then, that Kierkegaard's thought, according to its own logical development, has both a theoretical and a homiletical or upbuilding element. He analyzes human existence as a topic for reflection, but he also addresses his "reader" in a personal and challenging way, and through his "reader," himself. He invents a pseudonym who interprets the story of the creation of Adam and Eve, but he also writes an upbuilding discourse in which he speaks to his reader in a manner such as this:

> Just as knowing oneself in one's own nothingness is the condition for knowing God, so knowing God is the condition for the sanctification of a human being by God's assistance and according to his intention. Wherever God is in truth, there he is always creating. He does not want a person to be spiritually soft and to bathe in the contemplation of his glory, but in becoming known by a person he wants to create in him a new human being. (EUD, 325)

Kierkegaard's writings do not merely refer to the divine work of creation, they actually seek to bring their reader into the process of creation by opening her heart and mind to the God whose work is being described.[5]

When we turn to Kierkegaard's pseudonymous works, we find again the theme of continuing creation. A prime example is *Philosophical Fragments*, the first work of the pseudonym Johannes Climacus. For our purposes here, it is important to note that when Climacus describes the "learner" who is taught by the "god in time," he uses language that resonates with the event of creation:

> When the learner is untruth . . . but is nevertheless a human being, and he now receives the condition and the truth, he does not, of course, become a human being for the first time, for he already was that; but he becomes a different person . . . he becomes a person of a different quality or, as we can also call it, a *new* person. . . .
>
> Inasmuch as he was in untruth and now along with the condition receives the truth, a change takes place in him like the change from "not to be" to "to be." But this transition from "not to be" to "to be" is indeed the transition of birth. But the person who already *is* cannot be born, and yet he is born. Let us call this transition *rebirth*. . . . (PF, 18–19)

Climacus then argues that this idea of rebirth could only be thought by one who has been reborn; "it would be unreasonable to think that one who is not reborn should do it" (PF, 20). Therefore the basic distinction between the Socratic vision and Christian thought is found in the difference between recollection of an innate

---

5. See Michael Plekon, "Kierkegaard the Theologian: The Roots of His Theology in *Works of Love*," in *Foundations of Kierkegaard's Vision of Community*, ed. Connell and Evans (Atlantic Highlands: Humanities Press International, 1992), 4, 6.

truth of being, and new awareness in the present moment in time of a transformation of the person which has occurred in response to the teacher:

> —In *the moment*, a person becomes aware that he was born, for his previous
> state, to which he is not to appeal, was indeed one of "not to be." In *the mo-*
> *ment*, he becomes aware of the rebirth, for his previous state was indeed one of
> "not to be." If his previous state had been one of "to be," then under no circum-
> stances would the moment have acquired decisive significance for him, as ex-
> plained above. Whereas the Greek pathos focuses on recollection, the pathos
> of our project focuses on the moment, and no wonder, for is it not an exceed-
> ingly pathos-filled matter to come into existence from the state of "not to be"?
> (PF, 21)

The underlying vision here is the basic story of humanity as told by traditional
theological anthropology. In the beginning the human race was created by God in
a state of goodness. God gave humanity "the condition for understanding the truth"
(PF, 15). But human beings fell into sin through "their own fault." They thus forfeited the truth and are now continually "forfeiting the condition" for understanding it. The teacher is God who has entered into time in order to remind human
beings that they are in untruth through their own fault. The teacher thus makes
possible the resumption of the process of creation which was interrupted by sin.[6]

The next logical step in our survey of Kierkegaard's reflections on creation is
to examine more closely what he understands by the concept of "sin."

Fear and Angst

In 1757 David Hume published a small work entitled *The Natural History of Reli-*
gion. His aim was to put forward a naturalistic account of the origin of religion in
"human nature." For our purposes, it is of interest to consider Hume's description
of the basic motivations that led to the "invention" of religion. He suggests that
our ancestors, the primitive "barbarians," did not have the leisure necessary for
"contemplation of the works of nature." Thus they could not see the "design" that
"prevails throughout the whole." They were engaged in a desperate struggle to
survive. They were not attempting to understand nature philosophically, or scien-
tifically, or even religiously; they were not trying to *understand* but to *cope* with a
terrifying universe.[7] Primitive peoples were afraid of events that seemed beyond

---

6. The second work of Johannes Climacus, *Concluding Unscientific Postscript*, further
develops this line of thought through the concept of *becoming* (a Christian). See pp. 371–
372, 381–384, 411, 420–421, 587–588.

7. See M. Jamie Ferreira, "Religion's 'Foundation in Reason': The Common Sense of
Hume's Natural History," *Canadian Journal of Philosophy* 24 (1994): 565–582.

their control: storms, droughts, plagues, earthquakes, wars, and so forth. They imagined that there were a host of invisible powers behind these events, and they sought to appease these powers by "prayers and sacrifices, rites and ceremonies." Hume listed the basic motivations of the primitives as "the anxious concern for happiness, the dread of future misery, the terror of death, the thirst of revenge, the appetite for food and other necessaries."[8]

In 1844 a book was published in Copenhagen under the title *Begrebet Angest: En simpel psychologisk-paapegende Overveielse i Retning af det dogmatiske Problem om Arvesynden* [The Concept Angst:[9] A Simple Psychological-Demonstrative Reflection in the Direction of the Dogmatic Problem of Original/Hereditary Sin]. The pseudonymous author was Vigilius Haufniensis, "The Watchman of the Harbortown."

Haufniensis was not specifically responding to Hume, and most likely he had not read *The Natural History of Religion*; nevertheless, juxtaposing these two works allows an interesting comparison. Although Haufniensis does not advance a thesis on the origin of religion, he is very concerned with the question of the basic motivations that underlie human behavior. Haufniensis proposes that the most basic element of a theory of behavior should not be fear, as Hume had suggested, but angst, which is a different emotion. Animals can experience fear and terror. A gazelle can fear a cheetah and a rabbit can fear a hawk. But animals cannot experience angst, which is a uniquely human emotion. Hume portrays human beings as animals with sophisticated brains and the consequent ability to imagine and personify unseen powers. But Haufniensis suggests that the uniqueness of humanity consists in the presence of an emotion that differs qualitatively from fear, that arises not out of *external* threats to the individual's existence, but out of *internal* conditions:

> The concept of angst is almost never treated in psychology. Therefore, I must point out that it is altogether different from fear and similar concepts that refer to something definite, whereas angst is freedom's actuality as the possibility of possibility. For this reason, angst is not found in the beast, precisely because by nature the beast is not qualified as spirit. (CA, 42)

What does this mean, that animals are not "qualified as spirit"?

---

8. This and the previous quotations can be found in Hume, *The Natural History of Religion*, ed. H. E. Root (Stanford: Stanford University Press, 1957), 26–28.

9. In the text that follows, I use the term *angst* rather than *anxiety*, since the German word has entered into common English usage and is the direct equivalent of the Danish *Angest*. I modify the standard translations accordingly whenever I quote them. In referring to the title of the book, however, I use the term *Anxiety*. For a differing view supporting the use of "anxiety," see Gregory Beabout, *Freedom and Its Misuses: Kierkegaard on Anxiety and Despair* (Milwaukee: Marquette University Press, 1996), 15–18.

Haufniensis suggests that the lower animals have a set psychology that controls their response to their environment. Their world presents various threats, and they do their best to avoid these threats while they search for their sustenance. But human beings, lacking a set psychology, are free, which means that we are aware of possibilities open to us. We can shape the future through our choice of actions. It is out of this capability that angst arises. Freedom, which entails an awareness of future possibilities, constitutes an element of human nature that animals lack, an element that needs to be named: *spirit*.

Hume's *Natural History* is clearly an account of religion that presents an alternative to the biblical tradition; it is a *natural*, not a theological, history. Thus, there is no real place in Hume's account for Adam and Eve. They can only be ignored as the mythological human archetypes imagined by the ancient Hebrews. Adam and Eve do play a key role in Haufniensis's portrayal of the human condition, because his account is not naturalistic but theological. Hume's book attempts to give a plausible account of the origin of religion, regardless of whether or not the gods posited by religion exist. Haufniensis, on the other hand, assumes the existence of the Creator God described in the Bible, and he proceeds from that perspective. He assumes that human beings can gain a knowledge of God and of themselves through the stories in the Bible. Today we might describe Haufniensis as a "narrative theologian."

For Haufniensis, Adam and Eve represent the human race, which means that they symbolize *spiritual* existence, as distinct from *animal* existence. In them we see the future of the human race—the future not just in a chronological sense, but in a psychological sense as well. In them we see that human beings have a *future* that is open in a way it is not for the animals.[10] The future is the source of angst, because its indetermination leads to emotional ambivalence. Angst is de-

---

10. "It is quite possible to show that a very precise and correct usage of language links angst and the future together" (JP, 1: 98 [1844]). These remarks by Gregor Malantschuk are also appropriate at this point:

> Vigilius Haufniensis begins pondering original sin so far down the scale that he also touches on the difference between the animal and the human individual. He points to the underlying difference between animal and man as being that in the animal world the particular specimen of the species only repeats the characteristics of the species without contributing anything new to the development; whereas with man there begins a development which constantly creates new elements which alter the race and by changing the race preforms the new individuals. Vigilius Haufniensis believes firmly that the whole creative process which takes place in the single individual, which again influences the race, is due to man's connection with the eternal, which continually asserts itself more and more in the course of history. The essential difference between animal and man, then, is that the animal is but a transient, temporal being; whereas man is destined for eternity. Gregor Malantschuk, *Kierkegaard's Thought* (Princeton: Princeton University Press, 1971), 259

fined by Haufniensis as "*a sympathetic antipathy* and *an antipathetic sympathy*" (CA, 42).[11] Angst arises out of a conflict of emotions within the human being, a struggle between desiring and fearing the same thing. What is simultaneously desired and feared is the development of the self itself. That human beings lack a set psychology means that the human self is continually in the process of forma-tion. For human beings, the event of creation is not experienced as a completed action, but as a present reality. We do not simply exist, we are continually com-ing into existence—an awkward and uncomfortable position that can lead to negative consequences. The fact that we are coming into existence means that a possibility is open to us that is not open to the animals, the possibility of alienat-ing ourselves from the process of creation. We can, in other words, fall into *sin*, the term that indicates our propensity to fall out of harmony with our Creator, and with ourselves as well, through our own fault. Haufniensis's book thus begins with a consideration of the story of the fall of Adam and Eve into sin.

"Through the first sin, sin came into the world. Precisely in the same way it is true of every subsequent man's first sin, that through it sin comes into the world" (CA, 31). Adam and Eve made a "leap" into sin which allowed sinfulness to be-come a quality of human existence. Each person following them makes a similar leap. This leap into sin involves the loss of innocence and its replacement by guilt. Each person makes this "qualitative leap" as an individual (CA, 37). This leap is traditionally known as the Fall. But how is this aspect of human existence to be understood psychologically? This is Haufniensis's basic concern:

> Innocence is ignorance. In innocence, man is not qualified as spirit but is psy-chically qualified in immediate unity with his natural condition. The spirit in man is dreaming. . . .
>
> In this state there is peace and repose, but there is simultaneously something else that is not contention and strife, for there is indeed nothing against which to strive. What, then, is it? Nothing. But what effect does nothing have? It begets angst. This is the profound secret of innocence, that it is at the same time angst. Dreamily the spirit projects its own actuality, but this actuality is nothing, and innocence always sees this nothing outside itself.
>
> Angst is a qualification of dreaming spirit, and as such it has its place in psy-chology. Awake, the difference between myself and my other is posited; sleep-ing, it is suspended; dreaming, it is an intimated nothing. (CA, 41–42)

---

11. See also this related journal entry:

The nature of original sin has often been explained, and still a primary category has been lacking—it is *angst*; this is the essential determinant. Angst is a desire for what one fears, a sympathetic antipathy; angst is an alien power which grips the indi-vidual, and yet one cannot tear himself free from it and does not want to, for one fears, but what he fears he desires. (JP, 1: 94 [1842])

Haufniensis describes spirit as either dreaming or awake. Before the Fall, the spirit was dreaming in Adam and Eve. This is the state of innocence. But innocence is not entirely tranquil; it is the state out of which angst arises. Angst is that uneasiness that results from the individual's awareness that he could possibly be different than he is currently. He could have an ability or a knowledge that he does not now have. There is a possibility that is open to him, which could become an actuality. But what would be the consequence of this actuality? He does not know and is thus anxious. He is drawn to the possibility, but at the same time he is made uncomfortable by it.

Before the Fall, Adam and Eve lived in an innocence characterized by "the enormous nothing of ignorance" (CA, 44). When God spoke to the first couple and prohibited them from eating of the tree of the knowledge of good and evil, they could not understand what was said because they were ignorant of the distinction between good and evil. Perhaps they gained a presentiment that if they ate they would be able to do something that they could not presently do, but they did not know what this being able would mean. Likewise, when they were told that if they ate they would die, they had no way of knowing what it meant to die. They were ignorant of their mortality. "Because Adam has not understood what was spoken, there is nothing but the ambiguity of angst" (CA, 45).

Haufniensis's argument in his first chapter culminates in his reflections on the freedom of the human spirit:

> Angst is neither a category of necessity nor a category of freedom; it is entangled freedom, where freedom is not free in itself but entangled, not by necessity, but in itself. If sin has come into the world by necessity (which is a contradiction), there can be no angst. Nor can there be any angst if sin came into the world by an act of an abstract *liberum arbitrium* [freedom of indifference]. . . . To want to give a logical explanation of the coming of sin into the world is a stupidity that can occur only to people who are comically worried about finding an explanation. (CA, 49–50)

For Haufniensis, there can be no "science" of sin because sin arises out of freedom—a reality that transcends science. The "science" of psychology can reflect on the ground out of which sin arises, namely angst, but it can do no more than this. Science is an attempt to grasp logically the objectively perceivable world. But sin is subjective, and it is not logical. Therefore, the mode of knowing which is appropriate to the problem of sin is a subjective, existential mode. "How sin came into the world, each man understands solely by himself. If he would learn it from another, he would *eo ipso* misunderstand it" (CA, 51).

In the wake of Haufniensis's work, it becomes apparent that Hume's book lacks an awareness of angst. Hume occasionally uses the word "anxiety," but only as a synonym for fear. Angst as a uniquely human emotion, which involves the related concepts of (entangled) freedom, guilt, and the future development of the self, is not within his intellectual ken. Thus, he also lacks, from the theological perspective, a doctrine of sin. In place of a doctrine of sin, we find in his work little more than an *Enlightenment prejudice*: "primitive" people were ignorant, fearful, and barbaric; we modern philosophers are intelligent and serene. His writing expresses an unreflective self-righteousness and feeling of superiority. Haufniensis, on the other hand, strikes us as one who is writing about the human race out of *his own experience of freedom, guilt, and faith*. In articulating the story of the Fall of Adam and Eve, he is speaking about himself.

Our reading of Haufniensis's treatise has established the following points: (1) the most basic human emotion is not fear of external threats, but angst arising out of spiritual freedom; (2) the freedom of human beings is an expression of our situation as creatures who are continually coming into existence—we are continually being created; and (3) to fall into sin is to alienate ourselves from our Creator and to derail the divinely willed direction of our process of becoming.

Ernest Becker's Misinterpretation of Kierkegaard

Earlier, I pointed to Alasdair MacIntyre's writing as an example of the way in which Kierkegaard was misread in the twentieth century. Ernest Becker provides another example of misreading, which is even more significant for the central concern of this essay, namely, violence. One of the more widely read theorists of violence in recent decades, Becker claims in his work that his explanation of the roots of violence follows Kiekegaard closely. But when this claim is subjected to close scrutiny, it does not hold up. Becker would have been much more accurate if he had clearly stated that he was following the thought of Hume.

Becker's belief that his own thought is in basic accord with Kierkegaard's can be clearly seen in the following quotation:

> I am not going to attempt to repeat and decode Kierkegaard's breathtakingly penetrating and often difficult-to-understand analysis of the human condition. What I want to do instead is to try to present a summing-up of the main argument contained in his psychological works [*The Concept of Anxiety* and *The Sickness unto Death*], as pointedly and sparingly as possible, so that the reader can see "in a nutshell" what Kierkegaard was driving at. If I can do this without getting too involved because fascinated by Kierkegaard's genius, the reader should be struck by the result. The structure of Kierkegaard's understanding of man *is almost exactly a recap of the modern clinical picture of man that we have sketched in the first four chapters of this book*. The reader can then judge for himself how congruent the two pictures are at basic points (even though I don't present Kierkegaard in his stunning detail), why it is that today we are comparing Kierkegaard's stature in psychology to Freud's, and why I and others

are prepared to call Kierkegaard as great a student of the human condition as was Freud. The fact is that, although writing in the 1840's he was really post-Freudian, which conveys the eternal uncanniness of genius. (*The Denial of Death*, 68)

Becker asks his reader to judge "how congruent the two pictures are," assuming that the reader will see a close similarity between his perspective and Kierkegaard's. But he has made a claim that he cannot establish.

Becker's theory, that the "mainspring of human behavior" is the denial of death, is actually an updated version of Hume's anthropology. Both authors use *fear* as the cornerstone of their accounts, and both view human beings as essentially animals with sophisticated brains capable of self-consciousness. This is clearly seen in Becker's text:

> Man is a union of opposites, of self-consciousness and of physical body. Man emerged from the instinctive thoughtless action of the lower animals and came to reflect on his condition. He was given a consciousness of his part-divinity in creation, the beauty and uniqueness of his face and his name. At the same time he was given the consciousness of the terror of the world and of his own death and decay. . . . As we saw, the leading modern psychologists have themselves made it the cornerstone of their understanding. But Kierkegaard had already counseled them: "Further than this psychology cannot go . . . and moreover it can verify this point again and again in its observation of human life." (*The Denial of Death*, 68–69)

Becker is here implying that the "point" that psychology is verifying concerns awareness of one's mortality. But if we read the passage from which the Haufniensis quotation is taken, we can see that this is not the "point" at all. The basic idea of the passage is that innocence is ignorance. Angst arises within Adam in his state of innocence in response to the command, "Do not eat of the tree." He becomes anxiously aware that if he did eat of the tree he would become able to do something or know something that he cannot now. The word of judgment accompanies the prohibition: "If you eat you will surely die." But *Adam does not know what it means to die*" (CA, 45 [emphasis added]). Thus we can see that Becker badly misconstrued the meaning of the passage that he has quoted. For Haufniensis, it is essential that angst *precedes* rather than *follows* the knowledge of mortality. Angst arises out of the ground of human freedom before God, not out of the clash between a self-conscious psyche and a mortal body. Angst arises not out of *knowledge* but out of *ignorance*; it is not a rational phenomenon, but a prerational or subconscious phenomenon.

At the most basic level, the difference between the two perspectives can be summarized in this way: For Becker the mainspring of human behavior is the denial of death; for Kierkegaard, it is the denial of the fullness of life to which God is calling each person. Becker's ideal of mental health is to become oneself before Death; Kierkegaard's message is a call to become oneself before God. Everything that the two authors say about the human condition grows out of these starting points. The fundamental distinction between Becker's and Kierkegaard's thought can be seen in these two passages, the first from *The Denial of Death*, the second from *The Sickness unto Death*:

> Kierkegaard's torment was the direct result of seeing the world as it really is in relation to his situation as a creature. The prison of one's character is painstakingly built up to deny one thing and one thing alone: one's creatureliness. The creatureliness is the terror. Once admit that you are a defecating creature and you invite the primeval ocean of creature anxiety to flood over you. But it is more than creature anxiety, it is also man's anxiety, the anxiety that results from the human paradox that man is an animal who is conscious of his animal limitation. Anxiety is the result of the perception of the truth of one's condition. (*The Denial of Death*, 87)

[Kierkegaard:]

> There is much talk about human distress and wretchedness—I try to understand it and have also had some intimate acquaintance with it—there is so much talk about wasting a life, but only that person's life was wasted who went on living so deceived by life's joys or by its sorrows that he never became decisively and eternally conscious as spirit, as self, or, what amounts to the same thing, never became aware and in the deepest sense never gained the impression that there is a God and "he," he himself, his self, exists before this God—an infinite benefaction that is never gained except through despair. (SUD, 26–27)

Becker sensed that Kierkegaard's psychology has great importance for the task of understanding human behavior in the modern world. He erred, however, by insisting that Kierkegaard's thought would be best understood after it had been forced to conform to the outlines of the death-denial theory.

In chapter 3 I turn to *The Sickness unto Death* to demonstrate that it does lay the groundwork for an effective interpretation of political violence. Unlike Becker, however, I allow Kierkegaard's thought to breathe freely the air of the Christian theological tradition, rather than confining it within the straightjacket of secular social science.

3

EGO-PROTECTION IN KIERKEGAARD

When one denies God, he does God no harm but destroys himself;
when one mocks God, he mocks himself.

JP, 2: 1349 (1846)

The Analysis of Despair

Friedrich Nietzsche was born one generation later than Kierkegaard. Both authors,
in their later works, expressed stinging critiques of the established Lutheranism
into which they had been born. The most obvious difference between them, of
course, lies in Kierkegaard's desire to transform the Church, in contrast with
Nietzsche's desire to abolish it. Both authors diagnose what they see as the "sickness" of Christendom, but one sees the disease as terminal. Nietzsche believes that
Christianity is sick to its core, because it arises out of distrust of natural human
life on this earth. Kierkegaard believes that Christianity has been distorted and
perverted in the course of its development, but in its best form it points the way to
"true humanity" (PV, 108).

Despite these obvious differences between Kierkegaard and Nietzsche, I believe
that there is one important sense in which they were thinking along similar lines.
Both authors saw the comfortable existence of middle-class Europeans as an inadequate stopping point for the development of the human person. Both authors
longed for *a resumption of the process of creation*, which had been artificially cut off
by the spiritual sloth of the "mass man." For Kierkegaard, the process of creation
involves a divine call that draws the individual forward, while for Nietzsche, it is
precisely this notion of divine direction which must be overcome in the self-
creating will of the overman. But the similarity of perspective remains, at the
anthropological level, despite the complete difference at the theological level.

Nietzsche's desire to see a resumption of the process of creation is plainly evident in the words of Zarathustra, whose proclamation that "God is dead" is a pre-
amble to his central message: "*I teach you the overman*. Man is something that shall
be overcome. What have you done to overcome him?" Zarathustra's rhetoric continues along similar lines: "What is great in man is that he is a bridge and not an
end." "I say unto you: one must still have chaos in oneself to be able to give birth
to a dancing star. I say unto you: you still have chaos in yourselves." "Behold the
good and the just! Whom do they hate most? The man who breaks their table of

values, the breaker, the lawbreaker; yet he is the creator." "Companions, the creator seeks, not corpses, not herds and believers. Fellow creators, the creator seeks— those who write new values on new tablets." "Change of values—that is a change of creators. Whoever must be a creator always annihilates."[1] Here we encounter Nietzsche's *faith*, his vision for the future development of humanity. He longs for his readers to share his vision and cross over the "bridge" to a new perception of the world and themselves.

Kierkegaard's *faith* is also expressed through the medium of an alter ego. Anti-Climacus articulates Kierkegaard's critique of the established Church and the middle class of the nineteenth century. Like Zarathustra, he analyzes the spiritual sickness of the contemporary age. He also deplores the sloth and inertia that reveal the resistance of human beings to the potential development of their souls. Like Zarathustra, he longs to see a new creation. But he differs profoundly from Nietzsche's hero in basing his message on the New Testament, with its call to new life that comes from God.

Nietzsche begins *On the Genealogy of Morals* with the words, "We are unknown to ourselves, we men of knowledge." He is hoping that his book will act as a *revelation*, making manifest the hidden springs of human behavior and thought, which have remained buried under the weight of philosophical and theological tradition. His work has the form of an exercise in *alētheia*, an "unforgetting" of the truth of human life. *The Sickness unto Death*, by Anti-Climacus, has the same basic form, but a different content, since he believes that the pathway to truth lies in a deeper appreciation of theological tradition, rather than a rejection of it. He also seeks to give his readers a degree of self-knowledge that they do not now possess, as indicated in the subtitle: "A Christian Psychological Exposition for Upbuilding and Awakening." Anti-Climacus seeks to awaken his readers to the reality of despair—that basic existential alienation from God which renders impossible the living of a fully human life.

Anti-Climacus proposes that there are three principal forms that despair may take in different individuals. The first is that despair which underlies an individual's lack of conscious awareness of selfhood. The second is the despair of weakness, not willing to be oneself. The third is the despair of defiance, willing to be oneself, but in defiance of the Creator. In order to explicate these three forms, Anti-Climacus needs to begin with a definition of the self:

> The human being is spirit.[2] But what is spirit? Spirit is the self. But what is the self? The self is a relation which relates itself to itself, or it is the relation relat-

---

1. *Thus Spake Zarathustra*, trans. Walter Kaufmann (New York: Viking, 1966), 12, 15, 17, 23, 24, 59.

2. I have modified the Hongs' translation here from "A human being is spirit" in favor of a more literal rendering of *Mennesket er Aand*. The Hongs' phrasing has the unfortunate

ing itself to itself in the relation; the self is not the relation but that the relation relates itself to itself. The human being is a synthesis of infinitude and finitude, of the temporal and the eternal, of freedom and necessity, in short, a synthesis. A synthesis is a relation between two elements. So considered, the human being is still not a self. (my trans., cf. SUD, 13)

This passage has been described by one scholar as "gobbledygook" that is intended as a parody of Hegelian jargon.[3] The gobbledygook has a real purpose, however, in that it raises the question of how the self should be understood in Christian theological anthropology.

Anti-Climacus is suggesting that the self has three main dimensions or can be seen from three angles.[4] First, the self is a *synthesis* of opposing elements, such as infinitude and finitude, freedom and necessity. Second, the self is a *self-relation*; it has the ability to be conscious of itself. Third, the self is *related to the Power that established it*, God. These three dimensions, taken together, establish the way in which *the self is spirit*. Anti-Climacus develops his treatise along the lines that he has laid out in this definition of the self. The first section of *The Sickness unto Death* considers the self as a *synthesis* of opposing elements (pp. 29–42 in the Hong translation). The second considers the self as *self-conscious* (pp. 42–74). The remainder of the work, on the doctrine of sin, considers the self as *related to God* (pp. 77–131). It is also apparent that these three parts of *The Sickness unto Death* are another presentation of the theory of the spheres of existence: the aesthetic, the ethical, and the religious.

For Anti-Climacus, the possibility of despair is inherent in the possibility of misrelation in the synthesis of the physical, the psychical, and the spiritual. But the synthesis itself is not the misrelation, because if it were then despair would lie in human nature per se: "Where then, does the despair come from? From the relation in which the synthesis relates itself to itself, inasmuch as God, who constituted man a relation, releases it from his hand, as it were—that is, inasmuch as the relation relates itself to itself" (SUD, 16). Here we see again the doctrine of cre-

---

tendency to individualize a philosophically general statement. On this point, refer to the comments by Stephen Crites in his essay in the Connell and Evans volume, *Foundations of Kierkegaard's Vision of Community* (Atlantic Highlands: Humanities Press International, 1992), 149. Alastair Hannay chooses "The human being is spirit" in his translation, while another possibility can be seen in Walter Lowrie's "Man is spirit."

3. Louis Mackey, *Kierkegaard: A Kind of Poet* (Philadelphia: University of Pennsylvania Press, 1971), 134–137.

4. I am drawing here on John Glenn's insightful essay "The Definition of the Self and the Structure of Kierkegaard's Work," in *The Sickness unto Death*, ed. Perkins, International Kierkegaard Commentary (Macon: Mercer University Press, 1987), 5–6.

ation which is crucial in Kierkegaard's thought as a whole.[5] Human beings are unique among the creatures in that they are "released from God's hand." This letting go gives freedom, yet it brings with it the possibility of despair; individuals can fail to become true human beings in a way that is not possible for the other animals. A horse embodies horseness and a cat embodies catness because there is a sense in which they are always held in God's hand. There is nothing to block the fulfillment of God's intention for their character and essence. But this fulfill-ment can be blocked in the case of human beings, because they can themselves actively block it. This is the basic argument of *The Sickness unto Death* as a whole.

Anti-Climacus suggests that despair takes various identifiable forms, depending on which elements of the self are developed or not developed. Like Nietzsche, he views the immature self as a kind of chaos that has the *potential* to become ordered.[6] Un-like Nietzsche, however, he views the elements of the self theologically. Despair can thus be defined by the relations between infinitude and finitude, possibility and ne-cessity, and consciousness and unconsciousness. Anti-Climacus understands infini-tude as pointing toward the divine source of the self; possibility arises out of the di-vine gift of free will; and consciousness is ultimately awareness of one's existence before God. But when the human self is immature and is alienated from the Creator, these elements take on a life of their own and lead to various distortions and psy-chopathologies, which Anti-Climacus details in the first half of his book.

When Anti-Climacus begins to analyze despair "as defined by consciousness," he refers to the third main pair of elements within the self: the eternal/the tempo-

---

5. The idea of continuing creation in *The Sickness unto Death* is described by Vincent McCarthy in this way: "The elements of the synthesis will not come to equilibrium with-out a readjustment of the relationship to the Constituting Power—who is not a Watch-maker God, who creates and lets creation run its course, or even a Watch-repairman God, who must intervene once to repair a faulty mechanism. For Kierkegaard, while there are special moments of divine action, the Divine must be present and active at every moment, and an *ongoing* relationship to the Constituting Power becomes the key." See "'Psychologi-cal Fragments': Kierkegaard's Religious Psychology," in *Kierkegaard's Truth: The Disclosure of the Self*, ed. Joseph H. Smith (New Haven: Yale University Press, 1981), 260. Stephen Crites provides a similar perspective in Connell and Evans, eds., *Foundations of Kierkegaard's Vision of Community*, 154: "God is the primal ground, not of causality, not even of being, but of that possibility that is the ever-renewed birthplace of free spiritual relation." See also C. Stephen Evans, "Human Persons as Substantial Achievers," *Philosophia Reformata* 58 (1993): 110: "The doctrine of creation is crucial here. Creation makes it possible for Kierke-gaard to see persons as *beings* who are called to achieve. Without creation one would have only an achievement theory, which would amount to a rebellious expression of human autonomy. With creation, one can recognize human nature and human personhood as substantial realities."

6. See "The Soul as a Plurality," in Leslie Paul Thiele, *Friedrich Nietzsche and the Poli-tics of the Soul* (Princeton: Princeton University Press, 1990), 51–65.

ral. Anti-Climacus lays out a series of stages of consciousness, beginning with the least developed. The lowest form of despair, and also the most common, is ignorance of having an eternal self, ignorance of being intended as spirit. Life in this mode is dominated by the sensate and the psychical and never rises to the level of the truly spiritual. It is as if the human being were like a house with a basement and two floors; the basement is the level of the instinctual, the physical (programmed responses to external stimuli); the first floor is the psychical, the cultural (thought enters in, but only the thoughts of the "others"); the second floor is the spiritual, the inward (the realm in which the particular individual becomes aware of the eternal and the infinite). In the lowest form of despair, the individual, who, after all, owns the house, prefers to live in the basement and only makes brief forays to the first floor and then returns to the basement. He will become indignant toward and consider an enemy anyone who points out the existence of the second floor and the possibility of a visit there. Why? Because to do so murders his happiness (SUD, 43). The angst that underlies spiritlessness is recognized precisely by its sense of apparent security. Such "security" may derive from the person's attempt to rest in and merge with an abstract entity such as the "state," but this is only another expression of an underlying despair (SUD, 46).

Anti-Climacus suggests that there are two principal forms of conscious despair: despair in weakness and despair in defiance. The first form can be broken down once again into two subforms, despair over the earthly or over something earthly, and despair of the eternal or over oneself.

With the first subform, there is a consciousness of despair, but only as a result of adverse external factors. Despair is not perceived as originating in the self. Instead, something happens to the self, in the immediacy of its relation to the environment, which makes the self despair (SUD, 51). The individual submits to this "bad luck," plunges into despair, and hopes for a rescuer. If such help does arrive, if "good luck" comes his way, then he revives and is happy once again—he picks up where he left off, but without realizing that he has not yet become a self. The second subform under the category of despair in weakness is despair of the eternal or over oneself. The essential difference between this form and that just depicted is that there, the individual was in despair over the earthly or something earthly, while here the individual knows that it is weakness to despair over the earthly and yet remains entrenched in despair over his inability to do otherwise. He is in despair over his weakness (SUD, 61). He becomes more clearly conscious that his despair is *his*, that it is *he* who is attributing such significance to the earthly, that it is *he* who has lost the eternal and himself with it, but he remains paralyzed in this consciousness. "If a person is to despair over himself, he must be aware of having a self; and yet it is over this that he despairs, not over the earthly or something earthly, but over himself" (SUD, 62).

The next step in the intensification of despair is the cross-over from weakness (in despair not to will to be oneself), to defiance (in despair to will to be oneself).

The person is very definitely conscious of being an infinite self, but he despairingly wills to be an abstract form of the self, severed from the Power that established it (SUD, 68). The self wants "to be master of itself or to create itself," to shape its own nature and destiny, and thus must defiantly reject the concrete self that is contingent upon God.[7] Here we see once again the doctrine of creation, but as it is inverted by the demonic self, which attempts to be its own creator: "He does not want to put on his own self, does not want to see his given self as his task—he himself wants to compose his self by means of being the infinite form" (SUD, 68). In despair the self enjoys making itself, developing itself, being itself, and it gives itself honor for this magnificent achievement.[8]

In this way, Anti-Climacus has understood Nietzsche better than Nietzsche understood himself. "The more consciousness there is in such a sufferer who in despair wills to be himself, the more his despair intensifies and becomes demonic" (SUD, 71–72). The sense in which *The Sickness unto Death* describes Nietzsche is expressed well by Gregor Malantschuk:

> We must conclude that Nietzsche went the way of offense in every respect with such consistency and thoroughness that no one, in his own words, could ever rival him. That Nietzsche never managed to achieve that emancipation from a relationship with the eternal, which was precisely the aim of the overman, is, however, quite another matter. His unfinished war with the eternal can be taken as a direct confirmation of the truth of Kierkegaard's conception that man is a combination of the temporal and the eternal.[9]

---

7. These comments by Libuse Miller reveal a deep and accurate understanding of Kierkegaard:

> So the formula for despair in all its forms is to be in despair over oneself and in that despair to will to be rid of oneself. In the parlance of a more recent psychology, despair is the attempt to substitute an idealized, imaginary self for one's real self, precisely in order not to have to be, or to admit that one is, the real self, that particular *given* which one has been saddled with by "nature" without the slightest regard for one's own wishes in the matter. It is the "givenness" that is offensive when the relation to the Giver is negative, and in defiance the self tries desperately to be a self of its own choosing. Hatred of the real self is thus a hidden form of the hatred of God. . . . This is basically a contest of right and power between man and God; which of them has the right and power to create a self?

See *In Search of the Self* (Philadelphia: Muhlenberg Press, 1962), 256.

8. See Thiele, *Friedrich Nietzsche and the Politics of the Soul*, 86: "'The noble soul has reverence for itself.' The higher man, then, is the bearer of a higher egoism, a love of his own individuality."

9. See Gregor Malantschuk, in Howard A. Johnson and Niels Thulstrup, eds., *A Kierkegaard Critique* (Chicago: Henry Regnery, 1967), 127.

Nietzsche is the supremely *conscious* atheistic philosopher. Anti-Climacus suggests that at an earlier point the defiant person in despair might have wanted to be rid of his agony, but now it is too late, now he would rather rage against the universe than do anything else, and he must have his torment with him to prove his rightness. No one must be allowed to take it away from him. Eternity, truth, and goodness now become his greatest enemies because they, and only they, can separate him from his cherished justification over against the world and God. "What demonic madness—the thought that most infuriates him is that eternity could get the notion to deprive him of his misery" (SUD, 72).

Demonic despair is the most intense form of this last category: in despair to will to be oneself. The self, instead of willing to be a self-created image of its own perfection, wills to be itself in imperfection and misery, as an expression of its hatred and resentment toward existence. Defiance receives its highest potentiation in spite and malice, and these are directed most essentially toward the self itself. Thus Anti-Climacus speaks of the person who has "obtained evidence" against the goodness of existence, this evidence being "he himself." The corrupt self refuses to hear anything about repentance, healing, and transformation, because that would undermine his rebellion and defiance. The self that has ruined itself insists upon remaining in a ruined state:

> Rebelling against all existence, [the self] feels that it has obtained evidence against it, against its goodness. The person in despair believes that he himself is the evidence, and that is what he wants to be, and therefore he wants to be himself, himself in his torment, in order to protest against all existence with his torment. Just as the weak, despairing person is unwilling to hear anything about any consolation eternity has for him, so a person in such despair does not want to hear anything about it, either, but for a different reason: this very consolation would be his undoing—as a denunciation of all existence. Figuratively speaking, it is as if an error slipped into an author's writing and the error became conscious of its self as an error—perhaps it actually was not a mistake but in a much higher sense an essential part of the whole production—and now this error wants to mutiny against the author, out of hatred toward him, forbidding him to correct it and in maniacal defiance saying to him: No, I refuse to be erased; I will stand as a witness against you, a witness that you are a second-rate author. (SUD, 73–74)

With these words Anti-Climacus ends his psychological analysis of the forms of despair. It is difficult to imagine a more perceptive critique of Nietzsche. Eric Voegelin echoes this critique in his writings:

> Only in recent years have I developed the concept of the "egophanic revolt," in order to designate the concentration on the epiphany of the ego as the fundamental experience that eclipses the epiphany of God in the structure of Classic

and Christian consciousness. . . . The discovery of man had to be paid for by the death of God, as this phenomenon was called by Hegel and Nietzsche.[10]

From the point of view of *The Sickness unto Death*, we can see that Nietzsche is comprehended within Kierkegaard's authorship as the philosopher, par excellence, of individualistic aestheticism in defiance of God the Creator.[11]

The Definition of Sin

Karl Barth's small book *Christ and Adam* puts forward the thesis that if we want to know what "human nature" is, we cannot simply look around at human beings and observe their behavior. Nor can we study history in general to find the answers. All that we can see along this line of enquiry is the heritage of Adam, the fallenness of the human race. But fallenness does not define human nature, it is a perversion of human nature. If we want to know what human nature truly is, we have only one source of knowledge: Christ. In Barth's words, "the *special* anthropology of Jesus Christ . . . constitutes the secret of 'Adam' also, and so is the *norm* of *all* anthropology" (36). He then claims that Adam can only serve as a representative of the fallenness of the human race, as "one among others." But Adam "cannot be their lord and head; he cannot determine their life and their destiny" (115). Barth concludes that Christ is the definition of the universally human because "it is in His humanity that we have to recognize true human nature in the condition and character in which it was willed and created by God" (116).

In making this argument, Barth points in the direction of a distinctively theological approach to social theory. A secular approach to reflection on "human nature" will not place a priority on any one individual in relation to others; it will simply scan human history broadly in an attempt to discern intelligible patterns. Perhaps it will find such patterns, perhaps not. But a theological approach to anthropology begins with an acceptance of a special source of knowledge, a reve-

---

10. Eric Voegelin, *Autobiographical Reflections* (Baton Rouge: Louisiana State University Press, 1989), 67–68.

11. See Gregor Malantschuk, in Johnson and Thulstrup, eds., *A Kierkegaard Critique*, 124: "Nietzsche belongs to the class of people who have knowledge of the eternal but who wish to remain within the sphere of the aesthetic and make the aesthetic the one reality. It is therefore understandable that from this position he is forced to attack trends which go beyond the aesthetic. With Socrates and Judaism there arose an awareness of the eternal which placed the aesthetic on a lower plane, and it is interesting to note that Nietzsche is much concerned with these two phases in the history of the world and that he adopts a polemic and deprecatory attitude towards them—in complete contrast to Kierkegaard."

lation, which is embodied in a particular person. The person of Christ reveals true human nature; it is in contrast with him that we can understand fallen and distorted human nature.

I suggest that Barth is describing here, unwittingly, the basic anthropological vision at work in *The Sickness unto Death*. We turn now to the second half of Anti-Climacus's treatise, in which he presents his understanding of the Christian doctrine of sin, to see how these ideas are developed.

"Sin is: *before God, or with the conception of God, in despair not to will to be oneself, or in despair to will to be oneself.* Thus sin is intensified weakness or intensified defiance: sin is the intensification of despair" (SUD, 77). That despair is sin had been the implication of all that was said previously by Anti-Climacus; now it is out in the open. Gradations in the degree of consciousness, which had been the basis of earlier distinctions, were seen in the comparison of person with person; the distinguishing criterion was within the realm of the human. But now the criterion is the "theological self," the self directly before God, and the starting point is the truth that every sin, before it is a sin against others is, first and last, a sin against God:

> God is not some externality in the sense that a policeman is. The point that must be observed is that the self has a conception of God and yet does not will as he wills, and thus is disobedient. Nor does one only occasionally sin before God, or, more correctly, what really makes human guilt into sin is that the guilty one has the consciousness of existing before God.
>
> Despair is intensified in relation to the consciousness of the self, but the self is intensified in relation to the criterion for the self, infinitely when God is the criterion. In fact, the greater the conception of God, the more self there is; the more self, the greater the conception of God. Not until a self as this specific individual is conscious of existing before God, not until then is it the infinite self, and this self sins before God. (SUD, 80)

Anti-Climacus suggests that specific *sins* such as murder, stealing, debauchery, and so on, are merely surface forms of the deeper state that is *sin*. Sin in its most fundamental form is avoidance of obedience to God with regard to "every clandestine desire and thought"; it is an unwillingness to "hear and understand" the voice of God which communicates the divine will for the individual (SUD, 82). From this perspective, it becomes apparent that the opposite of sin is not virtue but faith, because faith is present when the self "rests transparently in God."

Philosophers such as Nietzsche sometimes claim to be offended by Christianity because it is so dark and gloomy and is always talking about sin and is "anti-life," and so on, but Anti-Climacus suggests that the actual source of this offense is the perception that Christianity is too high, its goal is too strenuous, it wants to make each human being into something so extraordinary that the mind cannot grasp it (SUD, 83). Christianity teaches that every single individual human being, regardless of occupation, gender, race, wealth, talent, age, and so forth, exists *before God*; every single individual is invited to live on the most intimate terms with God the Creator.

Anti-Climacus has led his reader to the point at which a decisive statement can be made. Christianly understood, *sin is not a negation but a position* (SUD, 96). Sin ought not to be understood only in negative terms, as "weakness, sensuousness, finitude, ignorance, etc." Sin is defiance of God. In this sense it is positive; it is a position taken by the individual. For Nietzsche, "sin" can only mean not willing to be oneself; "sin" cannot be a position, because there is no Creator against which one can take up a defiant attitude.

For Anti-Climacus, the state of sin, the continuation of sinful separation from God, is itself a new sin, and every moment this sin remains unrepented is also a new sin (SUD, 105). Thus Anti-Climacus describes the continuity of sin as the negative parallel of the continuity of faith. The sinner, as a consequence of his sin, is blind to sin's continuity, which is the true problem underneath the particular sins that are committed. Such blindness results in a "shallow triviality" that oscillates from day to day between despair and happiness without ever achieving a meaningful sense of "self-consistency" (SUD, 107).

For the believer, one who lives his life in the consistency of the good, even the slightest sin is feared profoundly, because it represents a breakdown of this consistency, and the loss of the infinite good. For the sinner, however, who is most dramatically illustrated by the demoniac, the inner consistency of sin must be maintained at all costs. When such a one is approached by the good, he pleads that the good pass him by, leave him alone, not speak to him, because he knows that the good is the ultimate threat to his continuation in sin (SUD, 108). That sin wants to become internally consistent is the manifestation of despair's intensification: the new sin of despairing over one's sin. Sin is like crossing the bridge to the other side of the canyon; despairing over one's sin is like burning the bridge to prevent the possibility of return. The first is the break with the good and the second is the break with repentance. Despair over sin is "an effort to give stability and interest to sin as a power by deciding once and for all that one will refuse to hear anything about repentance and grace" (SUD, 110).[12]

When the self is placed directly before Christ, despair is intensified once more and becomes the sin of despairing of the forgiveness of sins, which is offense:

> A self directly before Christ is a self intensified by the inordinate concession from God, intensified by the inordinate accent that falls upon it because God allowed

---

12. Karl Barth: "We know and rightly understand our sin only when we have realized it to be enmity against the grace of God. And we turn from our sin only when we return to the grace of God." *Church Dogmatics*, ed. G. W. Bromiley and T. F. Torrance (Edinburgh: T & T Clark, 1956–1969), II/1, 357.

himself to be born, become man, suffer, and die also for the sake of this self. As
stated previously, the greater the conception of God, the more self; so it holds
true here: the greater the conception of Christ, the more self. Qualitatively a
self is what its criterion is. That Christ is the criterion is the expression, attested
by God, for the staggering reality that a self has, for only in Christ is it true that
God is man's goal and criterion, or the criterion and goal.—But the more self
there is, the more intense is sin. (SUD, 113–114)

This passage parallels Barth's central idea in *Christ and Adam*. Christ is the individual's "criterion and goal." Christ defines true human nature. The distortion
of human nature that Anti-Climacus describes in his treatise is revealed most
clearly as a shrinking back from the words and example of Christ. More specifically, Christ's offer of divine forgiveness to the sinner calls him forward into
human maturity. By rejecting this call, he is preventing himself from becoming
an integrated, whole person before God.[13]

Still another intensification of sin is possible, the sin of dismissing Christianity
completely, of declaring it to be untruth. Here the self is at the highest intensity of
despair, which brings about a change in the "tactics." Instead of the way of simple
evasion, which characterized the lower forms of despair, now the corrupt self
switches over from "the defensive to the offensive." Now the struggle against God's
grace becomes an "offensive war"; now sin is attacking (SUD, 125). At this point
in his treatise, Anti-Climacus has led his reader to the place where the death of
Christ can be set in context:

> The existence of an infinite qualitative difference between God and man con-
> stitutes the possibility of offense, which cannot be removed. Out of love, God
> becomes man. He says: Here you see what it is to be a human being; but he adds:
> Take care, for I am also God—blessed is he who takes no offense at me. As man
> he takes the form of a lowly servant; he shows what it is to be an unimportant
> man so that no man will feel himself excluded or think that it is human status
> and popularity with men that bring a person closer to God. No, he is the insig-
> nificant man. Look this way, he says, and know for certain what it is to be a
> human being, but take care, for I am also God—blessed is he who takes no of-
> fense at me. Or the reverse: The Father and I are one; yet I am this simple, in-
> significant man, poor, forsaken, surrendered to man's violence—blessed is he
> who takes no offense at me. (SUD, 127–128)

---

13. See Abrahim Khan's article, "Kierkegaard's Conception of Evil," *Journal of Religion
and Health* 14 (1975): 64: "The Kierkegaardian literature indicates that, to be fully human,
man must secure the eternal within him, for man is 'compounded of the temporal and the
eternal.' He has within him something eternal, which he can lose. To 'lose the eternal tem-
porally' is to sin, and hence to deny oneself full human development."

What does it mean to take offense at Christ? It means to reject the call of creation, the divine pull that seeks to draw the individual forward into fullness of life. It is this rejection that led to the crucifixion of Christ, and the basic spiritual condition of the human race has not changed since his day.

Ego-Protection

The concept of "ego-protection" serves well to summarize the basic insights articulated in *The Concept of Anxiety* and *The Sickness unto Death*. Human beings do not have a determined psychology; we are continually coming into being. This situation leads to angst, the state out of which sin arises. The "leap into sin" involves a turning of the creature away from God in an effort to control the process of creation and lessen the discomfort of angst. "Sin" thus entails a hardening of the individual's psychological structure; the ego becomes a kind of "shell" within which the individual hides in an attempt to evade the possible further development of the self. In this state, the self seeks to protect itself from the future, that is, it continually seeks to fend off the possibility that it could "die to itself" and be reborn in a different, more mature formation.[14]

When the desire of the ego to protect itself from the possibility of its own growth becomes the dominant factor of the individual's character, then the individual is choosing to live in despair. The *demonic* is the term used to describe human existence when the attempt to avoid the possibility of the breakdown of the ego has reached the level of panic. Thus Kierkegaard says in the journals that "man prefers to be free from the kind of liberation which God and Christianity have in mind, yes, defends himself against it at any price." To be demonic is "to pray to be free from being saved"(JP, 2: 1277–1278 [1854–1855]). Consider also this passage:

> To despair over one's sin indicates that sin has become or wants to be internally consistent. It wants nothing to do with the good, does not want to be so weak as to listen occasionally to other talk. No, it insists on listening only to itself, on having dealings only with itself; it *closes itself up within itself*, indeed, locks itself inside one more inclosure, and *protects itself* against every attack or pursuit by the good by despairing over sin. It is aware of having burned the bridge behind it and of thereby being inaccessible to it, so that if in a weak moment it should itself will the good, that would still be impossible. Sin itself is severance from the good, but despair over sin is the second severance. This, of course, squeezes the uttermost demonic powers out of sin, gives it the profane toughness or perverseness that must consistently regard everything called repentance and grace not only as empty and meaningless but also as its enemy,

---

14. This is the principal thesis in the writings of Fritz Künkel and M. Scott Peck.

as *something against which a defense must be made most of all,* just as the good defends itself against temptation. (SUD, 109 [*emphasis added*])

Notice here the acoustic metaphor that is central to Kierkegaard's anthropology. The demonic insists on listening only to itself. It must close itself off from the voice of God, because that voice is the Word of creation. Even though the voice of creation is a quiet voice, it calls with a persistent, subtle invitation that puts pressure on the individual (pressure to move forward through the experience of angst). From the perspective of the demonic ego, this invitation must be drowned out. Another passage from *The Sickness unto Death* may be considered in this context:

> And now in our enlightened age, when all anthropomorphic and anthropopathic conceptions of God are inappropriate, it is still not inappropriate to think of God as a judge comparable to an ordinary district judge or judge advocate who cannot get through such a complicated and protracted case—and the conclusion is that it will be exactly like this in eternity. Therefore, let us just stick together and make sure that the clergy preach in this way. And should there happen to be an individual who dares to speak otherwise, an individual foolish enough to make his own life concerned and accountable in fear and trembling, and then in addition makes himself a nuisance to others—then *let us protect ourselves* by regarding him as mad or, if necessary, *by putting him to death.* If many of us do it, then there is no wrong. It is nonsense, an antiquated notion, that the many can do wrong. What many do is God's will. . . . It is just a matter of continuing to be many, a good majority who stick together; if we do that, *then we are protected* against the judgment of eternity. (SUD, 123–124 [emphasis added])

Here it is utterly clear that, for Kierkegaard, the basic motivation which underlies violence against a witness for the truth, such as Christ, is the human desire to avoid existence before God, because such an existence places a demand upon individuals to grow in spiritual maturity. It is this possibility of growth that is being fended off in the act of violence.

Another perspective on the theme of ego-protection appears in *For Self-Examination*, the location of Kierkegaard's memorable parable of the king who gives a royal edict, only to find that instead of being obeyed, it meets with a plethora of scholarly interpretations. For our purposes, the salient point of this passage is the motivation for the evasion:

> And God's Word—what is it intended to be and into what have we changed it? All this interpreting and interpreting and scholarly research and new scholarly research that is produced on the solemn and serious principle that it is in order to understand God's Word properly—look more closely and you will see that it is in order to defend oneself against God's Word. (FSE, 34)

This is Kierkegaard's critique of the established Church as he knew it. In his view, the Gospel has a great potential to transform individuals and societies. This potential is feared and resisted, not just by the "heathen," but more decisively by "Christians." Christians do not want to undergo the changes necessary if they were to follow the way of Christ. Therefore they evade recognizing themselves in the mirror of the Word. They seek to protect themselves: that is, they seek to preserve the present shape of their egos, because the angst of transformation is too much to bear.

Judge for Yourself! echoes the same theme. Here the focus has shifted from the commandments of Christ to the person of Christ. The sinful human race asks how it can "get rid of him." He can't simply be declared "insane" because he is too powerful for "the whole contemporary age; he has wounded them too deeply." The human race must defend itself against him with "the category of guilt." He will be condemned for blaspheming God (JFY, 176). Here, Kierkegaard is pointing to the psychological need to construe the scapegoat as *guilty*, as deserving exclusion from the community. Kierkegaard is identifying the underlying motivation of violence—the desire to defend oneself against the possibility of "being spirit" (JFY, 175).

To sum up: we have arrived at the insight that resistance to the possibility of spiritual growth gives rise to violence. It is not simply the case that individuals fail to become psychologically integrated; they are actively evading the possibility of becoming psychologically integrated. Sin is not a negation but a position. It is this active evasion, this willful sloth, that is the most basic root of the impulse to attack another human being. A more complete exposition of this insight is the subject of the next chapter.

4

THE KIERKEGAARDIAN
UNDERSTANDING OF VIOLENCE

Love to God and love to neighbor are like two doors that open
simultaneously, so that it is impossible to open the one without
opening the other, and impossible to shut one without also shutting
the other.

JP, 3: 2434 (1851)

We sometimes become most angry when he wants to do us the most
good.

TM, 270

"God is love." "In this world
love is hated."

"Ego-protection" is the attempt of human beings to evade the ongoing process of
creation. At root, this evasion stems from angst concerning the possibility of spiritual growth. *The state of sin that arises out of angst expresses a person's perception of
the Creator as a threat to the ego.* For Kierkegaard, this perception is mistaken. God
is love. God seeks to draw all human beings forward into genuine spiritual maturity. God desires and intends the maximum of human flourishing. Therefore, the
person who attempts to evade God's call because it is perceived as a threat is *mistaken at the core of his being.*[1] This mistakenness is so deep and so subtle that most
people live their lives without even being aware that this type of mistakenness is

---

1. See Karl Barth, *Church Dogmatics,* ed. G. W. Bromiley and T. F. Torrance (Edinburgh:
T. & T. Clark, 1956–1969), IV/1, 489: "It is inevitable that to the man who has become guilty
before God, but who has not fallen from Him and cannot escape from Him, God should
appear as an enemy when He encounters him." See also Keith Ward, *Religion and Creation*
(Oxford: Oxford University Press, 1996), 262: "Christians believe that all people are created by a God of supreme love, so that they might find their fulfillment in unity with divine
love. They are created with an inherent longing for love, for relationship with God, in which
true happiness lies. This means that the way of destructive self-regard is a form of pathology, an ignorance of what true fulfillment and happiness are and of the presence of God as
Creator."

possible. Kierkegaard's thought is a kind of archaeological enquiry, seeking to unearth and bring to light this deepest stratum of human disorder.[2]

Kierkegaard's theological archaeology of consciousness is developed most fully in his second authorship. We can see it, for example, in chapter 4 of "The Gospel of Sufferings" (UDVS, 264–288). In this discourse, Kierkegaard meditates on the story of the crucifixion, more specifically on the saying of the robber: "We are receiving what our deeds have deserved, but this one has done nothing wrong."

The words of the robber point to the goodness and truthfulness of Christ. In Christ it can be seen that God is love. Since this robber rightly acknowledges the character of God, he will be with Christ "in paradise." His sins will be forgiven; his spirit will be made whole. But the other robber, who mocked until the end, is a sign of the undoing of the human personality. He represents fundamental doubt concerning the love of God. In Kierkegaard's words, "It must be said of the person who gave up his faith in God's love that he is suffering the shipwreck of eternity's joy of living." The person who gives up on God, who believes that external circumstances can harm him in some decisive way—"that person has suffered damage in the innermost joint in a human being." Kierkegaard develops the nautical simile. Faith in the reality of God's love is "the divine joint in a human being. . . . If it holds it makes him the proudest sailing ship, but if it is loosened it makes a wreck of him and thereby makes the content of his whole life a futility and miserable vanity" (UDVS, 269).

In this discourse Kierkegaard suggests that when human beings adopt a fundamental attitude of mistrust toward God, when they do not believe that God is love, then they succeed only in undoing their own character. The motivation of "self-protection" paradoxically leads to a collapse of the spiritual integrity of the self. This is the case because the psychological soundness of the self is inherently dependent upon the openness of the self in its relationship with the Creator. We are reminded here of Christ's words, "He who saves his life will lose it" (Matt. 16:25).

In *Works of Love* we find further reflections on this theme: God's love for humanity, and humanity's distrust and evasion. In the discourse entitled "Love Is the Fulfilling of the Law," Christ is portrayed as the fulfillment of the law of God because his love for other human beings was constant and creative; "his love was

---

2. See John Milbank, *The Word Made Strange* (Cambridge: Blackwell, 1997), 230: "Whereas Augustine had discovered original sin to be pride and desire, Luther and then Kierkegaard claimed that the desire to command, desire to possess and prideful delight in domination of others all originate in a still more original *fear* that the unknown is not to be trusted, so requiring legal security in ourselves." Milbank's footnote to this sentence refers the reader to *The Concept of Anxiety*. See also Emil Brunner, *Man in Revolt*, 74: "Being-for-love is not one attribute of human existence among others, but it is human existence itself. Man is man to the exact extent in which he lives in love. The degree of his alienation from love is the degree of his inhumanity."

sheer action" (WL, 99). He loved the wayward and uncomprehending disciples; he loved Mary and Martha; he loved the blind and the demon-possessed; he even loved those who placed him on the Cross. In Christ's love there was no selfish desire to take what belonged to another. "What Christ required of him was solely the other person's benefit, and he required it solely for the sake of the other person" (WL, 100). The kind of love that Christ showed through his life is not the same as the kind of "love" that is common in the world. Kierkegaard expresses this idea in these summary sentences:

> Worldly wisdom is of the opinion that love is a relationship between persons; Christianity teaches that love is a relationship between: a person—God—a person, that is, that God is the middle term. . . . To love God is to love oneself truly; to help another person to love God is to love another person; to be helped by another person to love God is to be loved. (WL, 106–107)

The worldly conception of love renders itself untrue by removing God from the relationship of love. When God is removed in this way, human relationships can function as hiding places for the self which is afraid of spiritual growth. To allow God to be the middle term in the relationship is disastrous for the self which is afraid of the future, because God is the loving Creator whose desire is the continual upbuilding of the human being. Thus, from the point of view of the fearful ego, God's love is a threat. There is a kind of "logic" to be discerned here, although it is the "logic" of sin:

> These are the circumstances: the highest degree of self-love the world also calls self-love; the self-love of the alliance the world calls love; a noble, self-sacrificing, magnanimous, human love that still is not Christian love is ridiculed by the world as foolishness; but Christian love is hated, detested, and persecuted by the world. (WL, 120)[3]

In *Practice in Christianity*, the world's rejection of God's love is discussed in relation to John 12:32, "And I, when I am lifted up from the earth, will draw all to myself." The fourth discourse on this verse works with the idea that every human life is an examination (PC, 183). Christ, the prototype for what it is to be a human being, seeks to draw all people into the way of life which he himself has demonstrated. This drawing is an examination, a test of the ability of persons to love as Christ loved. The person who seeks to pass this examination, the Christian, will learn certain important truths in the course of his life. He will learn that the power that governs and directs human life is love (PC, 189). But in this world, there are

3. David Gouwens also addresses this theme in *Kierkegaard as Religious Thinker* (Cambridge: Cambridge University Press, 1996), 221–224.

forces that rebel against God's Governance. Thus, in this world the truth is victo-rious only through suffering (PC, 194). That the truth is persecuted is a "fright-ful" discovery, but it is the most valuable insight gained by the Christian as he journeys through life, drawn forward by the image of the loving one who died on the Cross. As the Christian seeks to walk in the pattern set by Christ, he will find that he is treated in the same way that Christ was treated:

> If this Christian did not have the prototype to look at, he would not persevere, he would not dare to believe there was any love within himself when people testify against him in this way. But the prototype, who eternally knew in himself that he was love, whom therefore no world, not the whole world, could shake in this certainty, has expressly manifested that love is hated, truth is persecuted. Be-cause of this image before his eyes, the Christian perseveres in abasement, drawn to him who from on high will draw all to himself. (PC, 197–198)

In *For Self-Examination* as well, we find the idea that love is not loved in this world. In part three, on the Holy Spirit, Kierkegaard comments on John 6:63, "It is the Spirit who gives life." Here we see very clearly the idea that spiritual/ psy-chological growth is a painful process. According to the New Testament, the new life that is given by the Spirit can only be received by those who have died to them-selves. The Spirit gives "a life on the other side of death." For Kierkegaard, the death of the old self is actually brought about by the Spirit: "The life-giving Spirit is the very one who slays you." We could rephrase this idea by saying that the process of creation is the cause of the angst experienced by the individual, but the same process calms that angst and calls the individual forward into greater maturity. Kierkegaard says that the self hangs onto nothing as tightly as its selfishness; the self does not want to go through the painful experience of having its selfishness dethroned (FSE, 76–78).

Kierkegaard continues the discourse by describing the way the Spirit brings to the believer who has died to the world three things: faith, hope, and love. The apostles, who had been given these gifts, discovered that loving the world as Christ did led to rejection and suffering. "Everything grew black around them" when they discovered that in this world "love is not loved, that it is hated, that it is mocked, that it is spat upon, that it is crucified in this world and is crucified while judging justice calmly washes its hands and while the voice of the people clamors for the robber." The apostles persevered, however, following Christ, and "resolved to love, to suffer, to endure all things, to be sacrificed in order to save this unloving world" (FSE, 84–85).[4]

---

4. See also JP, 1:612 (1849), which reinforces this idea: "Only the Christian is *hated*; he must be destroyed and in the basest way, as no criminal is destroyed." According to news accounts, the teenage boys who went on a shooting rampage in Colorado (Columbine High School, April 1999) killed some of their classmates because they were Christians.

I have been surveying Kierkegaard's theme, "In this world love is hated." Most fundamentally, the love to which Kierkegaard refers is the love of God for his creatures, that love which draws them forward into human maturity. When Kierkegaard says that this love is hated, he is suggesting that if we seek to understand the negative aspects of human behavior, we need to begin with a consideration of the relationship between the individual and God the Creator. When human beings express hatred toward other human beings, they are making manifest their state of inward alienation from God. The misrelation of the self to God has negative ramifications for the coherence of the self and for the relations of the self with others. Of course, the most dramatic and significant historical event which manifests this misrelation of the self with God is the crucifixion of Christ.

Kierkegaard's Understanding of the Cross

We return once again to *Works of Love*, this time to the discourse entitled "Our Duty to Love Those We See." The discourse begins with the assertion that the need for love is deeply grounded in the nature of human beings. The fact that human beings are created in the image of God entails that this need for love expresses the divine nature. Indeed, we see this need in the life of Christ:

> So deeply is this need rooted in human nature, and so *essentially* does it belong to being human, that even he who was one with the Father and in the communion of love with the Father and the Spirit, he who loved the whole race, our Lord Jesus Christ, even he humanly felt this need to love and be loved by an individual human being. (WL, 155)

Kierkegaard uses this observation to begin consideration of the relationship between Christ and Peter. Christ's love is abiding; it is not fickle and changeable from moment to moment. Christ loves others not because they are lovable, but because he consistently loves the person he sees, the actual human being with whom he is confronted at a given time. Kierkegaard draws from this the following formulation: "*When this is the duty, the task is not to find the lovable object, but the task is to find the once given or chosen object—lovable, and to be able to continue to find him lovable no matter how he is changed*" (WL, 159). In human terms, we would expect that Peter's betrayal of Christ would lead Christ to abandon Peter. In "the world" rejection is met with rejection. Yet Christ does not live according to the way of the world. He is the God—man; he is the incarnation of the divine love that governs human life.

In this context, Kierkegaard articulates an extraordinary redescription of the scene in which Christ is beaten and mocked:

If your life had been brought to the most crucial decision and you had a friend who on his own initiative loudly and solemnly swore loyalty to you, yes, that he was willing to risk his life for you, and then in the moment of danger he did not stay away (that would have been almost forgivable)—no, he came, he was present, but he did not lift a finger; he calmly stood there and looked on—yet, no, he did not stand calmly; his one and only thought was to save himself and on any condition; he did not even take flight (that would have been almost forgivable); no, he remained standing there as a spectator, which he made sure he could be, by denying you—what then? We shall not even trace the consequences; let us only describe the situation rather vividly and speak quite humanly about it.

So, then, you stood there accused by your enemies, condemned by your enemies; it was literally true that you stood surrounded on every side by enemies. The mighty, who perhaps could have understood you, had hardened themselves against you; they hated you. Therefore you now stood accused and condemned, while a blinded, raging crowd howled insults at you, even rejoicing insanely at the thought that your blood would be upon them and upon their children. And this pleased the mighty, who themselves usually held the crowd in deep contempt; it pleased them because it gratified their hatred that it was brute savagery and the lowest meanness that had found in you its quarry and its prey. You had reconciled yourself to your fate, were conscious of the impossibility of saying one single word, since derision was merely seeking an opportunity. Thus a magnanimous word about your innocence, as if it were defiance, would give derision a new occasion; thus the clearest proof of your integrity would make derision even more indignant and furious; thus a cry of pain, as if it were cowardliness, would give derision a new occasion.

In this way you stood cast out of human society and yet not cast out; after all, you stood there surrounded by human beings, but not one of them all saw in you a human being, although in another sense they did see in you a human being, because they would not have treated an animal as inhumanly. What horror, more terrible than if you had fallen among wild beasts, for I wonder if even the wild, nocturnal howling of bloodthirsty beasts of prey is as horrible as the inhumanity of a raging crowd. I wonder if one beast of prey in a pack can incite another to greater savagery than is natural for each one separately in the way that one human being in the impenitent crowd can incite another to even more than animal bloodthirstiness and savagery. I wonder if the spiteful or flashing eyes of the most bloodthirsty beast of prey have the fire of evil that is ignited in the individual's eyes when he, incited and inciting, rages with the wild crowd!

In this way you stood—accused, condemned, insulted; you sought in vain to discover a form that still resembled a human being, to say nothing of a kind face upon which your eyes could rest—and then you saw him, your friend, but he denied you. And the derision, which had been strident enough, now sounded as if echo had amplified it a hundred times! (WL, 168–169)[5]

The most extraordinary feature of this passage is the way in which it asks the reader to imagine *being in the place of Christ* as he was suffering the violence of the crowd. Normally, religious piety would preclude such a possibility. How could a person imagine being Christ, the Savior? One could perhaps imagine being a disciple, or a soldier, or a member of the crowd. Yet Kierkegaard has such a strong sense of the *humanity* of Christ that it is natural for him to establish a connection between the believer and Christ in a context such as this, an act of scapegoating. Because scapegoating is a phenomenon with many historical examples, it is not out of place to ask the Christian to imagine being a scapegoat. Indeed, according to Kierkegaard's understanding of Christian faith, this is precisely what disciples should expect if they are authentic witnesses to the truth. Kierkegaard is not asking his reader to imagine being the Savior of the world, but to imagine being in the place of one who is being killed unjustly, one who is receiving the violence of the crowd which is untruth. Kierkegaard is thus taking for granted the idea that truth is on the side of the victim. The Gospels do not portray an act of scapegoating from the point of view of the persecutors, but from the point of view of the victim. This passage from *Works of Love* presupposes this insight and brings it home to the reader in a powerful way. Here the reader is not merely being given a philosophical framework for the interpretation of history; the reader is actually brought to feel the truth of the Gospels by being transported into the place of the sacrificial victim. (It will become clearer in the next chapter why I am tempted to say that this passage is more Girardian than the writings of Girard himself. As a description of the psychology of the crowd at the moment of sacrificial frenzy, it is nothing less than astonishing.)

We turn next to the *Christian Discourses*, which also express Kierkegaard's interpretation of the Cross. In the first discourse of part IV, for example, Kierkegaard reflects on Luke 22:15, "I have longed with all my heart to eat this Passover with you before I suffer." A consideration of the sacrament of communion leads Kierkegaard to say that "*sin* is the corruption of the nations and of every human being" (CD, 258). "The whole world lies in evil," which is a truth that is not normally perceived by human beings; they must be taught this by a revelation. This is followed by a passage in which Kierkegaard imagines himself as a follower of Jesus, as he also is forced by the "savage glances" and the accusations of the crowd to betray Christ:

Above all, I will recall the experience of the Holy One when he walked here upon earth, what opposition he suffered from sinners, how his whole life was sheer

---

5. A parallel journal entry is found at JP, 3: 2926.

suffering of mind and spirit through belonging to the fallen human race, which he wanted to save and which did not want to be saved, that a living person chained to a corpse cannot suffer more tortuously than he suffered in mind and spirit by being embodied as man in the human race! I will bear in mind how he was mocked, and how everyone was received with great applause when he could think up a new insult, how there was no longer any mention, to say nothing of thought, of his innocence, of his holiness, how the only mitigating words that were spoken were the commiserating words: See what a man!

Suppose I had lived at the time of that dreadful episode, suppose I had been present in "the crowd" that insulted him and spat upon him! Suppose that I had been present in the crowd—I dare not believe that I among a whole generation would have been one of the twelve—suppose that I had been present! Well, but neither can I think it of myself that I would have been present *in order* to take part in the mockery. But just suppose that the bystanders became aware of me, that I was not taking part—ah, already I see those savage glances, see the attack turned for a moment against me; already I hear the cry, "He, too, is a Galilean, a follower; kill him, or make him take part in the mockery, in the people's cause!" . . . Good heavens, then I certainly would have taken part in the mockery—in order to save my life I would have screamed with the others, "His blood be upon me"—in order to save my life. . . . I would have acted no better than the crowd of people! (CD, 259–260)

Here again we find an acute sensitivity to the psychology of the lynch mob. The crowd has a need to kill its victim—a need that has arisen out of its own dynamics, without any reference to the actual guilt or innocence of the one being killed. The crowd demands *unanimity* and will turn anyone who does not support that goal into another victim. The one who does not cooperate in this lynching is seen as a dangerous threat—a threat to the crowd's interpretation of reality, which is actually a lie. The basic motivation of the mob is demonic fear of spiritual transformation.

There is a journal passage that is the most direct statement I have found in Kierkegaard of the thesis that the roots of violence are to be found in resistance to the possibility of spiritual growth. This passage is mentioned in the Introduction above, in which Kierkegaard asks why Christ was crucified:

How Did It Happen That Christ Was Put to Death?
I can answer this in such a way that with the same answer I show what Christianity is.
What is "spirit"? (And Christ is indeed spirit, his religion is of the spirit.) Spirit is: to live as if dead (to die to the world).
So far removed is this mode of existence from the natural man that it is quite literally worse for him than simply dying.
The natural man can tolerate it for an hour when it is introduced very guardedly at the distance of the imagination—yes, then it even pleases him. But if it is moved any closer to him, so close that it is presented in dead earnestness as

a demand upon him, then the self-preservation instinct of the natural life is aroused to such an extent that it becomes a regular fury, as happens through drinking, or as they say, a *furor uterinus*. In this state of derangement he demands the death of the man of spirit or rushes upon him to slay him. (JP, 4: 4360 [1854])[6]

Here we see, perhaps more clearly than anywhere else, that the basic motivation for violence is the impulse toward self-protection on the part of the immature ego. This impulse is in turn triggered by the demand of the spirit to live in ongoing communion with God the Creator, a continual pressure on the individual that produces angst. The human attempt to calm the angst by doing away with its source is the starting point of violence. The drama of human rejection of the possibility of spiritual growth is most clearly revealed in the crucifixion of Christ. This event has a key place in history because it manifests human sin as directed against the Creator and motivated by the desire to avoid the ongoing process of creation. It is clear, however, that other acts of violence in history, such as the killing of the prophets and the apostles, have the same basic motivation. The Cross is thus seen by Kierkegaard as an interpretive key, rather than as an utterly unique occurrence that could be placed fantastically on the outside of human history.

The Self's Violence toward Its Other

Our Kierkegaardian theory of violence needs to be refined one step further. We have established that the starting point of violence is resistance to the possibility of spiritual growth. But we can ask more specifically: Why does this resistance lead to the desire to do away with another human being? What is the connection between internal evasion and external violence?

Stephen Dunning's interpretation of *The Concept of Anxiety* is very helpful in this regard. He shows that Haufniensis's work analyzes angst as arising out of the ambiguous relationship between the self and the other. Using language that borders on René Girard's concept of mimetic desire, Dunning describes the "individual's search for self in the other," arguing that "the origin of anxiety is the search for self in another self." He continues: "Anxiety is a matter of the dialectic of self and other. It originates when the self seeks itself in an other, and it can be characterized as the state of a self that is other ('a stranger') to itself. Anxiety is the root and result of alienation, understood as a distorted relationship to oneself

---

6. Along similar lines, see JP, 3: 2921.

and to others."[7] Dunning turns our attention to the precise subject at the heart of a Kierkegaardian understanding of violence. The concept of angst expresses the misrelation of the self to itself, *which is inevitably expressed in misrelations with others in the world.* The "entangled freedom" of angst leads to the entanglement of human lives in the sin-distorted history of the human race.

Further light on this area of theological-psychological enquiry is found in Kierkegaard's early discourses entitled "The Expectancy of Faith" and "To Need God Is a Human Being's Highest Perfection." In the first discourse he describes the person who "battles with the future" as having a "dangerous enemy" since he is "battling with himself":

> The ability to be occupied with the future is, then, a sign of the nobility of human beings; the struggle with the future is the most ennobling. He who struggles with the present struggles with a particular thing against which he can use his total energy. Therefore, if a person had nothing else with which to struggle, it would be possible for him to go victoriously through his whole life without learning to know himself or his power. He who battles with the future has a more dangerous enemy; he cannot remain ignorant of himself, since he is battling with himself. The future is not; it borrows its power from him himself, and when it has tricked him out of that it presents itself externally as the enemy he has to encounter. No matter how strong a person is, no person is stronger than himself. . . . When a person struggles with the future, he learns that however strong he is otherwise, there is one enemy that is stronger—himself; there is one enemy he cannot conquer by himself, and that is himself. (EUD, 17–18)

This discourse leads the reader to consider the idea that there is a relationship between struggles against various "enemies" whom a person perceives in the external world, and the person's struggles with his own spiritual future. If warfare and violence seem to be interminable in human history, this may have something to do with the inability of the self to overcome itself.

In the other discourse Kierkegaard draws a contrast between the "first self," by which he means the hardened shell of the anxious ego, and the "deeper self," which is the more mature self God is calling into being. The first self perceives the possibility that the deeper self represents, and it recoils in the desire for self-protection:

> When a person turns and faces himself in order to understand himself, he steps, as it were, in the way of that first self, halts that which was turned outward in hankering for and seeking after the surrounding world that is its object, and

---

7. This and the previous quotes are found in Stephen Dunning, *Kierkegaard's Dialectic of Inwardness* (Princeton: Princeton University Press, 1985), 148–150.

summons it back from the external. In order to prompt the first self to this with-drawal, the deeper self lets the surrounding world remain what it is—remain dubious. This is indeed the way it is; the world around us is inconstant and can be changed into the opposite at any moment, and there is not one person who can force this change by his own might or by the conjuration of his wish. The deeper self now shapes the deceitful flexibility of the surrounding world in such a way that it is no longer attractive to that first self. Then the first self either must proceed to kill the deeper self, to render it forgotten, whereby the whole matter is given up; or it must admit that the deeper self is right, because to want to predicate constancy of something that continually changes is indeed a con-tradiction, and as soon as one confesses that it changes, it can, of course, change in that same moment. However much that first self shrinks from this, there is no wordsmith so ingenious or no thought-twister so wily that he can invalidate the deeper self's eternal claim. There is only one way out, and that is to silence the deeper self by letting the roar of inconstancy drown it out. (EUD, 314)

The first self, as resistance to creation, seeks to do away with (to kill) the deeper self and the possibility that it represents. It must either do this or admit that the deeper self is right and allow the claim of the eternal to come forward.[8]

The struggle between the first self and the deeper self is expanded upon in *Works of Love*. Here Kierkegaard describes preferential love as being, in reality, a form of infatuation with oneself. The person who thinks he has "fallen in love" with an-other is in error; he is actually in a solipsistic relationship with himself, because preferential love only loves the other insofar as the other fulfills the needs and desires of the self. Preferential love is not the genuine neighbor love that God com-mands; it is a form of egoism in which the neighbor is not truly encountered. The "first I" who loves in this manner is loving the "other I" in the other (WL, 57–58). In other words, preferential love does not allow an escape from the psychological prison of the immature ego.

But what Kierkegaard calls preferential or spontaneous love "can be changed into its opposite, into *hate*" (WL, 34–35). The individual who has not allowed his soul to become rightly ordered through hearing the command of God is an inher-ently unstable person. His self is entangled and conflicted. Therefore he may love the other one moment and hate the other the next, a vacillation that occurs be-cause he may solipsistically love himself one moment and suicidally hate himself the next. Just as love of the other under these conditions is actually love of one-

---

8. Bruce Kirmmse echoes this idea: "One's natural and spiritual selves are thus totally divided against one another. It is as though it were a struggle between two different people and the question was who one would become." See *Kierkegaard in Golden Age Denmark* (Bloomington: Indiana University Press, 1990), 466.

self, so also hate of the other is actually hatred directed toward the self.[9] At this point we have reached the most profound core of the Kierkegaardian understanding of "man's inhumanity to man."

The call of God is the call of creation. The deeper, truer, more mature form of selfhood is a possibility toward which God is always drawing the individual. But insofar as the individual is actively resisting the call of creation, he is existing in a state of inner conflict. He loves himself and seeks to maintain control over his own selfhood, and he hates the pressure that is being placed upon him to become a more mature person. He hates this possibility. Because it is impossible to kill a possibility, or to kill the Creator, the sinful human being becomes immensely frustrated at his inability to prevent his creation.[10] In his anger over his inability to kill his deeper self, he develops a need to kill other human beings. He subconsciously construes the other person as a representation of that which he is trying to kill within himself. Instead of addressing his internal alienation as his own problem, he projects his anger out into the world. To attack the Other, the Enemy, becomes a psychological need for the sinful person, as he seeks to avoid becoming *an other to himself*, that is, a new self. *The most basic root of ill will toward others is ill will toward the self that one is in the process of becoming.*

When an entire society is made up of persons who exist in this psychological state, the society as a whole acts on the basis of this spiritual sickness. The society develops a need to identify and attack an Enemy. The society selects scapegoats and sacrifices them as a way of reinforcing its impulse to ego-protection. George Steiner develops this insight perceptively in his work *In Bluebeard's Castle*, which shows clearly the influence of Kierkegaard on his thinking:

The Book of the Prophets and the Sermon on the Mount and parables of Jesus which are so closely related to the prophetic idiom, constitute an unequaled act of moral demand. . . . *We hate most those who hold out to us a goal, an ideal.* . . .

The genocide that took place in Europe and the Soviet Union during the period 1936–45 . . . was far more than a political tactic, an eruption of lower-middle-class malaise, or a product of declining capitalism. It was no mere secular, socioeconomic phenomenon. It enacted a suicidal impulse in Western civi-

---

9. Dostoevsky portrays this ambivalence profoundly, as René Girard notes: "Dostoevsky's art is literally prophetic. He is not prophetic in the sense of predicting the future, but in a truly biblical sense, for he untiringly denounces the fall of the people of God back into idolatry. He reveals the exile, the rupture, and the suffering that results from this idolatry. In a world where the love of Christ and the love of the neighbor form one true love, the true touchstone is our relation to others. It is the Other whom one must love *as oneself* if one does not desire to idolize and hate the Other in the depths of the underground." *Resurrection from the Underground: Feodor Dostoevsky*, trans. James G. Williams (New York: Crossroad, 1997), 129.

10. See CD, 66–67 and 172–173, on humanity's attempt to "kill God."

lization. It was an attempt to level the future—or, more precisely, to make history commensurate with the natural savageries, intellectual torpor, and material instincts of unextended man. (42–46)

In other words, the killing of the social Other results from the internal alienation and spiritual sloth of the individuals who make up the society.[11]

In this light we can discern that the psychology of violence is a precisely inverted image of the Great Commandment, "You shall love God with your whole heart, and your neighbor as yourself."[12] The violent person does not love God but lives with a fundamental distrust of God and the ongoing process of creation; he does not love the self that he is called to become; and he thus develops the need to turn his neighbor in the world into an enemy, an alien other which he must kill in order to preserve his own "life."

My approach to understanding the roots of violence is not entirely original. I am happy to say that a kind of "cloud of witnesses" argue along similar lines. It remains the case, however, that this approach has not permeated human consciousness in general. If it had, the world would be a very different place. I recall, for instance, a news story about a disgruntled employee at the Connecticut State Lottery office who went on a shooting rampage. The governor, interviewed on television, said, "We will never understand senseless acts of violence such as this." This sort of fatalism is not necessary.

I will present now a sampling of this theme in various authors, Owen Barfield discusses schizophrenia in the modern world in these terms:

---

11. This idea is echoed by Karl Barth: "It is because man is not at one in himself that we are not at one with each other. It is because inner consistency and continuity are lacking in the life of the individual that there is no fellowship among men." *Church Dogmatics* (Edinburgh: T. & T. Clark, 1957), II/2, 726–727. Sergio Cotta finds the roots of violence in the "dizziness" produced by modern nihilism and its exaltation of subjectivity in alienation from the human Other: "The Other, excluded from the participation in my own being and, therefore, from dialogue and no longer worthy of respect, is reduced either to raw material, a passive object of my calculating and dominating will, or to a nonredeemable enemy. No longer my like, he is really my hell, the source and target of a hatred that in reality is fueled by the innumerable defeats and frustrations of which the subject itself is the cause because it cut itself off from its indispensable *partner*." Sergio Cotta, *Why Violence*, trans. Giovanni Gullace (Gainesville: University Presses of Florida, 1985), 134. There are significant insights here, but I am uncomfortable with Cotta's phrase "excluded from the participation in my own being," given that the theory I am articulating locates the roots of political violence in an inability to separate the other from participation in my own (conflicted) being.

12. Stanley Moore suggests that "SK sees the transcendence of God, which he puts in the very sharpest of terms, as the eternal point of reference without which there is no love of neighbor, no genuine involvement, but only hatred, bloodshed, and chaos." See "Religion as the True Humanism," *Journal of the American Academy of Religion* 37 (1969): 20.

What the self of each of us feels isolated *from*, cut off *from*, by its encapsulation in the nakedly physical reality presented to it by the common sense of contemporary culture, is precisely its own existential source. The trouble is, that such an empirical self, founded as it were on its own physical encapsulation, is a false self, *without* reality. It is the kind of self which behaviorist psychology has to mention occasionally, in order to deny its existence. The true Self of everyone remains united—not co-extensive but united—with its original source in the spirit. And the mental illness now recognized as schizophrenia comes of the frantic efforts, sometimes aggressive, sometimes defensive, made by the imprisoned personality to fortify and preserve this fictitious self—which is really a nothingness—from destruction. Instead—and that way sanity lies—of taking the hint, as it were, and learning to abandon it in favor of the true Self. The resulting conflicts and the sickness, sometimes amounting to insanity, that those efforts may end in, arise from an invasion of this artificial self by the true, existential self. The personality remains subconsciously aware of its ultimate dependence on this real self for its very existence, while consciously resisting its still, small voice with every cunning device it can invent. The patient's unstable behavior is thus a disguised form of evasive action. . . .

And if it is etymologically no more than a pun, it is nevertheless a profound truth, that it is only by remembering our source that we can hope to "*re-member*" our true selves in a truly human community, instead of building up all manner of defenses and strategies to defend our empty artificial selves by fortifying them in their isolation.[13]

From a very different corner of the intellectual landscape, we find Jean-Paul Sartre analyzing anti-Semitism in this way: "The rational man groans as he gropes for the truth . . . he is 'open.' . . . But there are people who are attracted by the durability of a stone. They wish to be massive and impenetrable; they wish not to change. Where, indeed, would change take them? We have here a basic fear of oneself and of truth."[14] M. Scott Peck's *The Road Less Traveled* precisely echoes the Kierkegaardian understanding of violence. In a passage that reminds the reader of Anti-Climacus's description of the difference between the "despair of weakness" and the demonic "despair of defiance," Peck writes this:

Some ordinarily lazy people may not lift a finger to extend themselves unless they are compelled to do so. Their being is a manifestation of nonlove; still, they are not evil. Truly evil people, on the other hand, actively rather than passively avoid extending themselves. They will take any action in their power to protect their own laziness, to preserve the integrity of their sick self. Rather than

13. Owen Barfield, *History, Guilt, and Habit* (Middletown: Wesleyan University Press, 1981), 52–53, 62.

14. Jean-Paul Sartre, *Anti-Semite and Jew*, trans. George J. Becker (New York: Schocken, 1948), 18–19.

nurturing others, they will actually destroy others in this cause. If necessary, they will even kill to escape the pain of their own spiritual growth. As the integrity of their sick self is threatened by the spiritual health of those around them, they will seek by all manner of means to crush and demolish the spiritual health that may exist near them.[15]

Sebastian Moore echoes Kierkegaard's understanding of the cross:

What we are refusing is not, directly at least, "obedience to God" but some fullness of life to which God is impelling us and which our whole being dreads. Some unbearable personhood, identity, freedom, whose demands beat on our comfortable anonymity and choice of death. Further, something that at root we *are*, a self that is ours yet persistently ignored in favor of the readily satisfiable needs of the ego. . . . The crucifixion of Jesus then becomes the central drama of man's refusal of his true self.

Moore then argues that the presence of the exceptionally good person brings out a basic resentment in those who are rejecting the possibility of spiritual transformation. To be called to "full personhood" is a challenge to "our mediocrity"; its protection "will require murder."[16] Raymund Schwager, a Girardian theologian, says this:

As analyzed by Girard, the unfounded nature of aggression is the consequence of a groundless act, the willful falling away from God. . . . The reason why anger so easily leaps from one object to another is that ultimately it does not focus on any of these objects. It is, at bottom, resentment against God. Because the free rejection of God's love is groundless, humans must hide their own actions from themselves so thoroughly that they do not even notice the enmity they harbor in their hearts.[17]

Consider, finally, another Girardian theologian, James Alison:

The fact that people hate [Jesus] and seek to do away with him, *even though they have seen the works which he carries out*, suggests that these people are not just made uncomfortable by him, but that they are in fact locked into a profound aversion to creation itself. They are clinging on to a form, futile, useless, and shot through with death, of incomplete creation, and resisting being completely

---

15. See *The Road Less Traveled* (New York: Simon & Schuster, 1978), 377–378. Peck expands further on this idea in his next book, *People of the Lie* (New York: Simon & Schuster, 1983).

16. See *The Crucified Jesus Is No Stranger* (Minneapolis: Seabury Press, 1977), x, 13.

17. See *Must There Be Scapegoats?* trans. Maria L. Assad (San Francisco: Harper & Row, 1987), 199.

created. . . . Jesus' self-giving up to death *is* the fulfillment of creation, the putting of creation into a state of labor, so that we also, by our creative imitation of him in the midst of the order of death can come to be the fully created creatures which God always wanted us to be, and with us, the whole of creation.[18]

This passage more closely parallels my central thesis in this book than any other passage I have found in the secondary literature on Kierkegaard and Girard.

We can now summarize the elements of a Kierkegaardian understanding of the roots of political violence: (1) creation is an ongoing process; (2) human beings experience the event of creation as the feeling of angst; (3) the root of sin is the attempt to manage angst by turning away from the Creator in an effort to stop the process of creation; (4) sin is not simply immaturity, but willfully reinforced immaturity; (5) the individual who is seeking to avoid becoming an other to himself develops the need to attack other human beings and turn them into scapegoats; and (6) the crucifixion of Christ is the historical event that most clearly reveals the roots of violence.

Thus far in my exposition I have focused on Kierkegaard's understanding of the individual's resistance to the possibility of his own spiritual growth as the most basic root of violence. I have referred in passing to the crowd as the collection of individuals who are seeking to evade the call of God, but this concept, which needs to be more extensively developed, is the subject of chapter 5. There I bring Kierkegaard's thought into dialogue with the writings of René Girard, who has made a major contribution to the task of understanding "the crowd" from a point of view informed by the New Testament.

---

18. James Alison, *Raising Abel* (New York: Crossroad, 1996), 73–74.

5

KIERKEGAARD AND GIRARD

The reason why the world does not advance but goes backward is
that men consult only with each other instead of each one
individually consulting with God.

JP, 4: 4148 (1848)

A group of people who will function only as a crowd, as *numerus*,
also really function only as a machine.

LD, 269 (1848)

Creation and Lack

René Girard is, in my opinion, the most significant theorist of violence in the twentieth century. Since I am interpreting Kierkegaard as a theorist of violence, it makes
sense to bring his thought into dialogue with Girard's. There has not been a large
quantity of secondary material written on this subject,[1] and Girard's works themselves contain only a few passing references to Kierkegaard.[2] This deficiency is

---

1. Cesareo Bandera, "From Girard to Shakespeare, Kierkegaard, and Others," *South
Central Review* 12 (1995): 56–68; works that make some reference (usually in passing)
to Kierkegaard and Girard include Gil Bailie, *Violence Unveiled* (New York: Crossroad,
1995); Robert Hamerton-Kelly, *Sacred Violence* (Minneapolis: Fortress Press, 1992); David
McCracken, *The Scandal of the Gospels* (New York: Oxford University Press, 1994), "Scan-
dal and Imitation in Matthew, Kierkegaard, and Girard," *Contagion* 4 (1997): 146–162;
George Pattison, *Kierkegaard: The Aesthetic and the Religious* (London: Macmillan, 1992);
Marjorie Suchocki, *The Fall to Violence* (New York: Continuum, 1994); Eugene Webb, *Phi-
losophers of Consciousness* (Seattle: University of Washington Press, 1988), and *The Self
Between* (Seattle: University of Washington Press, 1993).

2. See *Deceit, Desire, and the Novel*, trans. Yvonne Freccero (Baltimore: Johns Hopkins
University Press, 1965), 58; *The Scapegoat* trans. Freccero (Baltimore: Johns Hopkins University Press, 1986), 173; *To Double Business Bound* (Baltimore: Johns Hopkins University
Press, 1978), 26–27; *The Girard Reader*, ed. James G, Williams (New York: Crossroad, 1996),
268; and p. xi of Girard's "Foreword" to Robert Hamerton-Kelly, *The Gospel and the Sacred*
(Minneapolis: Fortress Press, 1994): "Mimetic theory is too realistic and commonsensical
to be confused with one more nihilistic stepchild of German idealism. And yet, unlike the
positivistic social sciences, it is not blind to paradox; it can articulate the intricacies of
human relations just as effectively as a Kierkegaard or a Dostoievsky."

unfortunate, since, as I hope to show in the following pages, these two authors do in fact have much in common. To view them together is a very fruitful enterprise.[3]

Girard does not write as a theologian, but as a literary critic and social philosopher. He is clearly a religious thinker, however, in that he states his goal as interpreting human behavior using the Bible as his epistemological starting point (see Book II of *Things Hidden since the Foundation of the World*). There is thus a certain ambiguity in his argument, as the reader is not clear whether he is trying to meet secular social scientists on their own turf, or trying to reject that turf entirely in favor of the Christian narrative. A more extensive discussion of this issue constitutes chapter 6, but initially we need to focus on the relationship between creation and human psychology.

We have seen that the idea of creation as an ongoing event forms the foundation of Kierkegaard's psychology as it is reflected in the concept of angst, which is the unique human emotion arising out of the ongoing experience of coming into existence. Is there a parallel idea in Girard? He does not refer to creation per se, but his analysis of mimetic desire begins with the idea of a basic existential lack. He suggests that individuals often feel inferior, anxious, afraid, uncertain. In Girard's words:

> When modern theorists envisage man as a being who knows what he wants, or who at least possesses an "unconscious" that knows for him, they may simply have failed to perceive the domain in which human uncertainty is most extreme. Once his basic needs are satisfied (indeed, sometimes even before), man is subject to intense desires, though he may not know precisely for what. The reason is that he desires *being*, something he himself lacks and which some other person seems to possess. The subject thus looks to that other person to inform him of what he should desire in order to acquire that being. If the model, who is apparently already endowed with superior being, desires some object, that object must surely be capable of conferring an even greater plenitude of being. (*Violence and the Sacred*, 145–146)

The idea of the Fall of humanity is present in Girard's thought, though in a subtle form. The Fall occurs when individuals turn to others for their definition of successful existence. Adam and Eve allowed the Serpent to convince them that there was something they lacked, some power or ability they needed to become more complete as human beings. The Serpent thus turned them away from a "vertical"

---

3. Those readers who are not already familiar with Girard may gain a general orientation to his thought through these books: *The Girard Reader*, James G. Williams, ed.(New York: Crossroad, 1996); James G. Williams, *The Bible, Violence, and the Sacred* (San Francisco: HarperCollins, 1991); Eugene Webb, *Philosophers of Consciousness: Polanyi, Lonergan, Voegelin, Ricoeur, Girard, Kierkegaard* (Seattle: University of Washington Press, 1988), 183–225.

relationship with God, toward a "horizontal" relationship with other people and with the intramundane forces that shape human life. Girard's thought as a whole can be understood as a very brilliant extended analysis of the results of the Fall, when seen in this light as a turn to the "horizontal." It remains the case, however, that Kierkegaard's thought provides deeper insights into the vertical dimension of human existence, which is essential to an understanding of the Fall.

Girard's psychological theory begins with the feeling of existential lack, the engine that drives mimetic desire and rivalry. But why do human beings have this feeling of lack? This is the kind of fundamental question that "empirical" social science cannot answer, just as "empirical" physical science cannot say what preceded the Big Bang. Kierkegaard's thought suggests a theological answer to this question. We have this feeling of lack because we are unfinished creatures.[4] We are immature. We have not yet arrived at the *telos* of our existence. We are involved in the ongoing process of creation. With this key perspective, Kierkegaard's thought shows how Girard's secular and horizontal theory can be developed to reach down into the deeper theological level of insight.

Mimetic Desire in
Kierkegaard's Thought

Girard argues that this feeling of existential lack drives human beings to imitate others. The self experiences itself as a negativity in comparison to a successful model who represents a greater fullness of being. The self does not have a center within itself; it is not content, at home, at peace with itself. This feeling of lack impels the person out into the social realm, where it is thought that a greater fullness of being can be gained by acquiring the goods or the power that others have. Can we find a parallel understanding of mimetic desire in Kierkegaard's thought? Mimetic desire is indeed a phenomenon important to Kierkegaard, and it is abundantly illustrated in the passages quoted in the following discussion. From this perspective, Kierkegaard's writings can easily be placed alongside the works of Cervantes, Flaubert, and Dostoevsky, as another example of the vision of human existence which Girard calls the "unity of novelistic genius."[5]

---

4. See Robert Hamerton-Kelly, *Sacred Violence*, 166.

5. *Deceit, Desire, and the Novel*, 245. Geoffrey Clive makes a similar comment: "*The Sickness unto Death* . . . happens to be the best and only worthy companion to *Letters from the Underworld*. What cries out for interpretation in Dostoevsky's narrative is clarified and resolved by Kierkegaard's brilliant analysis. Not only content-wise but linguistically as well this is one of the great marriages of minds inexplicable on superficial grounds, in modern intellectual history." "The Sickness unto Death in the Underworld: A Study of Nihilism," *Harvard Theological Review* 51 (1958): 135–167.

In *Upbuilding Discourses in Various Spirits*, Kierkegaard includes three discourses on one of his favorite themes, the lilies of the field and the birds of the air. The first of these is a meditation on Christ's teaching concerning "contentment with being a human being." If it were not anachronistic, one would be tempted to say that Kierkegaard wrote this discourse in response to Girard's analysis of the human condition. We find in this discourse the parable of the worried lily. According to the story, there was a lily who lived in an out-of-the-way place along with some other flowers and some nettles. One day a little bird came along and told the lily that in another place he had seen there were many other lilies who were more beautiful than she. In comparison with these other Crown Imperial lilies, the solitary lily "looked like nothing." Upon hearing this, the lily became very worried and upset. "The little bird had told it that of all the lilies the Crown Imperial was regarded as the most beautiful and was the envy of all other lilies" (UDVS, 168). So the lily asked the bird to peck the soil away from her roots and carry her to this place where the more beautiful lilies lived. "Alas, on the way the lily withered." Kierkegaard explains the parable:

> The lily is the human being. The naughty little bird is the restless mentality of comparison (*Sammenligning*), which roams far and wide, fitfully and capriciously, and gleans the morbid knowledge of diversity; and just as the bird did not put itself in the lily's place, comparison does the same thing by either putting the human being in someone else's place or putting someone else in his place. (UDVS, 169)

The moral of the story is that human beings ought to be content with their unique personhood as it has been created by God. To not be content is to become sick with "worldly worry," which leads to the mentality of comparison. In this discourse Kierkegaard uses the Danish word *Sammenligning* (comparison) in a way that exactly parallels Girard's concept of mimetic desire.

In chapter 4 we encountered a passage from *Works of Love* that I described as an astonishing portrayal of the scene of the crucifixion. In Kierkegaard's next book, *Christian Discourses*, one particular discourse is equally as astonishing for readers who are familiar with Girard's thought. This discourse, on "The Worry of Lowliness,"[6] contains an anthropological analysis that clearly anticipates Girard's social psychology. Here, Kierkegaard describes three modes of being, which are represented by the bird, the heathen, and the Christian. The bird represents the realm of nature (not the "restless mentality of comparison"); the heathen represents

---

6. Walter Lowrie translates the title as "The Anxiety of Lowliness." This is acceptable, but it is misleading now, given that a reader is likely to assume that the same word is being used here and in Kierkegaard's important book, *The Concept of Anxiety*. The word being used here is not *Angest*, however, but *Bekymring*, which means "worry, trouble, concern."

human sin; the Christian represents the life of faith. Kierkegaard's description of the behavior of the "heathen" is almost identical to Girard's description of "bad mimesis":

> It indeed seems as if in order to begin to be oneself, a human being first of all must be fully informed about what the others are and by that find out then what he himself is—in order to be that. But if he falls into the snare of this optical illusion, he will never become himself. (CD, 39 [*trans. modified*])

The basic elements of mimetic desire are clearly revealed here. The individual lacks a coherent self, and therefore he must look to others to define his self for him. Social mediation is at the heart of this form of existence. This way of living is false however: it is an illusion, a sickness. Kierkegaard continues along the same lines, while opening up the theological dimension of human existence:

> From "the others" a person of course actually finds out only what the others are—it is in this way that the world wants to deceive a person out of becoming himself. "The others" in turn do not know what they themselves are either but continually know only what "the others" are. There is only one who completely knows himself, who in himself knows what he himself is—that is God. And he also knows what each human being is in himself, because he is that only by being before God. The person who is not before God is not himself either, which one can be only by being in the one who is in himself. If one is oneself by being in the one who is in himself, one can be in others and before others, but one cannot be oneself merely by being before others. (CD, 40)

Here Kierkegaard clearly reveals the system of mimetic desire as a vicious circle that has no stopping point within itself. Through mimetic desire, the blind lead the blind; the sick are models for the sick; the ignorant teach the ignorant. Particular individuals may take a more active role at certain times and a more passive, imitative role at other times. But this system is closed; there is no exit from it on its own terms. The only genuine way leading out of this system is the way of religious transcendence. Here Kierkegaard and Girard are in complete accord.

This lack of being at the center of the self, what does it signify? It is a hole, an absence, a nothing, where there ought to be a coherent personal identity established in relation to the Creator. In other words, mimetic desire is a system of nothingness, it is a form of nihilism. Kierkegaard puts his finger on this aspect as well, in his description of the "heathen":

> This enormous weight, "all the others," weighs upon him, and with the doubled weight of despair; it does not weigh upon him by dint of the idea that he is something—no, it weighs upon him by dint of the idea that he is nothing. Truly, no nation or society has ever treated any human being so inhumanly that on the condition of being nothing one has to bear the burden of all; only the pagan, the

despairingly lowly one, treats himself so inhumanly. He sinks deeper and deeper into desperate care, but he finds no footing for bearing his burden—after all, he is nothing, of which he becomes conscious to his own torment by dint of the idea of what the others are. More and more ludicrous—oh no, he becomes more and more pitiable or, rather, more and more ungodly, more and more nonhuman in his foolish striving to become at least something, something, even if it is ever so little, but something that in his opinion is worth being.

In this way the despairingly lowly one, the pagan, sinks under comparison's enormous weight, which he himself lays upon himself. . . . And yet he wants to belong to temporality on the most wretched conditions; he does not want to escape it. He clings tightly to being nothing, more and more tightly, because in a worldly way, and futilely, he tries to become something; with despair he clings more and more tightly to that—which to the point of despair he does not want to be. In this way he lives, not on the earth, but as if he were hurled down into the underworld. . . .

—like the trapped bird when it hopelessly and fearfully struggles to its death in the net, just so the lowly pagan, even more pitiable, desouls himself in the captivity of nothingness. (CD, 45–47)

In a passage such as this, Kierkegaard is providing an anthropological vision of the roots of nihilism. When human beings cut themselves off from God, the source of their being, then they become empty internally.[7] Since there is no coherent center of personal identity within them, they are forced to look outward, to the others, as models for being in the world. But this going out reveals a lack of inwardness, it reveals a nothingness, it is driven by despair. Kierkegaard's poetic description of the bird that beats itself to death in the net is a powerful depiction of the phenomenon of suicide in modern culture. By extension it can also be applied to deaths that result from drug and alcohol abuse.

Despair is, of course, the main theme of *The Sickness unto Death*. Despair is defined there as misrelationship with the eternal. Despair is the self-willed state of alienation from God, the "power" that has established the self. In this work as well, we find close attention to the phenomenon that Girard has analyzed as mimetic desire:

---

7. This idea is also affirmed by Eugene Rose:

To fight the very God Who has created him out of nothingness requires, of course, a certain blindness as well as the illusion of strength; but no Nihilist is so blind that he fails to sense, however dimly, the ultimate consequences of his action. The nameless "anxiety" of so many men today testifies to their passive participation in the program of antitheism; the more articulate speak of an "abyss" that seems to have opened up within the heart of man. This "anxiety" and this "abyss" are precisely the nothingness out of which God has called each man into being, and back to which man seems to fall when he denies God, and in consequence, denies his own creation and his own being.

See *Nihilism* (Forestville: Fr. Seraphim Rose Foundation, 1994), 69.

> Whereas one kind of despair plunges wildly into the infinite and loses itself, another kind of despair seems to permit itself to be tricked out of its self by "the others." Surrounded by hordes of men, absorbed in all sorts of secular matters, more and more shrewd about the ways of the world—such a person forgets himself, forgets his name divinely understood, does not dare to believe in himself, finds it too hazardous to be himself and far easier and safer to be like the others, to become a copy (*en Efterabelse*), to become a number, within the crowd. (SUD, 33–34 [*trans. modified*])

The word that Anti-Climacus chooses here, *en Efterabelse*, could be literally translated into English as "an after-aper," a mimicker. In this work it is very clear that despair is not simply an individualistic phenomenon. Despair, as a psychological state, has definite sociological consequences. Despairing persons gather together to form a society constituted by the system of mimetic desire. The basic motivation that drives this system is the attempt of the individual to escape from the possibility of living before God, in a relationship that involves the ongoing development of the self. "The crowd" is a phenomenon that arises out of spiritual evasion; thus it does not express the "nature" of human beings as they were intended by God in creation. The crowd is a perversion of nature; it is social sickness that replaces what ought to be social health. Anti-Climacus continues in the same vein:

> He [the person in despair] now acquires a little understanding of life, he learns to ape after the others, how they manage their lives—and he now proceeds to live the same way. In Christendom he is also a Christian, goes to church every Sunday, listens to and understands the pastor, indeed they have a mutual understanding; he dies, the pastor ushers him into eternity for ten rix-dollars—but a self he was not, and a self he did not become. (SUD, 52 [*trans. modified*])

"Christians" within Christendom live in the same way as the "heathen." In both cases the demands of genuine selfhood are being evaded in favor of an easier existence that consists of the imitation of others. Christendom is a strange phenomenon, because it is a place where people are constantly hearing sermons on biblical texts, given by pastors who are supposedly witnesses to the truth of Christianity, yet no one is actually hearing and responding to the message. The way of mimetic desire is still operating as the basic principle of society.

We have seen that Kierkegaard is certainly aware of the same phenomenon that Girard has described as mimetic desire. The basic motive underlying this form of life is a refusal to grow into authentic existence as a self before God. This attitude could be described as spiritual sloth or cowardice. We turn now to an essay in which Kierkegaard develops this idea further in relation to social existence.

"The Crowd Is Untruth"

While mimetic desire is noticed by Kierkegaard, he did not develop a theory of violence out of it, as Girard has done. This significant difference between them demonstrates Girard's substantial originality as a thinker. Kierkegaard's understanding of violence, as I present it, focuses more directly on the spiritual condition of individuals, rather than on social groups. It would be a mistake, however, to fall into the common trap of assuming that Kierkegaard is a "radically individualistic" thinker who has no understanding of social realities. In fact, "the crowd" is one of the most important themes in his authorship.

Kierkegaard's phrase "the crowd is untruth" perfectly summarizes Girard's social theory. For Girard, the untruth of the crowd consists in the way it seizes upon a victim and kills him to meet its own psychological needs. The crowd prevents itself from descending into a chaos of self-destruction by choosing a scapegoat whose death will create a new sense of social unanimity and cohesion. The central goal of Girard's writings is to reveal and condemn the moral and psychological falsity of this form of "salvation." He accomplishes this revelation by applying a hermeneutic of suspicion to social phenomena. If a society puts people to death because of their alleged guilt, or strangeness, or subhuman nature, Girard sees the operation of a mechanism that grinds up individuals for the sake of a supposed greater social good. The scapegoat mechanism is one side of the great either/or of human existence: either a society will sacrifice victims to meet the psychological needs arising out of its "ontological sickness," or human beings will follow the way of the Kingdom of God, which is the way of love of the neighbor.

We should not be surprised to find an almost identical analysis of the human condition in the writings of Kierkegaard (even though he did not explicitly connect the phenomenon that Girard has named "mimetic desire" with "the scapegoat mechanism"). One particular location in the authorship shows this with complete clarity, the essay on the theme "the crowd is untruth," which has been published in English as "Concerning the Dedication to 'The Individual'" (PV, 105–112). This essay anticipates Girard's sociological hermeneutic of suspicion just as precisely as the portion of *Christian Discourses* quoted previously in this chapter (CD, 45–47) anticipates Girard's psychology of mimetic desire. Kierkegaard expresses the great either/or of human existence in this way:

There is a view of life which holds that where the crowd is, the truth is also, that it is a need in truth itself, that it must have the crowd on its side. There is another view of life; which holds that wherever the crowd is, there is untruth, so that, for a moment to carry the matter out to its farthest conclusion, even if every individual possessed the truth in private, yet if they came together into a

crowd (so that "the crowd" received any *decisive*, voting, noisy, audible importance), untruth would at once be let in. (PV, 106 [*my trans.*])[8]

Human beings may inhabit two basic epistemological stances. One option is
the way of the crowd; it generates its own "knowledge," the knowledge it needs
in order to carry out its internal mechanism. According to the crowd's "truth,"
the one who is being killed deserves to die. But there is a fundamentally different
epistemological stance, which sees through the falsehood of the crowd. This alternative way of knowing allows human beings to disentangle themselves from
the crowd and recognize its mendacity. The gateway into this way of knowing is
repentance, a turning away from the crowd toward the divine source of truth. The
crowd's way of knowing grows out of its deeply entrenched lack of repentance.
Kierkegaard describes the crowd as rendering "the single individual wholly unrepentant and irresponsible" and as weakening "his responsibility by making it a
fraction of his decision" (PV, 107).

The attitude of unrepentance described here is the same spiritual condition that
we have previously discussed as resistance to the process of creation. It could be
described as *spiritual sloth*, or as *cowardice*, which is the term Kierkegaard uses in
this essay:

> Never at any time was even the most cowardly of all single individuals so cow-
> ardly, as the crowd always is. For every single individual who escapes into the
> crowd, and thus flees in cowardice from being a single individual . . . contrib-
> utes his share of cowardice to "the cowardice," which is: the crowd. Take the
> highest, think of Christ—and the whole human race, all human beings, which
> were ever born and ever will be born; the situation is the single individual, as
> an individual, in solitary surroundings alone with him; as a single individual
> he walks up to him and spits on him: the human being has never been born
> and never will be, who would have the courage or the impudence for it; this is
> the truth. But since they remain in a crowd, they have the courage for it—what
> frightening untruth. (PV, 108)

---

8. The following quotations from this essay are all my own translation. As an example
of the point of view that Kierkegaard is attacking, consider these words of Hitler supporters
Wilhelm Stuckart and Hans Globke: "According to the National Socialist conception, it is
not individual human beings, but races, peoples, and nations that constitute the elements
of the divinely willed order of this world. The individual is rooted in his Volkdom as a fate.
The community of the Volk is the primary value in the life of the whole as well as of the
individual" (from George Mosse, ed., *Nazi Culture* [New York: Grosset & Dunlap, 1966], 330).
It should also be noted that without referring to Kierkegaard at all, Zygmunt Bauman has
confirmed the central thesis of Kierkegaard's essay. He argues that normal social science
works with the assumption that morality "is born of the operation of society and maintained
by the operation of societal institutions." This assumption "failed the test" of the Holocaust
badly and is no longer philosophically tenable. See *Modernity and the Holocaust* (Ithaca:
Cornell University Press, 1989), 198.

As we have seen, spiritual cowardice, resistance to creation, is the central theme of a Kierkegaardian understanding of the roots of violence. People hide in the crowd precisely because they are attempting to avoid becoming individuals before God. This movement into the crowd results in a social configuration that is by its very nature violent:

> The crowd is untruth. Therefore was Christ crucified, because he, even though he addressed himself to all, would not have to do with the crowd, because he would not in any way let a crowd help him, because he in this respect absolutely pushed away, would not found a party, or allow balloting, but would be what he was, the truth, which relates itself to the single individual. And therefore everyone who in truth will serve the truth, is *eo ipso* in some way or other a martyr. (PV, 109)

Girard's thought raises the question of how violence can be brought to an end. Clearly, the answer lies in communication of a message that reaches out to the members of the crowd and seizes them. What is needed is a word that lifts the person out of his cowardice and draws him forward into genuine existence as a human being. This is the message of Christ, according to Kierkegaard:

> The witness for the truth—who naturally will have nothing to do with politics, and to the utmost of his ability is careful not to be confused with a politician—the godfearing work of the witness to the truth is to have dealings with all, if possible, but always individually, to talk with each privately, on the streets and lanes—to split up the crowd, or to talk to it, not to form a crowd, but so that one or another individual might go home from the assembly and become a single individual. (PV, 109)

Christ speaks as an individual to individuals. Genuine communication takes this form because it conveys existential truth. Truth in this sense is not a matter of impersonal facts or knowledge, but a matter of ethical and spiritual wholeness as a person. Such truth can only be communicated by one person to another person, who is called into existence by the act of communication. Since this event is the creation of the person, God the Creator is always the "middle term" in the act of communication:

> It [the truth] cannot work through the fantastical, which is the untruth; its communicator is only a single individual. And its communication relates itself once again to the single individual; for in this view of life the single individual is precisely the truth. The truth can neither be communicated nor be received without being as it were before the eyes of God, nor without God's help, nor without God being involved as the middle term, since he is the truth. It can therefore only be communicated by and received by "the single individual," which, for that matter, every single human being who lives could be: this is

the determination of the truth in contrast to the abstract, the fantastical, impersonal, "the crowd"—"the public," which excludes God as the middle term (for the *personal* God cannot be the middle term in an *impersonal* relation), and also thereby the truth, for God is the truth and its middle term. (PV, 110–111)

The way of the crowd is the exact opposite of the way of the Kingdom, which is expressed in the commandment to love one's neighbor as oneself. The spiritual untruthfulness of the crowd renders it unable to recognize and love its victims as neighbors. The commandment to love is thus identical with the call to disentangle oneself from the crowd and to become oneself before God. Kierkegaard speaks to this theme as well:

And to honor every individual human being, unconditionally every human being, that is the truth and fear of God and love of "the neighbor"; but ethicoreligiously viewed, to recognize "the crowd" as the court of last resort in relation to "the truth," that is to deny God and cannot possibly be to love "the neighbor." And "the neighbor" is the absolutely true expression for human equality; if everyone in truth loved the neighbor as himself, then would perfect human equality be unconditionally attained; every one who in truth loves the neighbor, expresses unconditional human equality; every one who is really aware (even if he admits, like I, that his effort is weak and imperfect) that the task is to love the neighbor, he is also aware of what human equality is. But never have I read in the Holy Scriptures this command: You shall love the crowd; even less: You shall, ethico-religiously, recognize in the crowd the court of last resort in relation to "the truth." It is clear that to love the neighbor is self-denial, that to love the crowd or to act as if one loved it, to make it the court of last resort for "the truth," that is the way to truly gain power, the way to all sorts of temporal and worldly advantage—yet it is untruth; for the crowd is untruth. (PV, 111)

Kierkegaard concludes his essay with the thought that "no one is prevented from being a single individual, unless he prevents himself" by hiding in the crowd. It is possible for each person to "become what he is, a single individual" (PV, 112). Cowardice, sloth, and violence are not inevitable expressions of the human condition. The way in which the crowd tyrannically abuses "the weak and powerless one" may seem to be an unalterable status quo, but it is not. It can never be anything other than what it is—untruth. And human untruth is a temporal phenomenon that cannot forever withstand divine truth, the divine truth that was embodied by *the single individual*—Christ.

This survey of Kierkegaard's essay on the crowd may seem to imply that there is a substantial difference between Kierkegaard and Girard with regard to their respective starting points, the individual vs. the culture. Is it not the case that Kierkegaard is only concerned with individuals and Girard is only concerned with societies? Are they not miles apart at this point?

Actually, at the heart of Girard's thought we find the idea that mimetic desire results from a *failure of individuality*. It should be clear by now that this idea precisely parallels Kierkegaard's understanding of sin. For Girard, a culture organized around the principle of mimetic desire contains no true individuals; there are only continually shifting patterns of doubling, rivalry, social unanimity and breakdown, possession and psychosis. Christ was a single individual, but only because he stood outside of the culture of mimetic rivalry. Human beings in general are not individuals; they are the failure of individuality, as noted in *Things Hidden*:

> JEAN-MICHEL OUGHOURLIAN: If we follow your reasoning, the real human *subject* can only come out of the rule of the Kingdom; apart from this rule, there is never anything but mimetism and the "interdividual." Until this happens, the only subject is the mimetic structure.
>
> RENÉ GIRARD: That is quite right. (199)

Kierkegaard's understanding of sin also works with this concept of the failure of individuality. In *The Sickness unto Death* he describes the man who "in a deeper sense lacks a self." "The greatest hazard of all, losing the self, can occur very quietly in the world, as if it were nothing at all. No other loss can occur so quietly; any other loss—an arm, a leg, five dollars, a wife, etc.—is sure to be noticed" (SUD, 32–33). The result of despair is the loss of the self; or, put differently, the failure to become a self. The psychological analysis in *The Sickness unto Death* focuses on the resistance of human beings to the possibility of existence as a *subject*. There is a direct linkage between this resistance and the formation of the crowd. The "crowd" is in fact the place where people hide from God, which means that they are evading the task of becoming a true self, an authentic individual, before God. From this point of view, Girard echoes Kierkegaard.

The category of "the individual" is obviously central to Kierkegaard's thought. Commentators go astray, however, if they notice this fact and immediately conclude that Kierkegaard was an "individualistic" thinker. It needs to be always remembered that the category of the individual has a definite historical reference: Christ. Christ is the single individual. When Kierkegaard addresses his reader, in an effort to disentangle the reader from the crowd, he intends to establish a relationship between the reader and Christ, who is the paradigm of individuality. The person who has become an individual, through relationship with Christ, is a person who hears the commandment: "You shall love your neighbor as yourself." This commandment opens up the way to a new kind of society,[9] a community of love and respect for all

---

9. Stanley Moore comments: "The point SK is most concerned to emphasize is that it is precisely by virtue of the transcendent God's command 'Thou shalt love thy neighbor,' it is only before God, that the neighbor *comes to be*." See "Religion as the True Humanism," *Journal of the American Academy of Religion* 37 (1969): 19.

people, in distinction from "the crowd"—a society of collective egotism.[10] Thus we can see that an attempt to drive a wedge between Kierkegaard and Girard with reference to the words *individual* and *culture* does not succeed. Both thinkers have an understanding of defective individuality and defective sociality, and both have a vision of authentic individuality and true community.[11]

There may also be a connection between Kierkegaard and Girard with regard to the psychological ambivalence of mimetic desire. For Kierkegaard's pseudonym Haufniensis, angst is the most fundamental human emotion, and angst arises out of ambivalence. Angst is "a sympathetic antipathy and an antipathetic sympathy" (CA, 42). The person is both drawn toward a possibility and repelled by it. I have argued that the possibility in question here involves the development of the self. Through the process of creation, the self can become an other to itself. The self can change, grow, develop, be transformed. This possibility produces angst. We can establish a link with Girard's thought by suggesting that this angst uncovered by Haufniensis is not radically individualistic but interpersonal and social. Haufniensis himself stresses the point that "the whole race participates in the individual and the individual in the whole race" (CA, 28). In other words, the angst of the individual inevitably involves him in an ambivalent relationship not only with himself, but with other human beings as well. The "other" whom the individual can become is often confused, in angst, with the actual human other. In this light, we can suggest that the system of mimetic desire, as it has been analyzed by Girard, is in fact an extended explication of the Kierkegaardian concepts of angst, fall, and original sin.

Offense/Scandal

As David McCracken points out, "scandal" is not a commonly addressed theme in contemporary philosophy and theology.[12] The two most notable exceptions to this rule are Kierkegaard and Girard. A comparison of Kierkegaard's concept of "of-

---

10. See John Elrod, *Kierkegaard and Christendom* (Princeton: Princeton University Press, 1981), especially 114–118.

Like Socrates in the *Gorgias*, Kierkegaard believed that social and political injustice is rooted in human inwardness and lack of character. The creation of a just social order hinges on the reorientation of the other in the individual's self-consciousness. Any genuine change bringing about a really new social order requires the transformation of human self-consciousness, and in Kierkegaard's view such a transformation can only occur through the power of ethics and religion. (118)

11. On this theme in SK, see Vernard Eller, *Kierkegaard and Radical Discipleship* (Princeton: Princeton University Press, 1968), 201–212.

12. McCracken, *The Scandal of the Gospels*, 8.

fense" with Girard's comments on "scandal" will be very helpful in further illuminating the connections between these two authors.

Girard points out that the Greek word *skandalon* plays a key role in the New Testament. The reader who pays close attention to this word is likely to understand the psychological and theological core message of the gospel revelation. The root meaning of the word *skandalon* is obstacle, stumbling block, or snare. It implies a tripping up of someone or a hindering of their forward progress. Girard suggests that in the New Testament the meaning of the word has been transposed from the physical realm to the spiritual, interpersonal realm. It is other people who scandalize someone, to the extent that he is both alienated from them and fascinated by them. In other words, the *skandalon* is the fruit of the system of mimetic desire with "all its empty ambitions and ridiculous antagonisms." The *skandalon* is the product of the fundamental ambivalence of mimetic desire: the other whom I seek to copy is the fascinating model of greater fullness of being, but at the same time he is the rival who blocks my forward progress toward acquisition of that goal. The model is both an *attractive* force and at the same time a *repelling* force. Thus he becomes "an inexaustible source of morbid fascination" (*Things Hidden*, 416).

The word *skandalon* appears in certain key verses in the Gospel of Matthew (to take just one biblical book as an example). Matthew 11:6 is the verse that was crucially important to Kierkegaard: "Blessed is anyone who takes no offense at [is not scandalized by] me." Those who hear Christ's message in faith are freed from the system of mimetic desire; Christ is not an object of morbid fascination for them, but one who leads the way to a truly human and loving life. In Matthew 16:23, when Christ rebukes Peter for misunderstanding the meaning of his ministry, he says: "Get behind me, Satan! You are a *skandalon* to me; for you are setting your mind not on divine things but on human things." Peter was offended at the idea that Christ would suffer and die; he expected Christ to be a worldly leader and king. Peter misconstrues Christ as a ruler within the worldly realm of mimetic desire, rather than correctly perceiving Christ as showing the way to a genuinely alternative form of life. In reality, Christ was not a *conqueror*, but a *witness to the truth* in a world of untruth. One might think that Peter would have learned something from this exchange, but he apparently did not. In Matthew 26:31, just before he is arrested, Christ says: "You will all become deserters [literally: be scandalized] because of me this night; for it is written, 'I will strike the shepherd, and the sheep of the flock will be scattered.' . . . Peter said to him, 'Though all [are scandalized] because of you, I will never [be scandalized by] you.' Jesus said to him, 'Truly I tell you, this very night, before the cock crows, you will deny me three times.'"

The New Testament term *skandalon* appears as the concept of *offense* in Kierkegaard's thought. It is clear in *The Sickness unto Death* that sin is offense. And what is the basic meaning of offense? To take offense before God is to actively refuse to move forward into the future that God intends for the person. To take offense is to refuse to become oneself before God. Anti-Climacus's presentation of offense parallels the understanding of psychological ambivalence that Girard describes as the relationship between the individual and his model:

> What is offense? Offense is unhappy admiration. Thus it is related to envy, but it is an envy that turns against the person himself, is worse against oneself to an even higher degree. The uncharitableness of the natural man cannot allow him the extraordinary that God has intended for him; so he is offended. . . .
>
> To understand offense, it is necessary to study human envy. . . . Envy is secret admiration. . . . Admiration is happy self-surrender; envy is unhappy self-assertion.
>
> It is the same with offense, for that which between man and man is admiration/envy is adoration/offense in the relationship between God and men. (SUD, 86)

This is another passage which has remarkable resonances for the reader who is familiar with Girard. Anti-Climacus points to the interpersonal dynamics of mimetic desire but situates them in the context of the vertical relationship between the person and God. Ultimately, it is love that constitutes the health of the human spirit. To take offense at God's voice is to be uncharitable toward oneself, and the outworking of this is seen in the world of interpersonal relationships.

The three primary theological virtues, as specified by St. Paul, are faith, hope, and love. The coordination of Kierkegaard's thought with Girard's enables us to see these virtues more clearly in contrast with their opposites:

faith	hope	love
offense/sin	despair	hate/violence

The Sickness unto Death is a treatise on offense, sin, and despair. I have suggested how it lays the groundwork for an understanding of the psychological roots of violence. Girard has shown that the *skandalon* lies at the heart of the Gospel message. Both thinkers are pointing to the way of Christ which entails moving beyond offense to faith. The person of faith lives in openness to God the Creator and is thus able to meet the future with hope rather than with despair and evasion. The person of faith develops a character-structure that is held together by love—love of self, neighbor, and God.

6

ARE SECULAR PERSPECTIVES ON
VIOLENCE SUFFICIENT?

The true Christian view, that universally human existence does not
explain Christianity and that Christianity is not simply another
factor in the world, but that Christianity explains the world . . . this
is not understood.

JP, 3: 3276 (1839)

G irard's thought raises a question that it does not answer clearly. Is
Girard putting forward a secular explanation of the roots of violence, or a theological one? That is, can his concepts of mimetic desire and the
scapegoat mechanism be accepted by nonreligious thinkers as a valid and convincing theory? Or is he relying so heavily on a biblical epistemology that his theory
is not actually secular at all? Is it a Trojan Horse if it is accepted by nonreligious
thinkers, or not? Paisley Livingston answers this question in the negative:

> My own approach to religious phenomena can be characterized rapidly as
> Durkheimian in the sense that I assume that explanations of such matters
> should be sought exclusively at the sociological and psychological levels of
> description. This means that I do not need Girard's hypothesis that the scien-
> tific project is a "byproduct" of the "subterranean" Revelation being wrought
> by the Holy Scriptures. My assumption is that many of Girard's original insights
> into human interaction and motivation are logically separate from such theo-
> logical claims.[1]

This last sentence raises questions of its own. Livingston speaks of "Girard's original insights." But Girard himself clearly states that what he is saying is not original
in the sense that he is simply presenting ideas that are found in Shakespeare,
Dostoevsky, the Bible, and so forth. His particular way of coordinating and packag-
ing ideas has an originality to it, but Girard would strenuously reject Livingston's
statement concerning originality.

Livingston also uses the phrase "logically separate" to distinguish sociological
claims from theological ones. This, of course, begs the question of how it has come
about that human minds are able to be "logical," that is, where our *logos* comes

---

1. Models of Desire (Baltimore: Johns Hopkins University Press, 1992), xvii–xviii.

from. The Christian tradition has maintained that human beings are rational, logical, because we are created in the image of God, who is the ultimate source of reason and logic. When we come to understand reality through the development of our reason, we are growing up into our divine source. In Voegelin's language, we are becoming attuned to the truth of the created order, becoming aware of the untruth of its fallen disorder, and becoming spiritually related to creation's transcendent source. Livingston seems to believe that all of this theological nonsense can be dispensed with; reality can be understood in wholly secular terms, and he claims that Girard's thought contributes to this secular understanding. That he could make this claim reveals the very real ambiguity in Girard's thought. Girard seems to want to have it both ways. He wants secular thinkers such as Livingston to agree with what he says, but he also wants to argue that the truth he is bringing into philosophical articulation can be traced back to the mysterious event of divine revelation. In other words, Girard seems to believe that his thought both is and is not a Trojan Horse for secularism.

In my opinion, Girard ought to drop the pretense of adhering to the methodological atheism of social science, which has decreed that religious postulates are unacceptable foundations for understanding human behavior.[2] He ought to write straightforwardly as a Christian apologist and argue that a theological mode of knowing is required for real insight into human behavior. His writing and speaking have tended to move in this direction in recent years, placing him in company with Eric Voegelin, John Milbank, Alasdair MacIntyre, and others. These authors are forging a new paradigm for the philosophy of social science in the twenty-first century, one that allows for what George Marsden has called "the outrageous idea of Christian scholarship."[3] This idea suggests that a religious psychologist, sociologist, or historian does not need to wear one hat as a believer, and another agnostic hat as a "scientist" or "scholar." She can interpret human behavior from within the perspective of a theological tradition, without being intimidated by the forced agnosticism of the Enlightenment paradigm.

I am arguing that Kierkegaard should also be considered as a dialogue partner here. In my view, Kierkegaard was a theological social theorist.[4] In other words,

---

2. A classic statement of this mode of thought is found in Peter Berger, *The Sacred Canopy* (Garden City: Anchor Books, 1969), 179.

3. George M. Marsden, *The Outrageous Idea of Christian Scholarship* (New York: Oxford University Press, 1997).

4. Michael Plekon comments: "Kierkegaard, at the end and in the end is both a theologian and a social thinker. I would argue that for him the roles were inseparable. . . . Only in our century is it difficult to imagine theology and social thought as intimately related, even fused in the thought of one individual. Yet this is precisely how we must understand Kierkegaard's enterprise of Christian proclamation and anthropological contemplation." See "Moral Accounting," *Kierkegaardiana* 12 (1982): 80.

he sought to interpret the "empirical" data of human psychology and culture using a theological interpretive framework. One cannot remove human existence *before God* from Kierkegaard's thought and have something left that is authentically Kierkegaardian. Attempts to detheologize Kierkegaard inevitably fail.

Yet is it possible, as Livingston believes, that there can be a viable secular understanding of human behavior? There can be, in the simple sense that thousands of social scientists and philosophers in the modern era have put forward their views on human behavior without basing them on religious ideas. But are these views ultimately satisfying and convincing? This is the question I raise in this chapter.

It will be helpful at this point to examine two books: *Violence: Reflections on a National Epidemic* by James Gilligan and *What Evil Means to Us* by C. Fred Alford. Gilligan's book is ambiguous in its approach to understanding violence, and a careful consideration of this ambiguity will clarify the issues involved here. A reader who picks up this book for the first time is likely to assume that its perspective will be fully secular. Gilligan worked for many years as a prison psychiatrist, and one would expect his writing to conform to the dictates of methodological atheism. The initial chapters of the book, however, surprise the reader, in that they are saturated by religious language and imagery.

Gilligan paints a Dantesque picture of criminal violence and the world of the prison. He does not shy away from speaking of "dead souls" who are wandering through "hell." He frames his discussion in terms of good and evil, guilt, myth, ritual, and tragedy. He refers to Dante, Dostoevsky, the Book of Job, Cain and Abel, Shakespeare, and Melville. Gilligan does not limit himself to the arid methodological atheism of the scientific guild, as he himself states:

> In my effort to understand the psychology of violent men, I often find myself turning to mythic and tragic literature. Only the Greek tragedies and those of Shakespeare, the horrors described in Thucydides and the Bible, map with fidelity the universe of human violence that I have seen in the prisons. . . . Compared to the tragedies I see and hear daily, the abstractions of the "social sciences" seem like pale imitations of reality, like the shadows in Plato's cave. (57–58)

A religious reader like me is particularly impressed by two of the author's key themes: the fragility of selfhood and the need to "hear" what violence is saying. Gilligan's comments on selfhood have a Kierkegaardian ring to them at times. He describes the most violent criminals as men who "already feel numb and dead by the time they begin killing." He continues:

> For the violent, "death" neither waits for the death of the body, nor is it incompatible with the continued life of the body. Death refers to the death of the self, which has occurred while the body is still living. So we speak of them as "the living dead," biologically alive yet spiritually and emotionally dead. (36)

These men find the death of the self so intolerable that they prefer physical death (their own and other people's) to the continuation of the living torment that the rest of us refer to as "life." It is no exaggeration to say that violent men come to hate life—their own and other people's. . . .

Those who kill others do so in part because they cannot stand to think that others are alive while they are not, and they cannot bear their living death, either. (38)

Gilligan is summarizing here his reflections on many shocking case histories, and he clearly notices the same spiritual condition that Kierkegaard calls "the sickness unto death." He sees very clearly that violence arises out of a malformation of the self that is so severe that the individual is merely a warped shadow of the full human being he was created to be, and his existence in this condition becomes antilife. He no longer has the capacity to value the lives of others or his own life. Gilligan perceives very clearly the close connection between the homicidal mentality and the suicidal mentality: "The suicide rate among men who have just committed a murder is several hundred times greater than it is among ordinary men" (41). He knows that these two mentalities are two sides of the same coin, which is exactly what we learn from Kierkegaard.

The second key theme in this book, listening to what is being said in violent acts, is extremely important. Gilligan argues that the key to understanding violence lies in gaining the ability to interpret it as a kind of language. In his words:

Actions can precede and serve as substitutes for conscious thoughts. They can take the place of thinking in words, if the behavior is never interpreted or translated into words and ideas. The philosopher and literary critic Kenneth Burke wrote that in order to understand literature, we must learn to interpret *language as symbolic action*. I am suggesting that in order to understand violence we must reverse that procedure and learn to interpret *action as symbolic language*—with a "symbolic logic" of its own. (61)

Gilligan describes the most violent people as having a "verbal inarticulateness" that prevents them from understanding and expressing their motivations and their feelings. Their violent actions are a way of saying what they are not capable of saying. Thus it is not very fruitful to ask a violent person why he committed the violent act. The question presumes that he knows the answer, but this is not the case. If he provides any answer at all, it will be distorted through the lens of his malformed self. A true understanding of the motives at work will not be found in the violent person himself. But this does not mean that such a true understanding cannot be obtained. It can be articulated by an observer who is not suffering from the same spiritual sickness, one who can formulate in speech the feelings, fears, and impulses of the sick one. Gilligan sees himself as filling this role.

As a dramatic example of this process of interpreting violent action, Gilligan recounts the story of "Ross L.," a twenty-year-old man who ran into a female former high school classmate at a convenience store. His car was broken down and he asked her for a ride, which she gave him. During the ride he pulled out a knife, stabbed her to death, and then mutilated her eyes and cut out her tongue. He did not rape her or steal the car. What was the motivation behind the killing and the mutilation? Gilligan's interviews with the young man found him to have a powerful sense of his own "wounded innocence." He continually complained about how the whole world was conspiring against him; people were always talking about him behind his back and insulting him; the girl he killed had "looked at him" in the wrong way, and so forth. Gilligan came to understand that this man had an overwhelming sense of shame, weakness, and inadequacy. His character structure had been built up as a massive attempt to suppress these feelings and convince himself that he was a "real man." Apparently, his violent action was triggered by the circumstance of having to depend for help on a girl because he did not have the financial resources or the mechanical know-how to fix his own car. After the crime he bragged about it to an acquaintance, apparently attempting to impress him.

Gilligan interprets the language of violence being spoken here in this way:

> "If I destroy eyes, I will destroy shame" (for one can only be shamed in the [evil] eyes of others); in other words, "If I destroy eyes, I cannot be shamed"; and "if I destroy tongues, then I cannot be talked about, ridiculed or laughed at; my shamefulness cannot be revealed to others."
>
> The emotional logic that underlies this particular crime, then, which I called the logic of shame, takes the form of magical thinking that says, "If I kill this person in this way, I will kill shame—I will be able to protect myself from being exposed and vulnerable to and potentially overwhelmed by the feeling of shame." (65–66)

In commenting on this case history and many others that are equally shocking and disturbing, Gilligan gives voice to the language of violence and finds that it is speaking most loudly concerning the reality of shame.

I return to the theme of shame in the following discussion, but I want to stress first the importance of the insight being expressed here. To be able to articulate the hidden language of violence is the most difficult task facing those who seek to understand the human condition. It is at the same time the most fruitful path for finding a way out of the nightmare of violence in human history. In this book I seek the same goal. I attempt to show that the psychological roots of violence can actually be understood and articulated.

While Gilligan's book contains many important insights into violence, I must conclude that it is tragically flawed. The key fault of the book is the author's only half-hearted attempt to open up the discussion onto a religious plane. As I quoted earlier, Gilligan asserts that considers the Bible to be a source of knowledge of human action, but this claim is not carried through seriously. Girard's strength as a thinker lies in his ability to make this claim and carry it through with substantial force, but we do not see the same real engagement with the scriptural texts in Gilligan. (We do not see any evidence of Gilligan having read Girard, either, which is a lack of erudition crippling to his enterprise.) Gilligan remains bound within a fundamentally secular, horizontal perspective in which individual and interpersonal psychology form the only avenue of understanding. That the self exists before God, and that this is crucial to understanding the human condition, is an insight that seems outside of Gilligan's intellectual ken. While his comments on the "death of the self" may have a Kierkegaardian ring to them, they lack a full theological awareness of the vertical dimension of selfhood.

This lack is evident at certain key points in the book. For instance, while discussing the effects of child abuse on the psychology of the child, he observes:

> The self cannot survive without love. The self starved of love dies. That is how violence can cause the death of the self even when it does not kill the body.
> The two possible sources of love for the self are love from others, and one's own love for oneself. (47)

A third possible source of love, the love of God, the source of our existence as human beings, is clearly beyond Gilligan's sphere of conception at this point in his text. His argument here is so close to a correct understanding of the health of the soul as being constituted by its ability to give and receive love, and yet so far from the truth because of its inability to see that the root of violence is the human being's alienation from the love of God, the Creator. At another point in the text, Gilligan argues that

> . . . all violence is an attempt to achieve justice, or what the violent person perceives as justice, for himself or for whomever it is on whose behalf he is being violent, so as to receive whatever retribution or compensation the violent person feels is "due" him or "owed" to him, or to those on whose behalf he is acting, whatever he or they are "entitled" to or have a "right" to; or so as to prevent those whom one loves or identifies with from being subjected to injustice. Thus, the attempt to achieve and maintain justice, or to undo or prevent injustice, is the one and only universal cause of violence. (11–12)

As the book unfolds, it becomes clear that Gilligan's "justice" is connected with the phenomenon of shame. The violent person who is overwhelmed by shame is attempting to establish "justice" from his point of view, one that is warped by the narcissistic malformation of his soul. But the theological vision I am articulating has a different take on this. What Gilligan calls "justice" is actually a desire for psychological stasis; it is an attempt to fend off the call of creation. The "justice" achieved by violent action reaffirms the world as it is perceived by the person whose alien-ation from God has closed him off from his own true future. The rage that arises out of shame is the fury of what Kierkegaard calls "the natural man," who feels oppressed by the demand that is placed on him to grow into spiritual maturity.

I do not mean to suggest that Gilligan's book is not worth reading. On the con-trary, I recommend it highly. It is very insightful and thought-provoking in a variety of ways. But a careful reading reveals the same flattened secular landscape that characterizes mainstream social science. The author's ambiguity toward secular and religious social theory is finally resolved in favor of the secular, as in various passages where Gilligan seems to choose as his guide through the hell of prison life not Vergil or even Dante, but Karl Marx. See chapter 7 of his book, for instance, in which his argument suffers a meltdown into socialist jargon. To make our way out of the hell of violence, we need better guides than Karl Marx, guides whose minds are open to the pull of creation.

C. Fred Alford's book is also worthy of consideration in this context. *What Evil Means to Us* reports on the author's numerous interviews with both prison in-mates and average citizens concerning the nature of evil. Alford is a political scientist with a strong interest in psychological approaches to understanding human behavior.

Alford interviewed 50 nonincarcerated people ranging in age from 18 to 80 and representing a wide variety of backgrounds and viewpoints. He spoke with each one individually for approximately two hours. He also organized a discussion group of prison inmates that met weekly for a year. This group ranged in age from 19 to 48 and included about 18 regular members, of whom 5 were women from the women's wing of the correctional facility. These sessions were co-led by Alford and a prison psychiatrist. He asked both types of interviewees open-ended ques-tions about evil such as: What's your definition of evil? Why do you think there is evil in the world? Has there always been? Will there always be? Is it evil to follow orders that hurt innocents? Is it evil to think evil? How does your religion help you understand evil? and so on.

After carrying out this lengthy research, Alford reflected on it and synthesized his thoughts for the book. His conclusions are striking from a Kierkegaardian perspective.

While for Gilligan the key word is *shame*, for Alford, it is *dread*, which immedi-ately brings to mind the title of the first English translation of Kierkegaard's *Begrebet Angest*, "The Concept of Dread." Alford sets up his project in this way:

> Dread is not the whole of evil, possibly not even its most important part, but it is its ground: the dread of being human, vulnerable, alone in the universe, and doomed to die.
>
> Evil is an experience of dread. *Doing* evil is an attempt to evacuate this expe-rience by inflicting it on others, making them feel dreadful by hurting them.

> Doing evil is an attempt to transform the terrible passivity and helplessness of suffering into activity.[5]

In this passage Alford seems merely to echo the perspective of Ernest Becker, whom he acknowledges as one of his sources. He goes on to say, however, that he differs from Becker in seeing dread as "rooted more in fear of life than of death" (10). This is the key shift in perspective which I am arguing is opened up for us in Kierkegaard's thought.

Alford's book is strewn about with many brilliant insights and memorable turns of phrase. He criticizes Elaine Pagels, for instance, for simplistically arguing that evil comes from a failure to accept "difference," as if "evildoers could do with a course in political correctness"(16). He provides an engaging analysis of the "paranoid-schizoid position," which underlies the most virulent and irrational forms of violence. In this psychological state, "we fear our doom at the hands of malevolent external persecutors who seek to destroy us and all the goods we possess"(40). His use of the first-person plural here is revealing. Alford does not engage in the common self-righteous exercise of placing evil at arms' length as a defense mechanism. He continually tries to break down that defense mechanism by teaching his reader that evil is a fundamental problem and possibility for all people. In commenting on the Oklahoma City bombing, he observes that "our inability to understand evil is a willful failure to know our own hearts"(8).

Alford's central argument hinges on what he calls "the paradigm of evil": the image of the torturer and his victim. The evil that human beings do is an attempt to overcome feelings of weakness, pain, and abandonment by generating those feelings in other people. "All evil has the quality of torture, inflicting dread on another so as to escape it oneself" (52). Alford describes evil as "cheating," as "bad faith," because it continually seeks to believe its own lie that one's doom can be avoided by inflicting doom on others.

When Alford speaks in a positive vein about the pathway out of violence, he continues to provide helpful and thought-provoking ideas. He writes:

> Morality depends on one's being able to make basic distinctions between self and other, distinctions so obvious they are often assumed to be given, available to all. In fact, they are made. Avoiding evil depends on how they are made. (47)

As I argue in chapter 8, when I comment directly on Naziism, this insight is absolutely essential. When we limit ourselves to thinking that the Nazis were violent toward the Jews because they saw the Jews as *different*, we do not see the situa-

---

5. C. Fred Alford, *What Evil Means to Us* (Ithaca: Cornell University Press, 1997), 3. Subsequent parenthetical references are to this book.

tion clearly. The root of violence is the inability of the immature self to actually see others as different, as separate from oneself. The paranoid-schizoid position is a self-contained psychedelic universe in which there are no distinct selves who can enter into relations with each other. There is only one immense, twisted, self-hating ego. In Alford's words:

> Identifying so completely and concretely with one internal object, the preda-tory stranger, the psychopath has no room for others. His relationships with others are not really object relationships at all, at least not human ones. Ex-cept as means, as tools strewn about the world, others do not truly exist. His is a great defense at a great price, the loss of an inner world, what it is to be truly human. (56)

Alford points the way to the real work that needs to be done if the human race is to move beyond violence: "Morality takes imagination, and moral imagination requires a concern for others whose existence and suffering is independent of our needs"(48).

At certain points in his book, Alford comes very close to what I argue is the best way of understanding violence. On the theme of resistance to psychological growth, for instance, he writes, "The hardman's goal is autarky, not to be touched by anything. Stasis—not being moved by anyone or anything—*is* transcendence, of a world that is always trying to put one through changes"(92). And his com-ments on envy (70–71), which are indebted to Melanie Klein, continue to be stun-ningly accurate:

> Klein argues that envy wants not merely to have all the goodness in the world for oneself but to destroy the good because one cannot be it. The very existence of goodness outside the self generates a destructive narcissistic rage that would destroy goodness because it is good. . . .
>
> If there were an adequate psychological definition of evil, this would be it. Evil is the special quality of badness called envy, the desire to destroy innocence and goodness for its own sake, because the very existence of innocence and goodness outside the self is an intolerable insult to the grandiose but empty self. . . .
>
> Evil is not just the devaluation of otherness because the other is scary and bad. Evil is the destruction of the other because the other is *good*, an even harsher truth that both Kant and Pagels fail to recognize.

We have here an intimation of what I have been trying to describe as the "call of creation." What we refuse is the possibility of becoming the truly good and lov-ing human beings that our Creator wants us to become. What we avoid is not our doom but our redemption and recreation. It is from the perspective of the ego hid-ing from God that this possibility looks like doom. But these are my words, not Alford's. Somehow, even though he is sniffing down the right trail, he does not quite bring everything together. Even though he claims to depart from Becker's view by focusing on fear of life rather than fear of death, in the actual development of his text he reverts again and again to the idea that evil arises from a refusal to recognize and accept one's own finitude: "the dread of being human, vulnerable, alone in the universe, and doomed to die" (3). We see here once again the lid placed on thought by the methodological atheism of social science; and we are not surprised when he describes Nietzsche as "the most profound student of evil" among philosophers (15). In sum, within the horizon of mainstream secular philosophy in our era, Alford's book is just about as good as it gets in understanding the roots of violence. But it can get better, if the horizon is truly opened up to comprehend the divine source of all life.

I suggest that the closure to transcendence inherent in methodological atheism prevents its theorists from fully understanding the phenomenon they are seeking to grasp. Concerning the religious vision of the relationship between humanity and its Creator, they presuppose that "we have no need for that hypothesis." Kierkegaard, however, does need the "hypothesis" of God and the work of creation in his effort to understand human beings.[6] His vision of the health and pathology of the human spirit is inherently and inescapably theological. In my view, this aspect of his thought gives him greater explanatory power than the secular theorists for a reason we can articulate in this way: *The most basic root of violence is the alienation of human beings from their Creator; thus, non-theological "explanations" of violence are actually caught up in and expressive of the same atmosphere of human alienation from God out of which violence arises.[7] As such, they are unable to master their subject; the "explanations" are themselves trapped in the tragedy of human history.*[8]

Eric Voegelin has criticized secular thought in its existential roots. In his view, modern thought is predominantly characterized by the attempt of intellectuals to disengage themselves from the demanding task of living in openness to the pull of

---

6. As David Gouwens notes: "Kierkegaard is a thinker for whom the religious and Christian concepts provide the governing concepts for his psychological reflection. He is a specifically *Christian* psychologist for whom the practice of psychology and of anthropological reflection is logically grounded in his belief in the truth of Christianity." See *Kierkegaard as Religious Thinker* (Cambridge: Cambridge University Press, 1996), 69; also pp. 70, 75, and 76 on the doctrine of creation in Kierkegaard. Along similar lines see Robert C. Roberts, *Taking the Word to Heart* (Grand Rapids: Eerdmans, 1993), 296–297, and C. Stephen Evans, *Søren Kierkegaard's Christian Psychology* (Grand Rapids: Zondervan, 1990), 39–40.

7. See Milbank's *Theology and Social Theory*, in which he claims that secular social philosophy is "complicit with an 'ontology of violence,' a reading of the world which assumes the priority of force and tells how this force is best managed and confined by counter-force." He describes Kierkegaard as providing an alternative mode of thought which is rooted in "an opening to transcendence" (4).

8. Ron Rosenbaum's article, "Explaining Hitler," *The New Yorker*, May 1, 1995, 50–70, is a haunting "secular" confirmation of precisely this point.

the divine. This shrinking back from existence before God leads to a shrunken, contracted self unable to comprehend reality effectively. The egocentric ego of the modern intellectual must invent a "second reality," a world without God, to have somewhere to live. The event of philosophical contraction can be seen in the writings of Hegel, Marx, Nietzsche, Heidegger, and others, and the consequences of the philosophical murder of God are evident in the attempts of Lenin and Hitler, and so on, to remake the world in their own diseased image. To the extent that present-day intellectuals are still in thrall to the "giants" of shrunken existence, they are unable to comprehend the violence of the twentieth century. The contracted self, analyzed by Kierkegaard and Voegelin as the "closed-up" self in alienation from God, is at the same time the root of violent actions and also the root of the inability of modern intellectuals to truly understand human behavior.[9]

9. On this theme in Voegelin, see the bibliography for "The Eclipse of Reality"; "On Classical Studies" and "Wisdom and the Magic of the Extreme" in *Published Essays, 1966–1985*; and *Science, Politics, and Gnosticism*.

7

THE PROBLEM OF CHRISTIAN VIOLENCE

> My position is that the whole prevailing official proclamation of
> Christianity is a conspiracy against the Bible—we suppress what
> does not suit us.
>
> JP, 6: 6688 (1850)

It is my view that the Christian intellectual tradition provides us with stronger resources for interpreting violence than any of the alternatives with which I am familiar. I am fully cognizant, however, that this belief is in tension with certain basic facts of Christian history. If it is the case that the New Testament reveals the roots of violence so profoundly, then why have Christians been so violent throughout their history? This is the central question I consider in this chapter. The first subsection presents brief summaries of violent events in the history of Christianity; I merely touch on certain notable highlights of this history, given that an exhaustive account would constitute a book in itself. The subsequent sections of the chapter suggest the ways in which Kierkegaard and Girard enable us to understand these events. I argue that both authors presuppose the paradigm for the interpretation of Christian history which forms the basis of Anabaptist thought. This paradigm holds that an ethically disastrous "fall" of Christian integrity took place during the age of Constantine. Christianity's apparent triumph over the world was in fact a defeat, from this point of view.

A Short History of
Christian Violence

1. As Christianity expanded into the Roman Empire during its first three centuries, it met with significant resistance from the governmental authorities, which often took the form of direct persecutions resulting in Christian martyrdoms. During this period, Christians were, generally speaking, the recipients of violence rather than the perpetrators of it. After Christianity became a tolerated and then an official religion, however, violent activity by Christians became much more common. The election of Pope Damasus I is a dramatic example of this development:

Immediately after the death of pope Liberius (366), some priests and deacons elected Damasus, while others in the basilica *Iulii* elected Ursinus, who was immediately consecrated by Paul, bishop of Tibur. The Damasians at once besieged the basilica for three days and dragged various victims out of it. Meanwhile Damasus had installed himself in the Lateran and been consecrated. Ursinus and others were exiled by the prefect of the city, but his followers occupied the basilica Liberiana, where they were besieged by the Damasians and a massacre took place.[1]

In this case rival factions of Christians did not hesitate to use violence to determine the outcome of a papal election.

2. Another notable incident during this period is the execution of Priscillian, a Spanish ascetic who began to preach semignostic doctrines and dabble in astrology and magic. His enemies in the Spanish church lobbied the Emperor Maximus and succeeded in obtaining his condemnation for heresy. Priscillian and one of his followers, the noblewoman Eucrotia, were beheaded in 384. This was the first case in which heretics had been formally tried, convicted, and executed through the cooperation of church and state, foreshadowing the extensive powers of the medieval Inquisition.[2]

3. In the year 390, the people of Thessalonica murdered the military commander of the city. The Christian Emperor Theodosius ordered a massacre of the city's inhabitants, which resulted in more than seven thousand deaths. Under pressure of excommunication, exerted by Bishop Ambrose, Theodosius publicly repented of his sin.[3]

4. The Crusades were a series of military expeditions organized by Western European Christians, during the twelfth and thirteenth centuries, in an effort to recover the Holy Land from the Muslim "infidels." The first Crusade was very successful militarily, achieving several victories over the "Turks" as the Western armies advanced toward Jerusalem. On July 1, 1097, one of the main Muslim armies was defeated and almost completely decimated by the Crusaders. Two years later the Crusaders reached Jerusalem and captured it after a relatively brief siege. In the course of taking the city, they massacred most of the inhabitants—men, women, and children. Jerusalem was described by observers as "awash in a sea of blood." The Crusaders saw their actions as expressing God's righteous judgment on the Muslim "infidels," who deserved to die for their rejection of Christ and their "desecration" of the Holy City. Various subsequent Crusades were carried out during the next two centuries, most resulting in military failure or short-lived Latin

---

1. A. DiBernardino, "Ursinus," *Encyclopedia of the Early Church.*

2. Tim Dowley, ed., *Introduction to the History of Christianity* (Minneapolis: Fortress Press, 1995), 150–151.

3. Ibid., 151.

kingdoms in the East. The net result of the Crusades was to further separate the Eastern and Western branches of Christianity from each other and to ensure the alienation of the Muslim world from Christianity—a situation that to a large extent persists up to the present.[4]

Between 1209 and 1229, a Crusade was organized against the Albigensian heretics in southern France. Because a significant portion of the nobility of that region had sided with the Albigensians, the fighting was long and drawn-out, resulting in tremendous loss of life. The Roman Catholic bishop of the city of Bezier, when asked by the besieging soldiers how to distinguish between the heretics and the orthodox, is reported to have said: "Kill them all, God will sort them out."

5. The Inquisition was the internal European institution that corresponded to the external Crusades. Its main function was to identify and punish the "infidels" within the Western world who were perceived as a threat to society. The Inquisition was organized in the first half of the thirteenth century, largely in response to the Albigensian heresy in France, but its power was soon extended into many areas of Europe. Typically, the Inquisitors would enter a city and establish a court. They would summon all heretics to come forward and confess their heresy. Those who did so were treated with relative leniency. Those who were accused of heresy by others and found guilty were punished more severely, sometimes with death (at the hands of the civil authorities, not the Inquisitors themselves). In 1252 Pope Innocent IV officially approved the use of torture by the Inquisition to extract "the truth" from defendants. Justification for this procedure was found in the tradition of *Roman law*. Methods of torture included the rack and placing hot coals on the soles of the feet. At the close of the court proceedings, the sentences of those found guilty were announced publicly in a ceremony referred to as an auto-da-fé—an "act of faith."[5]

In 1478 a relatively autonomous branch of the Inquisition was established with papal approval in Spain. It carried out a campaign against Jews and Muslims whose conversions to Christianity were thought to be insincere, against "witches," and in later decades against those accused of Protestant leanings. Tomás de Torquemada, the notorious Grand Inquisitor of Spain, burned at the stake thousands of alleged heretics between 1487 and 1498. The Spanish Inquisition was not formally dissolved until 1834.

The Dominican order provided most of the key inquisitors during the thirteenth century, and their leading theologian, Thomas Aquinas, attempted to justify the practice of executing heretics in his *Summa Theologiae*. To establish the legitimacy of executing heretics, he quotes Titus 3:10–11: "After a first and second admonition, have nothing more to do with anyone who causes divisions [a heretic], since

---

4. Ibid., 278–279.
5. Ibid., 321–324.

you know that such a person is perverted and sinful, being self-condemned." Thomas assumes that the phrase "have nothing more to do with" legitimates the killing of human beings. He argues that since forgers of money are put to death by the civil authorities it is even more imperative for heretics to be killed because "it is a much graver matter to corrupt faith."[6] The Church hopes for the conversion of the heretic, thus allowing him to respond to a "first and second admonition." But if he remains unrepentant, then the Church ceases to hope for his conversion and "looks to the salvation of others by excommunicating him and separating him from the Church, and furthermore delivers him to the secular tribunal to be exterminated thereby from the world by death." Aquinas quotes Jerome to support this course of action: "Cut off the decayed flesh, expel the mangy sheep from the fold, lest the whole house, the whole dough, the whole body, the whole flock burn, perish, rot, die."

The Waldensians were one of the groups particularly targeted for persecution by the Inquisition. Their principal crime was questioning the claim of the Roman Church to be the true Church of Christ. They sought to distinguish themselves from what they perceived as the avarice and moral laxity of the Roman Church by living in strict poverty and obedience to Scripture. They went from town to town preaching sermons from biblical texts. Their success in gaining converts in many areas of Europe alarmed the papacy and led to official attempts at repression by the Inquisition. These attempts did not succeed in wiping out the Waldensians, however, but only in forcing them into an underground or rural existence, which they maintained from the thirteenth century until the sixteenth, when many of their ideas entered into the mainstream of the Protestant Reformation.[7]

6. In the early fifteenth century, a somewhat similar reforming movement came into existence in Bohemia: the Hussites. Jan Hus, their leader, was greatly influenced by the writings of John Wyclif. He thus stressed Scripture as the supreme authority over popes and cardinals. He criticized corruption in the clergy, worship of images, and "superstitious pilgrimages." He was called before the Council of Constance in 1415 to defend himself against charges of heresy. Although he had been promised "safe passage," he was burned at the stake without being granted a full opportunity to defend his views.[8] During the sixteenth century, many Protestants were killed by the Roman Church for holding views similar to those of the Hussites. William Tyndale, for example, was burned at the stake by imperial authorities in 1536, his crime being unauthorized translation of the Bible into vernacular English.

---

6. St. Thomas Aquinas, *On Law, Morality, and Politics*, ed. William P. Baumgarth and Richard J. Regan (Indianapolis: Hackett, 1988), 256. [*ST* 2–II 11. 3.]

7. Dowley, ed., *Introduction to the History of Christianity*, 327–329.

8. Ibid., 336.

7. The magisterial reformers, Luther and Calvin, were not much different from the Roman Catholic leaders of the day with regard to their attitudes toward violence. Luther's teachings had indirectly contributed to the Peasants' Revolt in Germany in the 1520s. Luther called for suppression of the rebellious peasants in these well-known words: "Let everyone who can, smite, slay, and stab, secretly or openly, remembering that nothing can be more poisonous, hurtful, or devilish than a rebel. It is just as when one must kill a mad dog."[9] The Consistory in Calvin's Geneva burned at the stake the antitrinitarian heretic Michael Servetus in 1553. Calvin is reputed to have favored beheading as a more humane form of execution in this case. Nevertheless, he approved of the Consistory's decision and said that Servetus "cried like a Spaniard" as he was being burned.

8. The Catholics and the Protestants were united in their fear and loathing of the Anabaptists, who had the audacity to proclaim that Christians should not be in the business of killing. For teaching this they were killed. The following transcript of the trial of Anabaptist leader Michael Sattler effectively conveys the atmosphere of the time. After giving a speech to the court outlining the basic points of Anabaptist doctrine, Sattler concludes:

> Whereas, then, we have not acted contrary to God and the gospel, you will find that neither I nor my brethren and sisters have offended in word or deed against any authority. Therefore, ministers of God, if you have neither heard nor read the Word of God, send for the most learned men and for the sacred books of the Bible in whatsoever language they may be and let them confer with us in the Word of God. If they prove to us with the Holy Scriptures that we err and are in the wrong, we will gladly desist and recant and also willingly suffer the sentence and punishment for that of which we have been accused; but if no error is proven to us, I hope to God that you will be converted and receive instruction."
>
> Upon this speech the judges laughed and put their heads together, and the town clerk of Ensisheim said: "Yes, you infamous, desperate rascal of a monk, should we dispute with you? The hangman will dispute with you, I assure you!"
>
> . . . One of the prisoners also said: "We must not depart from the truth."
>
> The town clerk: "Yes, you desperate villain, you archheretic, I say, if there were no hangman here, I would hang you myself and be doing God a good service thereby."
>
> . . . The judges having returned to the room, the sentence was read. It was as follows: "In the case of the attorney of His Imperial Majesty vs. Michael Sattler, judgment is passed that Michael Sattler shall be delivered to the executioner, who shall lead him to the place of execution and cut out his tongue, then forge him fast to a wagon and thereon with red-hot tongs twice tear pieces from

---

9. J. M. Porter, ed., *Luther: Selected Political Writings* (Philadelphia: Fortress Press, 1974), 86.

his body; and after he has been brought outside the gate, he shall be plied five times more in the same manner. . . ."

After this had been done in the manner prescribed, he was burned to ashes as a heretic. His fellow brethren were executed with the sword, and the sisters drowned. His wife, also after being subjected to many entreaties, admonitions, and threats, under which she remained steadfast, was drowned a few days afterward.[10]

Scenes like this were repeated many times during the sixteenth century, resulting in the deaths of thousands of Anabaptists, who were perceived as dangerous heretics attacking the very foundations of Western Christian culture. Indeed, the Anabaptists were attacking these foundations, insofar as they were generated by the scapegoat mechanism rather than the teachings of Christ.

9. Violence between Catholics and Protestants occurred sporadically during the sixteenth and early seventeenth centuries, erupting finally on a grand scale in the Thirty Years War (1618–1648).[11] During this period the Catholic armies of the Holy Roman Empire battled with the Protestant armies of Bohemia, Germany, Denmark, and Sweden. Success and defeat ebbed and flowed for both sides for many years. Most of the fighting took place in Germany, resulting in widespread devastation. Historians estimate that the overall population of Germany was reduced by 15 to 20 percent. Later in the war, the Catholic armies of France fought with the Catholic armies of the Empire, for motives that were more political than religious.

10. The U.S. Civil War took place between 1861 and 1865. Historians estimate that 620,000 persons died in the war. On both sides Christian soldiers were ministered to and encouraged by chaplains who claimed that God was on their side.

Reintroducing Christianity into Christendom

The brief historical survey just completed raises important questions regarding the role of Christianity in history. How can people who claim to be followers of Christ commit acts of torture, burn other human beings alive, and slaughter each other in huge numbers? There is so great a contradiction here between the behavior of Christians and the teachings of the New Testament that a critical interpretation

---

10. "The Trial and Martyrdom of Michael Sattler," in *Spiritual and Anabaptist Writers,* ed. George Hunston Williams (Philadelphia: Westminster Press, 1957), 141–144.

11. Dowley, ed., *Introduction to the History of Christianity,* 427.

of this history is essential for the continued viability of Christian existence.[12] Such an interpretation is at the heart of the writings of both Kierkegaard and Girard.

In my view, Kierkegaard and Girard may be accurately placed in the tradition of thought that is most commonly associated with the Anabaptists.[13] This does not mean that they are Anabaptists in every sense of the word, but that their basic paradigm for interpreting the history of Christianity assumes that a crucial "fall" occurred during the age of Constantine. From the Anabaptist point of view, the alleged "triumph" of Christianity over the Roman Empire was in fact just the opposite. What took place at the end of the patristic era was the subtle alteration of Christianity from a religion that grew out of the teachings and example of Christ into one that "baptized" ways of thinking and acting that were fundamentally pre-Christian and anti-Christian. The violent social structures that had led to the crucifixion of Christ and the deaths of Stephen and the other early martyrs were actually adopted by Christianity itself, and in the process Christianity lost its integrity and coherence as a community of persons seeking to imitate Christ.

Anabaptist thought argues that as Christianity spread into the Roman Empire during its first three centuries, a very gradual change occurred in the meaning of conversion. The earliest Church had been made up of individuals who had undergone a conversion experience and had in most cases radically changed their previous ways of thinking and acting. Often, this commitment to the way of following Christ led to persecution and martyrdom. As Christianity became more and

---

12. John Howard Yoder's writings contribute to this critical assessment of Christian history.

> Can one gain new light upon the relevance of a Free Church vision of ethics by claiming that it also leads to a new way of interpreting events in the past? Decision in the present is often very much the product of how the past has been recounted to us. If we are then to open up a new future it must be the extension of a rereading of the past. Historiography must be rehabilitated by being taken back from the grasp of the military historians and the chroniclers of battles and dynasties, and informed by other criteria to judge a society's sickness or health. . . . Is there such a thing as a "peace church historiography"?

See *The Original Revolution* (Scottdale: Herald Press, 1971), 161. Yoder's vision is taken up and set in a very broad context by Nancey Murphy and George F. R. Ellis, *On the Moral Nature of the Universe* (Minneapolis: Fortress Press, 1996).

13. This argument has been made, with regard to Kierkegaard, by Vernard Eller. See *Kierkegaard and Radical Discipleship* (Princeton: Princeton University Press, 1968). In the journals, Kierkegaard says that it is nonsense "to believe that true Christianity is found in 'the Church' with its large numbers. The spirit of Christianity is opposed to nothing more than to this, this human mediocrity, this animal-man's faith in human numbers. No, whatever true Christianity there is to be found in the course of the centuries may be found in the sects and the like" (JP, 3: 2687). See also WL, 67–68, on the theme of love for enemies, and JP, 3: 3086, on infant baptism.

more "successful," however, and eventually "triumphed" over the Roman Empire by becoming its official religion under the emperor Constantine, the meaning of discipleship was subtly changed. It now became possible to conceive of the idea of "converting" large groups of people through their prince or tribal chieftain, whose commitment to the faith was enforced on his subjects from the top down. The process of becoming a Christian had shifted subtly but radically from the New Testament understanding of becoming a disciple of Christ to simply being born in a geographical area that had been ostensibly "Christianized." It was this new, less rigorous understanding of conversion that became the norm as Christianity continued to spread in the following centuries into Western Europe, Russia, and eventually the New World. As one historian has noted, "a Christian civilization had arisen ahead of all possible processes of individual conversion."[14] Tolstoy expressed a similar view:

> Never, I believe, has the discord between the mode of life of our societies and the religious ideals they have formally adopted been so great: they continue to live a life which is in effect pagan.
>
> In my opinion this disagreement is so marked because the Christian view of life at the moment of its formation went far beyond the moral and intellectual level of the peoples who acknowledged it at that time. That is why the code of conduct which it recommended was too greatly opposed not only to the habits of individual people but to the whole social organization of pagans, who had become Christians in name only.
>
> Thus it is that these peoples became attached to a false Christianity, represented by the Church, whose principles differ from those of paganism only in a lack of sincerity.[15]

A thin veneer of Christian religiosity had been spread over a large geographical area, but most of the individuals who were now labeled Christians had not undergone the process of spiritual and ethical development which is the norm in the New Testament vision of discipleship. The world was still "the world," even though it was now a "Christian" world.

In the preceding paragraph I included ironic quotation marks to point to a discrepancy between the historical reality of Christianity and what Christianity ought to be. By this point in the discussion, it should be clearly understood that *Kierkegaard's message to "Christendom" arises out of his awareness of this discrepancy.* His main concern as an author is to reject and denounce the form of Christianity

---

14. John McManners, *The Oxford Illustrated History of Christianity* (Oxford: Oxford University Press, 1990), 267.

15. Leo Tolstoy, *The Law of Love and the Law of Violence*, trans. Mary Koutouzow Tolstoy (New York: Holt, Rinehart and Winston, 1970), 2–3.

that resulted historically from the less rigorous understanding of conversion. From Kierkegaard's point of view, the supreme irony of Christian history is found in the failure of the Christian Church to firmly hold onto the teachings and revelatory power of its own Scriptures. Kierkegaard uses the following descriptive analogy:

> Imagine this. Suppose that a coachman sees an absolutely remarkable and utterly faultless five-year-old horse, an ideal horse, snorting and as full of mettle as any he has seen, and he says: "Well, I cannot bid on this horse, nor can I afford it, and even if I could it is quite unsuitable for my use." But after a dozen years, when that remarkable horse is spavined and spoiled etc., the coachman says: Now I can bid on it, now I can pay for it, and now I can make enough profit from it, from what is left in it, so that I can properly see my way to spending a little for its board.
>
> It is the same with the state and Christianity. Of the lofty Christianity which entered into the world, every state is obliged to say: "I cannot buy this religion; not only that, but I will say: God and Father, save me from buying this religion; it would surely be the ruin of me." But when after a few centuries Christianity had become spavined and decrepit and on its last legs, spoiled and muddle-headed, then the state said: See, now I can bid on it; and smart as I am I can see very well that I can use it and profit from it enough so that I can properly see my way to spending a little to polish it up.
>
> If only Christianity, in return for the refurbishing, would play on the state the practical joke of becoming itself again: "Ugh! God and Father, save and preserve us—any state can see that this religion is my ruin." The coachman is sure that he made a shrewd buy; he runs no risk of the twenty-year-old nag's getting back its five-year-old mettle again, which according to the unanimous opinion of all coachmen would not serve a coachman any more than the state is served by—the eternally young Christianity. (JP, 4: 4232 [1854])

Kierkegaard believed that as Christianity spread into the West and began to preach a less rigorous message, it was gradually reduced to almost the same level of spiritual immaturity that had characterized the Roman Empire. At the level of spiritual reality, it is much more accurate to say that the Roman Empire triumphed over Christianity than the opposite:

> Woe, woe to the Christian Church when it will have been victorious in this world, for then it is not the Church that has been victorious but the world. Then the heterogeneity between Christianity and the world has vanished, the world has won, and Christianity has lost. (PC, 223)

In the wake of the fall of Christianity, the individual who adheres to the New Testament vision realizes the need for missionary efforts directed toward Christendom itself. Kierkegaard saw himself as such a missionary, which led him to describe the overall goal of his writings in words such as these: "Christendom

has abolished Christianity without really knowing it itself. As a result, if something must be done, one must attempt again to introduce Christianity into Christendom" (PC, 36). The same theme is reiterated in *The Point of View for My Work
as an Author*:

> *The single individual*—this category has been used only once, its first time, in a
> decisively dialectical way, by Socrates, in order to disintegrate paganism. In
> Christendom it will be used a second time in the very opposite way, to make
> people (the Christians) Christians. It is not the missionary's category with
> regard to the pagans to whom he proclaims Christianity, but it is the mis-
> sionary's category within Christendom itself in order to introduce Christian-
> ity into Christendom. (PV, 123)

Clearly, the New Testament expresses a demanding ethical vision of the life of
Christians. Do the "thousands and thousands" of European Christians live according to this vision? Kierkegaard believes that the answer to this question is no.
Christendom constitutes a "crowd" that "makes for impenitence and irresponsi-
bility" in the individuals who comprise it (PV, 107). The way the crowd acts is
diametrically opposed to the way of love of the neighbor that Christ taught and
lived. From this perspective, Kierkegaard's *Works of Love* can be seen as not only
an ethical discourse, but also an implicit critique of Christendom as an ethical
debacle. Kierkegaard feels that he must explain the meaning of the Great Commandment because Christians do not understand it and live according to it. "Aesthetic" Christians live according to "spontaneous" love, which grows out of alienation from God. Thus Christians engage in the same persecution and mistreatment
of scapegoats which was made manifest in the crucifixion of Christ. Kierkegaard
had learned this through personal experience in the "*Corsair* Affair."[16]

For Kierkegaard, Christendom exists in a state of profound self-contradiction.
On the one hand, it gives lip service to the ethics of the New Testament, but on
the other, it is maintained by the same structures of violence that killed the
prophets and Christ. Kierkegaard points to the verses in the New Testament that
describe the situation of Christendom with complete clarity: "'If we had lived in
the days of our ancestors, we would not have taken part with them in shedding
the blood of the prophets.' Thus you testify against yourselves that you are descen-
dants of those who murdered the prophets" (Matt. 23:30–31). He thus describes
Christendom as "the greatest possible attempt" to serve God by "building the tombs
of the prophets" while saying "If we had lived. . . ." He says that Christianity is
"played" as a game in "Christendom." He likens the clergy to "dramatically cos-

---

16. For an overview of this period in Kierkegaard's life, see the "Historical Introduction" to *The Corsair Affair*, trans. and ed. Howard and Edna Hong (Princeton: Princeton
University Press, 1982).

tumed" artists who "make their appearance in artistic buildings." They "feign to be much, much better than those who put them to death, to be creatures altogether different from those monsters—indeed, they are building the tombs of those righteously put to death and adorning their graves" (TM, 133–134). Kierkegaard is even more direct in the *Journals and Papers*:

> Christendom has repeated the parable of the vineyard workers who killed the lord's messengers and finally also his son, "because this is our vineyard." . . . Once in a while someone comes along who either is a true Christian or is so concerned for the truth that he makes no secret of what is understood by being a true Christian. He is shouted down as a traitor . . . and killed. It is also treason to disclose this whole web of lies by being honest. Therefore they kill him. They say, as did those in the vineyard: "Let us kill him, since the vineyard is ours". (JP, 1: 383 [1849])

I have established three main points in Kierkegaard's interpretation of the history of Christianity: (1) Christianity underwent a profound spiritual "fall" during its early centuries; (2) This "fall" resulted in a massive ethical debacle in which Christians lost the ability to live in a loving way; (3) The established Church, in its alliance with the state, is in fact an aesthetic illusion. Kierkegaard's thought seeks to reach people who are living under this illusion so that they may be led into genuine discipleship to Christ. Thus he begins with the aesthetic, outlines the sphere of the ethical, and finally points toward the religious, which entails the imitation of Christ in one's personal existence: "*Imitation*, which corresponds to Christ as the prototype, must—if there is to be any meaning in Christendom—must be affirmed again, but in such a way, as we said, that something has been learned from the error of the past" (JFY, 190).

Girard's Critique of
Sacrificial Christianity

When we turn to Girard's thought, we find that his interpretation of the history of Christianity parallels Kierkegaard's. Mimetic desire as a pattern of life is generally equivalent to that which Kierkegaard describes as the aesthetic sphere of existence. Kierkegaard calls this "paganism," the way in which human beings live by default if they have not risen to one of the more mature forms of existence: the ethical or the religious. Girard works with the assumption that the default setting for human life is mimetic desire, which leads to a certain social structure formed around violence. He sees Judaism and Christianity as constituting an *exodus* through history that leads out of socially sanctioned violence into a fundamentally different way of life, one that is nonviolent: the way of the Kingdom. The New Testament in particular points the way out of conflictual mimesis, into love of the neighbor.

The actual historical road that Christianity has traveled, however, is a tragedy. Christianity began with the impetus of a great revelation, but over the course of its first centuries it relapsed into pre-Christian modes of existence. Christianity reverted to "a sacrificial form" that betrayed the nonsacrificial insights of the Gospels concerning the structural falsity of human culture. The fact that Christianity became a persecuting religion in the Middle Ages is proof that the revelatory power of the Bible was being resisted by Christians:

> Thanks to the sacrificial reading it has been possible for what we call Christendom to exist for fifteen or twenty centuries; that is to say, a culture has existed that is based, like all cultures (at least up to a certain point) on the mythological forms engendered by the founding mechanism. Paradoxically, in the sacrificial reading the Christian text itself provides the basis. Humankind relies upon a misunderstanding of the text that explicitly reveals the founding mechanism to re-establish cultural forms which remain sacrificial and to engender a society that, by virtue of this misunderstanding, takes its place in the sequence of all other cultures, still clinging to the sacrificial vision that the Gospel rejects. (*Things Hidden*, 181)

The "sacrificial reading" of the Gospels to which Girard refers involves an understanding of the crucifixion of Christ as a sacrifice demanded by God the Father so that his wrath toward humanity may be appeased. Girard considers this vision of the character of God to be a holdover of the primitive notion of the gods as invisible divine beings who must be placated through acts of human sacrifice. From his point of view, this is a mistaken interpretation of the Gospels; in reality, they reveal a nonviolent God who neither demands nor commands violent acts. The Gospels reveal that violence has a human, not a divine, origin:

> Jesus is the only man who achieves the goal God has set for all mankind, the only man who has nothing to do with violence and its works. The epithet "Son of Man" also corresponds, quite clearly, to the fact that Jesus alone has fulfilled a calling that belongs to all mankind.
>
> If the fulfillment, on earth, passes inevitably through the death of Jesus, this is not because the Father demands this death, for strange sacrificial motives. Neither the Son nor the Father should be questioned about the cause of this event, but all mankind, and mankind alone. The very fact that mankind has never really managed to understand what is involved reveals clearly that the misunderstanding of the founding murder is still being perpetuated, as is our inability to hear the Word of God. (*Things Hidden*, 213)

It is interesting that Kierkegaard had developed a similar perspective on the crucifixion of Christ:

> Rarely does one make a real attempt to understand how it was that Christ (whose life in one sense could not possibly have collided with anyone since it

had no earthly aims) ended his life by being crucified. Perhaps one fears getting to know anything of the implicit proof of the existence of evil in the world. *So one pretends as if Christ himself and God's providence ordained it this way.* . . . The fact that Christ was willing to sacrifice his life does not at all signify that he sought death or forced the Jews to kill him. Christ's willingness to offer his life simply means a conception of the world as being so evil that the Holy One unconditionally had to die—unless he wanted to become a sinner or a mediocrity in order to become a success in the world. (JP, 1: 305 [*emphasis added*] [1847])

Here also, violence is understood as having a human, not a divine, origin.

It is clear that Girard cannot tell the story of the history of Christianity in a triumphalistic way, because it is the story of an insight that humanity was not able to absorb and hold on to, an insight that was too difficult because it demanded too much personal awareness and cultural self-criticism. Thus historical Christianity developed a "persecutory character" that was reinforced by the sacrificial reading of the Bible (*Things Hidden*, 225). Girard analyzes an example of this persecutory mode of action in the first chapter of *The Scapegoat*, which treats the work of the fourteenth-century French poet Guillaume de Machaut. Machaut's work tells the story of the violence that Christians directed toward Jews in the wake of plague-induced paranoia. In Machaut's account, the Jews are blamed for causing the plague by poisoning the drinking water. They received recompense for their evil, however, as "heaven-sent justice righted these wrongs by making the evildoers known to the population, who massacred them all" (*The Scapegoat*, 1). Girard shows through this work that the scapegoat mechanism can be seen in full force during the "Christian" Middle Ages, exactly as if the Gospels had never been written.

Girard's thought has been influenced profoundly by Dostoevsky, whose parable of the Grand Inquisitor lies behind Girard's account of the history of Christianity. Christ's work had to be "corrected" by the Grand Inquisitor because the freedom and maturity to which he called humanity was too heavy to bear. Humanity prefers to remain in a state of "eternal infancy" in defiance of the truth that God seeks to communicate through the Bible (*Things Hidden*, 242). In the history of Christianity, the scapegoat mechanism has succeeded in preserving itself from possible destruction by coopting the greatest threat to its existence. The scapegoat mechanism inoculated itself against the power of revelation by turning the Gospel texts into a vaccine.

Girard is attempting to dismantle sacrificial Christianity, so that genuine New Testament Christianity may come into existence. In his words: "this sacrificial concept of divinity must 'die,' and with it the whole apparatus of historical Christianity, for the Gospels to be able to rise again in our midst, not looking like a corpse that we have exhumed, but revealed as the newest, finest, liveliest and truest thing that we have ever set eyes upon" (*Things Hidden*, 235–236). We have already seen that a virtually identical motive is at work in Kierkegaard's thought. He also seeks to unleash the transforming power of the Bible, which has been buried under the weight of Christendom's spiritual falsehood and sloth. Both Kierkegaard and Girard stress the idea that the Bible calls persons to spiritual and ethical maturity. But insofar as human beings are sinners, we resist the possibility of becoming mature; we prefer to remain infantile. To a great extent, the history of Christianity is the history of the resistance of immature "Christians" to the possibility that they could actually become followers of Christ. Phenomena such as the Inquisition, and the Crusades represent the leading edge of this effort by "Christians" to prevent their own spiritual growth.[17]

Kierkegaard as a
Political Philosopher

From Kierkegaard's point of view, there is a basic either/or set of possibilities that is open to each person. *Either* the person avoids living before God and becomes a participant in the crowd, *or* the person exists as a single individual before God, which places him in the position of suffering the violence of the crowd. The latter possibility is obviously martyrdom, which is the inevitable role of the person who hears and responds to the divine voice of creation. Here again we can see how those who accuse Kierkegaard of "radical individualism" have fundamentally failed to grasp his message. The martyr is not a person who is seeking his own individualistic salvation completely apart from all other human beings. The martyr is in an intense relationship with others, as he seeks their conversion and redemption:

> I want to make the crowd aware of their own ruin, and if they are unwilling to respond to the good, then I will constrain them with evil. Understand me—or do not misunderstand me. I do not intend to strike them (alas, one cannot strike the crowd)—no, I will constrain them to strike me. Thus I will still be constraining them with evil. For if they strike me first—they will surely be-

---

17. Stanley Windass comments: "For all our apparent easy-going materialism, the majority of us are still warriors at heart, or in fantasy; almost any crowd can soon be aroused by an orator or a propagandist who can evoke from the depths the archetypal images of the fight to death against the arch-foe in human form. This is indeed the world without the Gospels. The least appropriate, and yet the commonest attitude of Christians in the present world crisis." See *Christianity versus Violence* (London: Sheed and Ward, 1964), 149. He also expresses well how Christians *ought* to think and act: "The horror that the Christian feels is not that of being killed, but that of killing; not that of being a martyr, but of being a murderer; not the fear of suffering with Christ, but that of crucifying him afresh in the person of our fellow men. This is the backbone of our tradition, and must be the backbone of an informed Christian conscience" (129).

come aware—and if they kill me—then they will become unconditionally aware, and I will have won absolute victory.

Men are not so corrupt that they actually desire evil, but they are blind and really do not know what they are doing. Everything centers on drawing them out into the area of decision. A child can be somewhat unruly toward his father for a long time, but if the father can only get the child to make a real attack, the child is far closer to being saved. The revolt of the "masses" is victorious if we step aside for it so that it never comes to know what it is doing. The crowd is not essentially reflective; therefore, if it puts a man to death, it is *eo ipso* brought to a stop, becomes aware, and deliberates.

The reformer who, as they say, fights a power (a pope, an emperor, in short, an individual man) has to bring about the downfall of the mighty one; but he who with justice alone confronts "the crowd," from which comes all corruption, must see to it that he himself falls. (JP, 5: 5979 [1847])

"They are blind and do not know what they are doing." We can see that Kierkegaard's goal is the development of consciousness, self-awareness. His basic presupposition is that the crowd does not have the resources within itself to lift itself into a clear perception of reality. "Progress" in understanding the truth can only happen when the crowd is faced with the truth as it is embodied in the person they are killing. Thus the true Christian, the one who seeks to bring the light of God into the darkness of human history, must give himself to the task of bearing witness to the truth at the cost of his own life.

Any standard history of political philosophy in the West contains chapters on Machiavelli, Hobbes, Locke, Rousseau, Hegel, and so forth, but none on Kierkegaard. Why is this? The answer is plain. Mainstream political philosophy is written to guide and shape the state and its rulers, those who hold the reins of power in the world. It is not written from the point of view of the martyr, the one who suffers in his own person the effects of the power of the state or the crowd. But a "political philosophy" could be written from this perspective. It would be rooted in an understanding of authentic personal existence; it would articulate a critique of inauthentic existence as a form of "hiding" from the truth of oneself; and it would be inspired by a vision of continuing creation, a perception that the goal of human personal and social maturity can be reached through the openness of the human spirit to the divine Spirit. Political philosophy in this vein is not a mere possibility; it is a fait accompli in the New Testament, Anabaptist theology, Kierkegaard, Bonhoeffer, Voegelin, Girard, and similar writings.

8

POLITICAL VIOLENCE IN THE
TWENTIETH CENTURY

We human beings think as follows: this business of Adam's fall, that
happened a long, long time ago and is forgotten, and nowadays we
are nice people—for God this happens with Adam today. We human
beings make ourselves believe that this business of Christ being put
to death, this villainy of the human race, that all this happened
1,800 years ago, long ago, and is forgotten; now we are nice people—
for God this happens today.

> JP, 1: 698 (1854), cf. CD, 277–278

If, then, according to our assumption, the greater number of people
in Christendom only imagine themselves to be Christians, in what
categories do they live? They live in aesthetic, or, at the most, in
aesthetic-ethical categories.

> (PV, 25)

In this chapter I continue my historical application of the theory of
political violence developed above. I show how the writings of
Kierkegaard and Girard help us to understand the two most significant examples
of large-scale violence in the past century, Naziism and Stalinism. The basic presupposition of this book should be very clear by now: *we do not lack the philosophical categories that are necessary for comprehending political violence.* We need not live
in a fog of confusing "scientific" theories and/or simplistic question-begging answers to the problem of the roots of political violence. The intellectual tools needed
for adequate comprehension have already been forged by those authors who have
allowed themselves to become attuned to the right order of the human soul.

Naziism

In her book *The Roosevelt I Knew*, Frances Perkins describes how, during World
War II, President Roosevelt had become acquainted with a young Kierkegaard
scholar, Howard A. Johnson, who encouraged the president to read some of
Kierkegaard's writings. Roosevelt did so (apparently he read at least *The Concept
of Dread*), and Perkins recounts a conversation with him:

Some weeks later I happened to be reporting to Roosevelt on problems concerning the War Labor Board. He was looking at me, nodding his head, and, I thought, following my report, but suddenly he interrupted me. "Frances, have you ever read Kierkegaard?"

"Very little—mostly reviews of his writings."

"Well, you ought to read him, " he said with enthusiasm. "It will teach you something."

I thought perhaps he meant it would teach me something about the War Labor Board.

"It will teach you about the Nazis," he said. "Kierkegaard explains the Nazis to me as nothing else ever has. I have never been able to make out why people who are obviously human beings could behave like that. They are human, yet they behave like demons. Kierkegaard gives you an understanding of what it is in man that makes it possible for these Germans to be so evil. This fellow, Johnson, over at St. John's, knows a lot about Kierkegaard and his theories. You'd better read him."[1]

What did Roosevelt see in Kierkegaard that helped him to understand the Nazis? I cannot answer this question directly, but I can suggest the way in which Kierkegaard has helped me to reflect on the character of Hitler and his supporters.

In his writings, Kierkegaard paints a picture of the *aesthetic* sphere of existence.[2] Persons who live in the aesthetic sphere eschew the ethical and the religious dimensions of human existence; instead, they dwell in a solipsistic world of self-expression, always seeking interesting experiences. They live in and for the moment, reinventing themselves every year or day or hour. They have no stability; indeed, they perceive stability as *boredom*. If their efforts to flit from one interesting experience to the next fail, however, boredom is precisely the state into which they fall, because they have no inner core of selfhood. They live on the surface of reality, as vacuous personalities who lack purpose, vision, and integrity. Clearly, the aesthetic sphere of existence is a form of human immaturity, but it can become demonic when individuals who live in this sphere feel the pull of creation, only to reject it in favor of a despairing reassertion of their current way of thinking and acting. When the aesthete becomes demonic, the solipsism at the root of the aesthetic sphere reveals its true character as a rejection of ethical responsibility. The solipsistic person uses and manipulates others to meet his own psychological needs. When an entire society is made up of individuals who are living in this manner, the society begins to use and manipulate others to meet its psychological needs; and organized societies have so much more power than individuals or

1. Frances Perkins, *The Roosevelt I Knew* (New York: Viking, 1946), 148.

2. See *Either/Or*, vol. 1, and *Stages on Life's Way*, "In Vino Veritas." A general introduction to the spheres of existence is found in Gregor Malantschuk, *Kierkegaard's Way to the Truth*, trans. Mary Michelsen (Minneapolis: Augsburg, 1963).

minority groups within the society that the potential for demonic violence is very great.

The Nazis inhabited the aesthetic sphere; indeed, they took the aesthetic sphere to a demonic extreme without equal in world history. Naziism was essentially a repudiation of Western liberal political philosophy in favor of a reversion to pre-Christian Germanic primitivism. This comment by Sigmund Freud is very perceptive:

> We must not forget that all those peoples who excel today in their hatred of Jews became Christians only in late historic times, often driven to it by bloody coercion. It might be said that they are all "mis-baptized." They have been left, under a thin veneer of Christianity, what their ancestors were, who worshipped a barbarous polytheism. They have not got over a grudge against the new religion which was imposed on them; but they have displaced the grudge on to the source from which Christianity reached them. The fact that the Gospels tell a story which is set among the Jews, and in fact deals only with Jews, has made this displacement easy for them. Their hatred of Jews is at bottom a hatred of Christians, and we need not be surprised that in the German National-Socialist revolution this intimate relation between the two monotheist religions finds such a clear expression in the hostile treatment of both of them.[3]

In addition to further supporting the thesis of the previous chapter, Freud suggests that Christians need to take responsibility for the dire consequences of their attempt to spread a thin veneer of religiosity over a very wide area. When a false, watered-down form of Christianity is foisted on a culture, it is likely to be rejected in a backlash of demonic violence. If Christians themselves are victims of this violence, they need to honestly admit their part in generating it through their theologically inadequate form of evangelism.

Naziism represents this sort of demonic backlash in which nominal Christianity was rejected. One form of insincere religiosity was replaced by another, worse form, in which the nation-state attempted to worship itself aesthetically. Thus a key element of the Nazi seizure of power was a rejection of the traditional understanding of government by laws.[4] The traditional notion of human existence being

---

3. Quoted in Aryeh Maidenbaum and Stephen A. Martin, eds., *Lingering Shadows: Jungians, Freudians, and Anti-Semitism* (Boston and London: Shambhala, 1991), 388; from *Moses and Monotheism* [Standard Edition, 105–106].

4. See Mosse, ed., *Nazi Culture* (New York: Grosset & Dunlap, 1966), 320. See also Robert Hartman's Introduction to Picard's *Hitler in Our Selves*, trans. Heinrich Hauser (Hinsdale: Henry Regnery, 1947):

> There was always at least the theoretical possibility, foreseen by apocalyptic seers, that a man would arise who would concentrate all his energies on breaking down moral laws, a man of the moment and of momentary satisfactions, who would whip

guided and bounded by a legal system, which serves to protect human life, was jettisoned in favor of a reinvention of society according to the will of a dictator. This was a rejection of the ethical sphere of existence in favor of the arbitrary will of the aesthetic personality. The German people turned away from the moral law as it had traditionally been understood and surrendered their moral responsibility to the person of Adolf Hitler. Their unquestioning aesthetic worship of him meant that his will was allowed to define reality. Since he himself was a demonic aesthete, the German state was left without a moral conscience. In place of a conscience, the thinking of the German people was controlled by such aesthetic phantoms as "blood," "soil," "race," and "fatherland." Hitler himself makes the point that the ethical sphere must be rejected:

> The Volkish view recognizes the importance of mankind in its racially innate elements. . . . Thus it by no means believes in an equality of the races, but with their differences it also recognizes their inferior and superior values, and by this recognition it feels the obligation in accordance with the Eternal Will that dominates this universe to promote the victory of the better and stronger, and to demand the submission of the worse and the weaker. . . . It cannot grant the right of existence to an ethical idea, if this idea represents a danger for the racial life of the bearers of higher ethics; for in a hybridized and negrified world all conceptions of an idealized future of our mankind, would be lost forever.[5]

Hitler was an aesthete in the literal sense that he was a painter. When he turned to politics and came into power, Germany became the canvas on which he would create a new reality—a pure, noble, master race.[6] He devoted a large part of his time and energy to his grand architectural plans for the building of the Third Reich, and he encouraged artists and writers who were "loyal to the blood" to use their talents in the service of Germany. In 1937 he presented to the world an "Exhibition of German Art," which consisted of paintings depicting nature scenes, German peasants, the ideal Aryan family, and so forth. In another building nearby, a contrasting "Exhibition of Degenerate Art" was presented as an example of the poisoning of modern art by "Jewish" influences. The "rebirth" of art in Nazi Germany is described in this way by Goebbels:

---

up desires and hypostatize their satisfaction into a creed of world salvation—a savior of the moment, a saint of the transitory, a comforter of restlessness. Such a man would be a disease of all continuity, a destroyer of human community, a threat to the world (14).

5. Quoted in Mosse, ed., *Nazi Culture*, 5–6.
6. There is a fascinating conversation between Ron Rosenbaum and Berel Lang on the subject of "evil as art" in Rosenbaum's *Explaining Hitler*, 214–219.

Today we can assert with joy and satisfaction that the great development is once again set in motion. Everywhere people are painting, building, writing poetry, singing, and acting. The German artist has his feet on a solid, vital ground. Art, taken out of its narrow and isolated circle, again stands in the midst of the people and from there exerts its strong influences on the whole nation.[7]

Goebbels then speaks words that are chilling to post-Holocaust readers:

The people seek joy. They have a right to it. We have the duty of giving this joy to them. . . . In this hour, we all look reverently upon you, my Führer, you who do not regard art as a ceremonial duty but as a sacred mission and a lofty task, the ultimate and mightiest documentation of human life.[8]

Along with the aesthetic sphere of existence, another Kierkegaardian category provides an important insight into Naziism: angst before the good. In *The Concept of Anxiety*, Haufniensis speaks of angst before the evil and angst before the good as the two principal forms of an individual's relationship with the reality of sin. Angst before the good is the category Haufniensis uses to interpret "the demonic" as a psychological state. When an individual, in the wake of the leap into sin, continues to reinforce this leap in defiance of the good, a new state arises that is most strikingly manifested by the demoniacs of the Gospels. Haufniensis argues that in the state of innocence, freedom was a possibility that remained unactualized, remaining the "nothing" that induced angst in the individual. With the demonic, freedom is still the "nothing" that induces angst, but in the opposite relation; for the demonic, freedom has been forfeited and can only appear as an external threat that inspires angst. Innocence is a state disposed toward freedom, while the demonic is a state that flees from freedom. The demonic wants to close itself off completely from the good, but it cannot ever do this finally and ultimately. Demonic angst resurges in the moment of contact with the good, as illustrated by Jesus' encounters in the Gospels:

The demonic is closed-upness and the involuntarily revealed. These two definitions indicate, as they should, the same thing, because closed-upness is precisely the mute, and when it is to express itself, this must take place against its will, as the freedom which is the ground underlying unfreedom revolts upon coming into communication with the freedom without; it now betrays unfreedom, and the individual betrays himself against his will in angst. . . . The demonic does not close itself up with something, but closes itself up, and in this lies the profundity of existence, that unfreedom makes a prisoner precisely of

---

7. Quoted in Mosse, ed., *Nazi Culture*, 154.
8. Ibid., 157–158.

itself. Freedom is constantly communicating[9] (even if we consider the religious meaning of the word [i.e., communion], no harm is done), unfreedom becomes more and more closed-up and wants no communication. . . . Closed-upness is precisely the mute; language, the word, is precisely that which saves, that which saves from the closed-upness of empty abstraction. . . . A demoniac in the N.T. says therefore to Christ, when he approaches: Τί ἐμοὶ καὶ σοί [What have I to do with you? (Mark 5:7 || Luke 8:28)]; he continues that Christ has come to destroy him (angst before the good). Or the demoniac begs Christ to go another way. (my trans., cf. CA, 123–124)

For Haufniensis, the root of sin is a lack of inwardness. Inwardness signifies an open relationship between the individual and God. A lack of inwardness produces a finitizing of the spirit. This is the essence of the demonic, because the human spirit is intended in its creation by God to be related to the eternal. "Inwardness is therefore eternity or the constituent of the eternal in man" (CA, 151). But sinful human beings seek to evade the development of inwardness within them. They seek "to kill" the eternal, which they cannot succeed in doing (CA, 152). "Men are not willing to think eternity earnestly but are anxious about it, and angst can contrive a hundred evasions. And this is precisely the demonic" (CA, 154).[10]

The "good" signifies that wholeness of human personality which God intends as the *telos* of each person's life. The good means redemption, healing, and being drawn forward into maturity (in the sense of *Practice in Christianity*'s "From on

---

9. Ronald L. Hall elaborates on this theme in his essay "Language and Freedom: Kierkegaard's Analysis of the Demonic in *The Concept of Anxiety*," in *The Concept of Anxiety*, ed. Perkins, International Kierkegaard Commentary 8 (Macon: Mercer University Press, 1985), 153–166.

10. Rolf Fjelde, translator of Ibsen's *Peer Gynt*, has articulated the following description of the "troll" as a personality type, which closely parallels Kierkegaard's understanding of the demoniac:

What is it to be a troll? . . . He exists, in fact, in the widest array of forms. In recent history he ran the death camps; and today as in Ibsen's time, he maneuvers spitefully and secretly against recognition of the best, or mouths the tribal chant of a complacent nationalism. Instinctively he dislikes the open and gravitates toward caves, back rooms, closed thoughts and feelings. Yet with all his affinity for dark places, he shies away from the darkest place of all, himself. There he lives indolently on the surface, cutting corners, following fashions, getting by on compromise, accepting himself through custom and habit, rather than making the painful struggle to realize himself in truth and freedom. His mind, shapeless and indulgent at the core, is like a distorting prism; and with his passion for conformity, he must coerce all others to see things on his own bias. Above all, behind whatever disguise he wears, he finds his own ideas, his own prejudices, his own way of life, his clan, his class, his nation-state-enough. (Foreword to Henrik Ibsen, *Peer Gynt* [Minneapolis: University of Minnesota Press, 1980], xvii–xviii).

high he will draw all to himself"). To live in angst before the good is to take offense at the possibility of spiritual growth. The angst-ridden personality fears the
future and seeks to avoid the pain entailed by the process of personal development.
The voice that cries out "Have you come to destroy us?" is not the true self, the
person whom God is creating, but the panic-stricken immature ego, the voice of
uncreation, which Karl Barth refers to as "nothingness" (see *Church Dogmatics*,
III/3, 305–306). This voice is heard in Hitler's paranoid delusions concerning the
desire of "Jewry" to destroy the German people. For Kierkegaard, a demoniac is a
person whose highest priority is fending off divine grace, which is seen by the
immature ego as a "destroying" force. Divine grace is the pull of creation. In his
effort to evade grace, the demoniac tries to become the God of his own universe.
As his own God, he defines good and evil as he sees fit and attempts to rearrange
the whole world for his own self-protection.

When a society consists of demonic aesthetes, it cries out for a "leader" who
will facilitate its flight from the future. It wants to be "led" by a charismatic individual who knows what it wants and can articulate its goals and bring them to
fruition. Kierkegaard is fully aware of this phenomenon:

> The crowd is untruth. There is therefore no one who has more contempt
> for what it is to be a human being than those who make it their profession to
> lead the crowd. . . . For to win a crowd is not so great a trick; one only needs
> some talent, a certain dose of untruth and a little acquaintance with human
> passions. (my trans., cf. PV, 108–109)

Approximately one hundred years after these words were written, they came true.
Adolf Hitler was a master at winning a crowd in precisely this way. He knew exactly what he was doing, as we can see in this passage from *Mein Kampf*:

> The mass meeting is also necessary for the reason that in it the individual, who
> at first, while becoming a supporter of a young movement, feels lonely and
> easily succumbs to the fear of being alone, for the first time gets the picture of
> a larger community, which in most people has a strengthening, encouraging
> effect. . . . In the crowd he always feels somewhat sheltered. . . . When from his
> little workshop or big factory, in which he feels very small, he steps for the first
> time into a mass meeting and has thousands and thousands of people of the
> same opinions around him, when, as a seeker, he is swept away by three or four
> thousand others into the mighty effect of suggestive intoxication and enthusi-
> asm, when the visible success and agreement of thousands confirm to him the
> rightness of the new doctrine and for the first time arouse doubt in the truth of
> his previous conviction—then he himself has succumbed to the magic influ-
> ence of what we designate as "mass suggestion."[11]

---

11. Quoted in Veith, *Modern Fascism* (St. Louis: Concordia, 1993), 149.

The comments here are so insightful that one might almost think that Hitler had read Girard. A passage such as this suggests that Hitler was cynically manipulating the German people to achieve his ends. He understood the mass psychology of crowds and employed his knowledge very effectively. He knew what "tricks" were needed to "win a crowd."

Hitler knew very clearly that the key to mobilizing a crowd is to give it an *enemy* to fight against and kill. Immature aesthetes are looking for an outlet for their rancor and violence. The leader gives them what they want:

> He who would win the great masses must know the key which opens the door to their hearts. Its name is not objectivity—that is, weakness—but will power and strength.
>
> One can only succeed in winning the soul of a people if, apart from a positive fighting of one's own for one's own aims, one also destroys at the same time the supporter of the contrary.
>
> In the ruthless attack upon an adversary the people sees at all times a proof of its own right, and it perceives the renunciation of his destruction as an uncertainty as regards his own right, if not as a sign of its own wrong. . . .
>
> The nationalization of our masses will only be successful if, along with all the positive fighting for the soul of our people, its international poisoners are extirpated.[12]

These words by Hitler point to a key aspect of the program of Nazi violence. The Jews must be seen as *irreversibly evil*. They cannot be reformed or educated or healed of their "sickness." They must simply be eradicated, as Thomas Merton indicates:

> In the use of force, one simplifies the situation by assuming that the evil to be overcome is clear-cut, definite, and irreversible. Hence there remains but one thing: to eliminate it. Any dialogue with the sinner, any question of the irreversibility of his act, only means faltering and failure. Failure to eliminate evil is itself a defeat. Anything that even remotely risks such defeat is in itself capitulation to evil. The irreversibility of evil then reaches out to contaminate even the tolerant thought of the hesitant crusader who, momentarily, doubts the total evil of the enemy he is about to eliminate.[13]

The idea of the irreversibility of evil presents itself as an interpretation of the true nature of the victims, but in reality it reveals the spiritual state of the victimizers. *It is they who want to be irreversible.* They are demoniacs who fear the possibility of

---

12. Quoted in Mosse, ed., *Nazi Culture*, 8–9.

13. See Thomas Merton's introduction to *Gandhi on Non-Violence* (New York: New Directions, 1965), 13.

repentance more than anything else. This inward state becomes manifest in the world in their program of external violence. Those who see their "enemies" as intractably evil are expressing their absolute commitment to maintaining their current mode of existence. A society made up of such persons will generate a utopian ideology that excludes certain people as unassimilable.[14]

Kierkegaard enables us to see that the engine that drives political violence is the internal alienation of human beings. When the self is in conflict with itself, with its own possibilities, the conditions for conflict in the world are generated. What is needed is "rest" in the Augustinian sense—feeling at home with oneself before God. When this rest is lacking, when restlessness tears apart the hearts of individuals and the fabric of society, a void opens up which is filled in by the demonic. The *difference* between persons, which is the basis of the demonic vision of the world, is an expression of the spiritual state of feeling different from oneself, not being unified and at rest within oneself.

On the basis of Kierkegaard's religious psychology, we are able to articulate an understanding of *the scapegoat* in relation to the aesthetic sphere of existence. The demonic aesthete seeks to avoid becoming an other to himself; more specifically, he seeks to avoid becoming an ethical and religious self. This other which he seeks to fend off is his "shadow," not the shadow of the past, but the shadow of the future, *his own future*. He develops a need to attack his shadow as an external object. He seeks out a scapegoat who (unconsciously) represents himself as a mature person. When an entire society is made up of aesthetes who are hiding from their own future, identifying and killing scapegoats will become central to its existence as a society. It will constitute a "crowd" of "non-persons," that is, people who are evading the possibility of becoming true individuals before God. The nonpersonality that lies at the heart of the crowd's existence will express itself in violence that renders the social other a nonperson, a dead thing. This action, killing the other, manifests the basic desire of the aesthete to kill off the possibility of his own spiritual growth.

---

14. Zygmunt Bauman describes this situation very clearly:

Stalin's and Hitler's victims were not killed in order to capture and colonize the territory they occupied. Often they were killed in a dull, mechanical fashion with no human emotions—hatred included—to enliven it. They were killed because they did not fit, for one reason or another, the scheme of a perfect society. Their killing was not the work of destruction, but creation. They were eliminated, so that an objectively better human world—more efficient, more moral, more beautiful—could be established. A Communist world. Or a racially pure, Aryan world. In both cases, a harmonious world, conflict-free, docile in the hands of their rulers, orderly, controlled. People tainted with the ineradicable blight of their past or origin could not be fitted into such an unblemished, healthy, and shining world. Like weeds, their nature could not be changed. They could not be improved or re-educated. *Modernity and the Holocaust* (Ithaca: Cornell University Press, 1989), 92–93

Thinkers such as Jean-Paul Sartre and Richard Rorty have said that if Naziism had won, then "fascism would be the truth for man."[15] They can only say this because they themselves are trapped under the rubble of the Enlightenment's destruction of Western spiritual culture. From thinkers such as Kierkegaard and Girard, who embody this culture, we can learn definitively that fascism is nothing other than the untruth of man, regardless of its worldly success.

Stalinism

In his writings, Kierkegaard also paints a picture of the *ethical* sphere of existence, which can be contrasted with the aesthetic sphere.[16] The ethical person does not live only in the immediate moment but is conscious of herself as subject to duties that extend through time. She is not a simple solipsist but knows herself to be a member of a community, a social body that places claims on her and for which she is responsible. The ethicist proceeds through life with confidence in her ability, on the whole, to live ethically and justly. She sees herself as a competent person whose maturity places her in a position to instruct those who are immature. She is able to judge and teach aesthetes, so that they may become mature and stable, as she is.

Just as the aesthetic sphere of existence can become a social principle, so also can the ethical sphere be embodied in a society. This is natural and normal, given the intrinsic nature of the ethical sphere. People who have similar understandings of morality and similar degrees of self-confidence will gather together into a group that prides itself on its moral probity. They see themselves as superior to other groups or individuals whom they perceive as existing in a less mature mode of life. Those who inhabit the ethical sphere may develop a personality structure characterized by what Haufniensis calls "angst before the evil" (CA, 113–118). As is the case with those who inhabit the aesthetic sphere, the development of the self can become blocked and stalled by angst. In this case, the ethicist seeks to control the process of creation by continually comparing himself with others who are "inferior" to himself. He becomes fixated on the "evil" of others and fears more than anything else an awareness of his own fallibility—an awareness of his solidarity with the human race.[17]

---

15. Jean-Paul Sartre, *L'Existentialisme est un Humanisme* (Paris: Nagel, 1946), 53–54; Richard Rorty, *Consequences of Pragmatism* (Minneapolis: University of Minnesota Press, 1982), lxii.

16. See *Either/Or*, vol. 2, and *Stages on Life's Way*, 87–184.

17. Karl Barth: "Far more than the conservative, the revolutionary is *overcome of evil*, because with his 'No' he stands so strangely near to God. This is the tragedy of revolution. Evil is not the true answer to evil." *The Epistle to the Romans*, trans. Edwyn C. Hoskyns (London: Oxford University Press, 1968), 480.

In our century, Marxism/Leninism/Stalinism represents an extreme, demonic form of the ethical sphere of existence. Here a philosophical ideology concerning human "progress" becomes the basis for a dichotomizing worldview that labels some as counter-revolutionaries. Such egotistical, aesthetic individuals must be eliminated to purge society of its negative elements so that it may advance toward a utopian state. This theme is very clearly stated in the writings of Marx:

> The bourgeoisie, wherever it has got the upper hand, has put an end to all feudal, patriarchal, idyllic relations. It has pitilessly torn asunder the motley feudal ties that bound man to his "natural superiors," and has left remaining no other nexus between man and man than naked self-interest, than callous "cash payment." It has drowned the most heavenly ecstasies of religious fervor, of chivalrous enthusiasm, of philistine sentimentalism, in the icy water of egotistical calculation. . . . In one word, for exploitation, veiled by religious and political illusions, it has substituted naked, shameless, direct, brutal exploitation.[18]

Marx thinks of himself, of course, as not at all brutal and exploitative, but ethical and just. The basic self-righteousness of Marx's approach to political thought was imitated by Lenin and received its practical outworking in his control of the Soviet Union, as we can see in this quotation:

> Thousands of practical forms and methods of accounting and controlling the rich, the rogues and the idlers should be devised and put to a practical test by the communes themselves, by small units in town and country. Variety is a guarantee of vitality here, a pledge of success in achieving the single common aim—to cleanse the land of Russia of all sorts of harmful insects, of crook-fleas, of bedbugs—the rich, and so on and so forth. In one place half a score of rich, a dozen crooks, half a dozen workers who shirk their work . . . will be put in prison. In another place they will be put to cleaning latrines. In a third place they will be provided with "yellow tickets" after they have served their time, so that all the people shall have them under surveillance, as harmful persons, until they reform. In a fourth place, one out of every ten idlers will be shot on the spot. In a fifth place mixed methods may be adopted, and by probational release, for example, the rich, the bourgeois intellectuals, the crooks and hooligans who are corrigible will be given an opportunity to reform quickly. The more variety there will be, the better and richer will be our general experience, the more certain and more rapid will be the success of socialism, and the easier will it be for practice to devise—for only practice can devise—the best methods and means of struggle.[19]

---

18. *The Marx-Engels Reader* (New York: Norton, 1978), 475.
19. *The Lenin Anthology* (New York: Norton, 1975), 431–432.

The "ethical" person who has become demonic seeks to avoid becoming an other to himself; he seeks to avoid becoming aware of his own sinfulness. This other whom he seeks to fend off is his "shadow." While the aesthetic demoniac is attacking the shadow of the future, the "ethical" demoniac is attacking the shadow of the past, the shadow of that egocentric person whom he has transcended. He develops a need to attack his shadow as an external object. He seeks out a scapegoat who (unconsciously) represents himself as an immature, egoistic person. By killing this other, he is trying to prevent himself from becoming aware of his own fallibility—his own humanity.[20]

At this point the story of the killing of millions of human beings by Stalin's regime can be inserted into the argument. There is no need for me to retell it in detail.[21] One of the standard historical works on this subject, Robert Conquest's *The Great Terror*, estimates that the terror-famine of 1932–1933 led to 6 to 7 million deaths.[22] During the years 1937–1938, about 1 million people were executed outright, about 2 million more died in prison camps, and about 8 million more were being held in camps, of whom probably only 10 percent survived. Estimates of the total number of deaths that resulted from Stalin's reign are usually placed at 20 million, which is most likely a conservative figure.[23] We will never know the exact number, because Stalin's regime did not keep meticulous records of its killing activities.

Stalin biographer Isaac Deutscher argues that the basic motive behind the purges was Stalin's intense paranoia concerning even the remotest possibility that

---

20. Fritz Künkel's *In Search of Maturity* (New York: Charles Scribner's Sons, 1948) provides insights into the social-psychological dynamics that we have been considering. The following quotation, as an example, sheds light on Naziism and Stalinism: "To the majority of mankind both groups are equally ridiculous; but in their own eyes they are the only 'righteous' people in the world; and to each other they are the arch-enemy and abomination. From the psychological point of view the very fact that they exist together and that they are not able to redeem each other, means that both of them are doomed" (175). He continues: "Each idolater is imperiled by the potential collapse of the group . . . therefore, in defending his Idol he defends his own immaturity; and in cursing the rebellious infidel he tries to prevent his own relapse into the process of development. Therefore he is as ruthless as a drowning man fighting for his last chance of life" (177). He goes on to describe group egocentricity as a "dead, mechanical apparatus, unconsciously designed to protect the group against its own creativity" (183–184). From the point of view we have been developing, he has hit the nail on the head.

21. An overview of the purges is provided by Isaac Deutscher under the title, "The Gods Are Athirst." See *Stalin: A Political Biography* (New York: Oxford University Press, 1966), 345–385.

22. Robert Conquest, *The Great Terror: A Reassessment* (New York: Oxford University Press, 1990), 20.

23. *Ibid.*, 485–486.

an alternative to his own personal dictatorship might be suggested.[24] He thus ordered the killing not only of key old-guard Bolsheviks, but also of virtually anyone who had ever come in contact with them. This is another example of the thesis I have been developing. The most basic motive for violence is psychological self-protection. For Stalin to have admitted his crimes and released the reins of power would have amounted to a psychological breakdown. He feared this possibility more than anything else. He was driven to demand the deaths of others so that he could avoid becoming an other to himself, that is, a mature human being. For Kierkegaard, to be mature is equivalent to being repentant.[25]

The faint glimmering of the possibility of repentance can be seen in Central Committee member Nikolai Bukharin. In the wake of Stalin's brutal efforts at "rapid socialization" during the early 1930s, Bukharin began to realize that immoral actions were dehumanizing the Party. He commented: "In 1919 . . . we executed people, but we also risked our lives in the process. In the later period, however, we were conducting a mass annihilation of completely defenseless men, together with their wives and children."[26] Bukharin was concerned about the psychological effects that the terror was producing in those who were doing the terrorizing. He knew that some had committed suicide and others had gone insane. Those who remained "sane" became, in Bukharin's words, "professional bureaucrats for whom terror was henceforth a normal method of administration, and obedience to any order from above a high virtue."[27] Bukharin himself was executed during the Purge Trials of 1938, a victim of the Bolshevik system he had helped to create.

The central irony of this historical episode is the way in which Marxist ideology, inspired by an ethical goal, becomes a justification for actions that are grossly unethical on a grand scale. The irony comes to birth in the fundamental decision to separate means from ends—the decision to kill in order to create a just and peaceful society. Here also, Kierkegaard was prescient:

What means do you use to perform your work; is the means just as important to you as the end, just exactly as important? If not, you cannot possi-

---

24. *Stalin*, 375. Robert Tucker argues that Stalin's "supreme aim" was the furtherance of his own "glory" as the ruler of the expanding Soviet empire. The dark side of this obsessive search for "glory" was Stalin's complete indifference to the suffering of his victims. See Tucker's Foreword to *Stalin's Letters to Molotov 1925–1936*, ed. Lars Lih et al. (New Haven: Yale University Press, 1995), xi-xii.

25. See UDVS, 15: "Repentance and regret belong to the eternal in a human being." Gil Bailie echoes this idea in *Violence Unveiled* (New York: Crossroad, 1995): "Contrition is the specific Christian form of lucidity" (40).

26. Quoted in Boris Nicolaevsky, *Power and the Soviet Elite*, ed. Janet D. Zagoria (Ann Arbor: University of Michigan Press, 1975), 18.

27. Ibid. See also Robert Conquest, *The Great Terror*, 22.

bly will one thing; in that case the indefensible, the irresponsible, the self-serving, the heterogeneous means enters in, disturbing and defiling. (UDVS, 141)

Political Religion as Unbelief

Naziism and Stalinism were not merely political events, they were at root religious phenomena.[28] This historical and sociological argument has been effectively articulated by Nikolai Berdyaev, Eric Voegelin, and Jacques Ellul, among others.

We can see this theme very clearly anticipated by Kierkegaard. He commented that the Reformation began as a religious movement and became political, while "now everything appears to be politics but will turn out to be a religious movement" (JP, 6: 6256 [1848]). Kierkegaard longs for the appearance of true Christian pastors to "split up the crowd and turn it into individuals." Such pastors will "suffer the rudeness of the sick without being disturbed." "For the generation is sick, spiritually, sick unto death." People think that their problems will be solved by the installation of a new government, but in reality "it is the eternal that is needed." It is not clear to what extent Kierkegaard was personally aware of the writings of Marx, but he was certainly cognizant of the ideas being articulated by socialists such as Marx. Thus, at approximately the same time that the *Communist Manifesto* was written, Kierkegaard commented on "that frightful sigh (from hell) uttered in socialism: God is the evil; just get rid of him and we will get relief. Thus it says what it needs itself." He continues:

> "Christian" pastors are what will be needed, also with respect to one of the greatest of all dangers, which is far closer than one can possibly believe—namely, that when the catastrophe spreads and turns into a religious movement (and the strength in communism obviously is the same ingredient demonically potential in religiousness, even Christian religiousness), then, like mushrooms after a rain, demonically tainted characters will appear who soon will presumptuously make themselves apostles on a par with "the apostles," a few also assuming the task of perfecting Christianity, soon even becoming religious founders themselves, inventors of a new religion which will gratify the times and the world. . . . The most dangerous [attacks come] when the demoniacs themselves become apostles—something like thieves passing themselves off as policemen. (JP, 6: 6257 [1848])

---

28. This subsection heading is an allusion to §17.2 of Karl Barth's *Church Dogmatics* I/2, which bears the title "Religion as unbelief." Barth describes religion as "the realm of man's attempts to justify and sanctify himself before a capricious and arbitrary picture of god" (280).

We can see in such passages that Kierkegaard was fully aware of the potential for modern political regimes to become religious—exactly what happened in the twentieth century as demoniacs like Hitler and Stalin were worshiped by their "congregations."

Russian philosopher Nikolai Berdyaev acutely analyzes Soviet Communism as a religious phenomenon in his work *The Russian Revolution*. He describes Communism as not a merely social or political entity, but at root a spiritual movement. He suggests that Communism opposes Christianity precisely as an alternative religion with its own claim to give meaning to reality, its own dogmas, its own morality, its own catechisms, and its own cult.[29] The technical details of Marxist economics cannot by themselves inflame and inspire people to political action:

> What does rouse enthusiasm is Marx's messianic faith. It finds its complete expression in the idea of the proletariat's messianic vocation. The aspect of Marxism which looks forward to the future Socialist society and to the great mission of the proletariat has nothing in common with science—it is a faith, "the substance of things to be hoped for, the evidence of things that appear not." Marx's "proletariat" and his perfect Socialist society are "invisible things," an object of faith. Here we are in contact with a religious idea. (63–64)

Marx claimed that the traditional Christian notions of good and evil were outmoded and repressive. Yet in his thought the concepts of good and evil were merely transposed onto the "proletariat" and the "bourgeoisie." In this way he preserved religious notions of the elect and the damned. According to Berdyaev, this is an example of an "unconscious survival of dualistic Manichean tendencies," which is typical of revolutionary ideologies. Further, the Marxist theory of the end of capitalist society in a violent cataclysm is an example of an eschatological worldview (69–70).

Eric Voegelin articulated an interpretation of the religious nature of Naziism in 1938. He had intimate knowledge of his subject, as evidenced by his need to flee for his life to the United States. Like Berdyaev, he points out the need for political religions to designate a "Devil" figure against which a battle may be fought:

> We have already spoken about the Catholic Church as the Satan corresponding to the Leviathan. Kant's Devil is human instinct. Fichte sketched Napoleon as the monstrous figure of Satan. Religion and metaphysics belong to the positivist apocalypse as Evil; the bourgeoisie to the proletariat; the minority, above all the Jews as the "opposing race," to the select racist apocalypse. (*Political Religions*, 61)

Voegelin compares Naziism to the religion of the ancient Egyptians under Akhenaton. In both cases, "God" speaks to the people through the intermediation

---

29. *The Russian Revolution* (Ann Arbor: University of Michigan Press, 1961), 55–56.

of the Pharaoh/Führer. The sacred hero is the unique spokesman who conveys the divine will to the people (70).

In *The Ecumenic Age* Voegelin analyzes Marxism, which is ostensibly atheistic, as another form of corrupted religion:

> The revolution in "history" is made to substitute for the theophanic event in reality. The turbulence of the encounter between God and man is transformed into the violence of an encounter between man and man. In the imaginary reality of the ideologists, this killing of men in revolutionary action is supposed to produce the much desired transfigurative, or metastatic, change of the nature of man as an event in "history." Marx has been quite explicit on this point: Revolutionary killing will induce a Blutrausch, a "blood-intoxication"; and from this Blutrausch "man" will emerge as "superman" into the "realm of freedom." The magic of the Blutrausch is the ideological equivalent to the promise of the Pauline vision of the Resurrected. (253–254)

Like Berdyaev, Voegelin articulates a very sharp critique of political religion as a "falling away from God" that opposes true faith. He claims that in the modern era humanity's belief in its own inherent ability to define the good and improve the world is in fact "anti-Christian," it is a "turning away." He describes political religion as a worldly spirituality that "blocks the way to the reality of God" (*Political Religions*, 79).

Jacques Ellul has also made a significant contribution to this line of thought in his work *The New Demons*. He argues that the twentieth century has seen the rise of political movements that are precisely parallel to the earlier religious orders they seek to "transcend." He claims that to notice these parallels is not just a "journalistic" exercise, but the clear conclusion of contemporary sociology. He points to phenomena such as these:

> The outward works of Lenin, his establishment of a party on the model of the Jesuit Order and in the image of the Order of the Knights of the Sword (he said so himself), the accentuation of the role of the proletariat and elevation of the writings of Marx; the outward works of Stalin, establishing a liturgy, dogmatics, an inquisition of heretics—all those things went to confirm this religion very rapidly. It is organized by the exact procedures followed by Christianity itself. It ended in the "materialistic replica, a striking morphological similitude, of Roman Catholicism." (168)

In addition to Soviet Communism, he also puts forward Naziism and Maoism as his principal examples. He points out that no one laughed when Hitler claimed that he had been "sent by the Almighty" to establish a Reich that would last for "a thousand years." His faithful followers saw him as a "saving and transcendent divinity" for whom one could die (171). German schoolchildren recited this "grace" before meals:

Führer, my Führer, bequeathed to me by the Lord,
Protect and preserve me as long as I live!
Thou hast rescued Germany from deepest distress,
I thank thee today for my daily bread.
Abideth thou long with me, forsaketh me not,
Führer, my Führer, my faith and my light!
        Heil, mein Führer![30]

Girard confirms and deepens this line of thought already articulated by Kierke-gaard, Berdyaev, Voegelin, and Ellul. Girard is advancing a theory of the origin of culture in acts of violence. Thus he enables us to understand the increased need for killing at precisely those times in history when charismatic leaders are attempt-ing to establish a *new culture* such as the Thousand Year Reich or the Communist utopia. In commenting on Soviet Russia, for example, Girard analyzes the primi-tivity of the sacrificial culture:

> The system of scapegoats is carried so far under Stalin that it reminds one of a primitive society gone mad. In *The Gulag Archipelago*, for example, Solzhenit-syn recounts that the presence of a suspect in a building in Moscow entailed sometimes the arrest of all of the tenants and sometimes of all the inhabitants of the street. It is a little like the societies which see in the birth of twins a mani-festation of contagious violence because it is mimetic. Their members think therefore, very "logically," that the mother must have violated some interdict, that she has probably committed adultery. Sometimes the fear of violence is such that the suspicion extends to the whole family and even to the neighbor-hood, to the whole district. Instead of sending the whole world to the Gulag, one particularly requires purification rituals, which is certainly preferable. Stalinism also makes one think, *mutatis mutandis*, of the demented multiplica-tion of human sacrifices in precolumbian America.[31]

He argues that Naziism is an overt rebellion against Christianity in favor of a primi-tive sacrificial culture:

> The true "grandeur of National Socialism"—an expression effectively em-ployed by Martin Heidegger in his *Introduction to Metaphysics*—has consisted, it seems to me, in combating overtly the project of a society without scapegoats or sacrificial victims, that is, the Christian and modern project which Nietzsche has been paradoxically the first to notice. National Socialism strove to render this project null and void. They return deliberately to the system of scapegoats, which is more compellingly culpable than the ancient unconsciousness. Neo-paganism can only conduct itself this way. They want to renew the myth by

---

30. In Mosse, ed., *Nazi Culture*, 241.
31. *Quand Ces Choses Commenceront* (Paris: Arléa, 1994), 17–18, my translation.

taking the Jews as victims, and they want also to renew the primitive myth which was repressed in the Germanic forest.[32]

Girard's thought demonstrates that politics, culture, and religion are all inextricably connected. This is true not simply in the ancient world, but in the "modern" world as well. Girard demonstrates that "modernity," as we usually conceive it, is essentially an illusion. We are not living in a postreligious age, but one in which religion is taking different forms. Human beings are inherently religious; the question simply concerns the forms of religiosity dominant at a given time.

"Modernity" can be defined as simply a period of time—the recent past. But if modernity is given a more substantive definition, concerning the maturity of present-day human beings in contrast with our primitive and superstitious ancestors, then we must ask what constitutes genuine maturity. Is maturity to be equated with scientific and technological "progress"? Have we "come of age" if we can produce televisions, computers, precision-guided nuclear warheads? Is maturity to be equated with ways of acting that are described as "free" in relation to the "repressive" moral beliefs of the Puritans? Is maturity to be equated with having a "higher standard of living" than 99 percent of the human race throughout its history? Is maturity to be equated with advanced academic degrees? Is it a political system in which the majority rules through representative elections?

For Girard, changes in technological abilities, political forms, personal mores, and so forth, are of little importance as long as societies continue to be driven by the dynamics of mimetic desire. The scapegoat mechanism is just as powerful in our time as it was during the time of the Aztecs. Our sacrificial high priests are named Hitler and Stalin. Girard is suggesting that the concept of maturity makes sense only when it is equated with the possibility that human beings can escape from the system of mimetic rivalry and become genuine *subjects*, whom Kierkegaard calls *single individuals*.

For Kierkegaard and Girard, if modernity is understood to mean human intellectual and moral maturity, in distinction from the immature cultic violence of the primitive world, then *Christianity is modernity*.

Hitler, Stalin, and the Gospel

The basic presupposition of this book is that *human disorder has an intelligible order*. Though the ultimate springs of evil will always remain a mystery, human pathology can be understood to a great extent. Therefore, we need not despair of the possibility of understanding historical characters such as Hitler and Stalin. *The*

---

32. Ibid., 19, my translation.

categories for understanding violence are not lacking. This point has been made very effectively by Eric Voegelin, in an essay entitled "The German University and the Order of German Society: A Reconsideration of the Nazi Era."[33]

Voegelin argues that it is not necessary to live through certain historical events to understand them. Someone could have lived as a contemporary of Hitler in Germany without having any real intellectual grasp of what was occurring at that time. However, a person living in another time and place may have a very deep understanding of Hitler and the Holocaust. Voegelin maintains that understanding "requires qualities of knowledge and of intellectual development, of character and of intelligence."[34] It has been my basic argument throughout the preceding pages that Kierkegaard and Girard are two authors who possess exactly these qualities of intellectual insight.

Voegelin analyzes the moral disease of Naziism as a manifestation of estrangement from the spirit of God. The essence of this estrangement is "not-wanting-one's-being-to-be-altered."[35] He is here pointing to the same phenomenon I have been describing as *resistance to the process of creation.* These words of Voegelin could serve as a summary of the message of *The Sickness unto Death*:

> By spirit we understand the openness of man to the divine ground of his existence: by estrangement from the spirit, the closure and the revolt against the ground. Through spirit man actualizes his potential to partake of the divine. He rises thereby to the imago Dei which it is his destiny to be.[36]

For Voegelin, the closure of the human spirit against the call of the divine entails a need for human beings to become their own ground of being. Revolt against the divine basis of reality results in philosophical narcissism, which leads to moral "illiteracy."

With Voegelin's essay in mind, along with the themes I have drawn out of Kierkegaard and Girard, I would articulate a theological interpretation of Naziism and Stalinism along the following lines: Naziism and Stalinism, which differed from each other in many ways and warred with each other, were as one in constituting the great twentieth century revolt against the call of the eternal. The most basic belief that undergirds the revolt is that Christ is a person of the past. He has been left behind. He is no longer necessary. He is a hindrance to us. The events of the twentieth century have shown us, however, that *the person who thinks he has Christ behind him, in actuality has Christ in front of him, in the person he is kill-*

33. See Eric Voegelin, *Published Essays 1966–1985* ed. Ellis Sandoz (Baton Rouge: Louisiana State University Press, 1990), 1–35.

34. *Published Essays 1966–1985*, 2.

35. Ibid., 6.

36. Ibid., 7.

ing. Whenever and wherever scapegoats are killed by the social mechanism of spiritual evasion, the crucifixion of Christ is recurring. Thus the violence of the twentieth century demoniacs cannot ever accomplish its goal of sealing off Christ in the past; it can only take the story of the Cross and magnify it a million times, until human sinfulness becomes absolutely impossible to ignore.[37] The Gospel revelation of the roots of human violence is only made clearer and clearer as time goes by. This is one of Girard's key insights.

Kierkegaard portrays the alienated individual as disjointed and disunified. He is unable on his own to hold together the infinite and the finite, the eternal and the temporal, grace and contrition. Christ is the one in whom the paradox is held together, the disjointed is joined.[38] We are touching here on the heart of Kierkegaard's thought. *The Sickness unto Death* analyzes the order of human disorder, but at the same time it intimates a vision of the potential wholeness of the human spirit in relationship with Christ. Human beings fall into traps on the right side or on the left side when they live in the finite to the exclusion of the infinite, or when they seek freedom to the exclusion of necessity, or when they live in the temporal while ignoring the eternal. The goal of human life, then, is the difficult task of holding together these paradoxical elements in a creative synthesis. The highest and truest pathway in life can be compared to walking along a narrow mountain ridge. It is always possible to fall off the ridge to the right or to the left, but the successful walker continues forward maintaining a balance.

The Christian vision of mature human existence calls persons to the difficult task of recognizing that they are, in Luther's words, *simul justus et peccator* [simultaneously justified and a sinner]. The Christian message leads its hearers to recognize their sin before God. It calls for remorse and contrition. It accomplishes a thoroughgoing defeat of human self-righteousness. At the same time, the Christian message brings forgiveness and healing to the sinner. It lifts the weight of sin and calls the repentant individual forward into new life. The message brings about honesty in relation to the past and openness in relation to the future. When we consider Naziism and Stalinism, we can see that they reveal, against their will,

---

37. See Gil Bailie, *Violence Unveiled*, 274: "Perhaps the *anthropological* role of the Christian church in human history might be oversimplified as follows: To undermine the structures of sacred violence by making it impossible to forget how Jesus *died* and to show the world how to live without such structures by making it impossible to forget how Jesus *lived*."

38. See Picard, *Hitler in Our Selves*, trans. Hernrich Hauser (Hinsdale: Henry Regnery, 1947), 264–265. See also Reinhold Niebuhr: "The Christ is the redeemer who reveals God in His redemptive vitality, above and beyond the revelation of the created order. 'The world was made by Him' indeed. He is the pattern, the logos of creation. But He is also the revelation of the redemptive will which restores a fallen world to the pattern of its creation" (*The Nature and Destiny of Man* [New York: Charles Scribner's Sons, 1941], 1: 28).

this fundamental dialectic of Christian theology.[39] The greatest fear of the Nazi is grace, redemption, transformation. The greatest fear of the Communist is recognition of his own participation in the immorality of human history. Together, they reveal the consequences of deafness to the forgiving and recreating word of God.

The epitome of spiritual deafness is seen in historical phenomena such as Nazism and Stalinism, which express a panic-stricken need for "enemies" against which one must battle to the death (i.e., their death). The existence of such "enemies" reveals more about the person who fears them than it does about the objects of the hatred. Thus, the crux of Christian ethics, and the true strength of Christian proclamation in history, lies in the way Christ leads persons out of the hell of enemy-hatred and into the realm of reality, in which the other is simply another creature of God. As Dostoevsky's Father Zossima says, Hell is the suffering of being unable to love other human beings.[40] Christ's life and message transforms the alien other into our neighbor by ending our spiritual evasion and opening up our spirit to the call of the Creator.

---

39. A similar point is made by Eugene Rose: "In the end a Proudhon, a Bakunin, a Lenin, a Hitler, however great their temporary influence and success, must fail; they must even testify, against their will, to the Truth they would destroy. For their endeavor to *Nihilize* creation, and so annul God's act of creation by returning the world to the very nothingness from which it came, is but an inverted parody of God's creation" (*Nihilism* [Forestville: Fr. Seraphim Rose Foundation, 1994], 70).

40. Fyodor Dostoyevsky, *The Brothers Karamazov*, trans. Constance Garnett (New York: Macmillan, 1928), 343.

9

CONCLUSION: THE HEALING
OF THE SOUL

Those who are well have no need of a physician, but those who are
sick. Go and learn what this means, "I desire mercy and not
sacrifice." For I have come to call not the righteous but sinners.

Matt. 9:13

God is not my Father or any man's Father in a special way (frightful
presumptuousness and madness!); no, he is Father only in the sense
of being the Father of all. When I hate someone or deny that God is
his Father, it is not he who loses but I—then I have no Father.

JP, 2: 1413 (1850)

The essence of sin is alienation between the human being and God.
The opposite of sin is a harmonious and loving relationship between
the human being and God. The event that makes possible the transition from the
one to the other is the Atonement, the reconciliation between humanity and God.
Christian tradition teaches that this reconciliation took place in a decisive way
when Christ was crucified and raised from the dead. But it is clear from the long
history of human violence up to the present that human beings are still living apart
from the reality of the Atonement. Whatever took place on the Cross, however
Atonement is understood, it is clear that we have not allowed that reality to enter
into us and transform us into persons who live in joyful harmony with God. If the
past two thousand years have taught us anything, it is the utter stubbornness and
wickedness of the human heart.

I said just now "however Atonement is understood" because there is not just
one single understanding of the meaning of Atonement within the Christian tradition. Ever since Gustav Aulén's *Christus Victor* was published in 1930, the ransom theory of Atonement has been close to the surface of theological discussion
in the West, and this theory has always been foundational for the Eastern Orthodox tradition built upon the Fathers such as Irenaeus and Gregory of Nyssa.[1] This

---

1. Gustaf Aulén, *Christus Victor: An Historical Study of the Three Main Types of the Idea of
the Atonement*, trans. A. G. Hebert (New York: Macmillan, 1969).

perspective holds that the Fall entailed the entrapment of humanity within the snare of the Devil, sin, and death. The work of God in saving humanity involved God becoming man in Christ so that "He might destroy sin, overcome death, and give life to man."[2] Through the work of Christ on the Cross, God the Father overcame the Devil's grip on humanity and won us back for eternal life. The Devil, "who had taken man captive was himself taken captive by God, and man who had been taken captive was set free from the bondage of condemnation."[3] The major emphasis of this view of Atonement is placed on God's victorious campaign against his foe, Satan.

A major alternative theory of Atonement in the West was formulated by Anselm in the eleventh century, shifting attention away from the Devil. In *Cur Deus Homo* (Why God became Man), Anselm sketched what has come to be known as the satisfaction theory of Atonement. In conversation with an interlocutor named "Bozo," Anselm argues in this manner:

> Surely we argue conclusively enough that it was fitting for God to do the things we speak of, when we say that the human race, that very precious work of his, was altogether ruined [by the Fall]; that it was not fitting for God's plan for man to be entirely wiped out; and that this same plan could not be put into effect unless the human race were delivered by its Creator himself.[4]

It is important to note that both Bozo and Anselm agree on the point that it is incorrect to say that on the cross God was "giving up the innocent to death for the guilty."[5] In other words, this is not a penal substitution theory.

Anselm defines the "justice or rectitude of the will" as "every inclination of the rational creature" being subjected to God's will at all times. Sin is the exact opposite of this; it is the failure of human beings to subject themselves continually to the will of God. This failure "takes away from God what belongs to him and dishonors God."[6] The restoration of God's lost honor is something that human beings must do but cannot. Nor can they restore the original goodness and justice in which they were created. Therefore God's creation is threatened with frustration and dissolution. Anselm argues that this situation is "not fitting," "unseemly," "incongruous." God must and does act to repair this situation by becoming man in the person of Christ. Only God can complete this work of restoring his honor, but the work must be done by man; "otherwise man does not make satisfaction."[7]

2. Irenaeus, *Adversus Haereses*, III, 18.7, quoted in Aulén, 19.

3. Irenaeus, *Adversus Haereses*, III, 23.1, quoted in Aulén, 20.

4. Eugene R. Fairweather, ed., *A Scholastic Miscellany: Anselm to Ockham* (Philadelphia: Westminster Press, 1956), 105.

5. Ibid., 111, 118.

6. Ibid., 119.

7. Ibid., 151.

Christ achieves this satisfaction through complete obedience to God's will, even to the point of death. With the garden of Gethsemane in the back of his mind, Anselm thus argues: "Nothing that man can suffer for God's honor, freely and not as an obligation, is more bitter or harder than death. Nor can a man give himself more fully to God than he does when he surrenders himself to death for His honor."[8] Thus Christ makes the payment needed to restore God's honor and cancel the debt of the human race. His death satisfies God's justice and opens up the way of salvation once again, reestablishing the right and fitting order of the universe.

The penal substitution theory of Atonement is distinct from Anselm's, though it is easy to confuse the two. The substitution theory stresses the idea that Christ, the innocent one, took upon himself the penalty for sin that human beings deserve. John Calvin favored this view. He begins by placing great stress on the sinfulness of human beings:

> With regard to our corrupt nature and the wicked life that follows it, all of us surely displease God, are guilty in his sight, and are born to the damnation of hell. But because the Lord wills not to lose what is his in us, out of his own kindness he still finds something to love.[9]

Christ's arraignment before Pilate has great significance for Calvin. Pilate both acknowledges Christ's innocence and also condemns him to death as a criminal. In this image we see that to make the proper satisfaction for us "a form of death had to be chosen in which he might free us both by transferring our condemnation to himself and by taking our guilt upon himself."[10] Calvin marshals the familiar phrases from the Bible:

> But when we say that grace was imparted to us by the merit of Christ, we mean this: by his blood we were cleansed, and his death was an expiation for our sins. "His blood cleanses us from all sin."[I John 1:7.] "This is my blood . . . which is shed . . . for the forgiveness of sins." [Matt. 26:28; cf. Luke 22:20.] If the effect of his shedding of blood is that our sins are not imputed to us, it follows that God's judgment was satisfied by that price. On this point John the Baptist's words apply: "Behold, the Lamb of God, who takes away the sin of the world" [John 1:29].[11]

Calvin's view of Atonement is perhaps best summed up in this sentence: "For, in some ineffable way, God loved us and yet was angry toward us at the same time,

---

8. Ibid., 161.
9. John Calvin, *Institutes of the Christian Religion* (Philadelphia: Westminster Press, 1960), I:505.
10. Ibid., I:509.
11. Ibid., I:531.

until he became reconciled to us in Christ."[12] The wrath of God the Father is turned away from us by being turned toward his Son on the Cross.

The power of this vision has exerted great force down through history to the present day. It is seen particularly in the preaching of Protestant Christianity from the Reformation to Jonathan Edwards to Billy Graham. It forms the theological backbone of Handel's *Messiah*, as we can see particularly in the chorus, "All we like sheep have gone astray; and the Lord hath laid on him the iniquity of us all."

Another possible theory is described by Aulén under the heading of the subjective theory of Atonement. This view was formulated by Abelard, a younger contemporary of Anselm. Abelard rejects the ransom theory by not giving credence to the idea that the Devil has any legitimate rights or authority over humanity. He also rejects penal substitution by arguing that it is "cruel and wicked" that God would "demand the blood of an innocent person as the price for anything, or that it should in any way please him that an innocent man should be slain—still less that God should consider the death of his Son so agreeable that by it he should be reconciled to the whole world!" Abelard proposes that the correct understanding of Atonement holds that Christ's death on the cross shows the boundless love of God for us; when we behold this love, we are inwardly changed, redeemed, "enkindled by such a gift of divine grace."[13] This view has been reaffirmed by modern liberal theologians who have viewed the ransom theory as being too primitive and mythological, Anselm's theory as being too feudal and judicial, and the penal substitution theory as being suspect because of its picture of a legalistic and sadistic God whose thirst for blood sacrifices must be quenched.

These four views of Atonement—the ransom, satisfaction, penal substitution, and subjective theories—are not the only ones possible. An exhaustive account of all of the different perspectives on Atonement throughout the history of Christian thought would take up many hundreds of pages and would entail dozens of different subtheories. Supporters of all of these positions draw on key biblical verses because the Bible does not articulate one simplistic theory of Atonement. The Bible contains a rich tapestry of images and ideas that overlap and cross each other like the warp and woof of a cloth. George Lindbeck has argued that it is a very modern prejudice to insist that things should be otherwise. Premodern biblical interpreters were very comfortable developing these different strands of thought on the meaning of the Cross, as they thought and witnessed within differing historical contexts. Lindbeck points out that "Westerners and Easterners, Roman Catholics

---

12. Ibid., I:530.
13. This and the previous quotation are found in Fairweather, ed., *A Scholastic Miscellany*, 283.

and Protestants have never anathematized each other because of differences over Christ's saving work."[14]

Christians have anathematized each other on other theological points, however, and killed each other in large numbers, which indicates to me that the Bible has not been well understood by these Christians. A person who believes that he is living in obedience to Christ his savior while killing other people is actually living in a very profound delusion. We may be able to avoid this kind of delusion if we adopt an attitude of humility in our understanding of the Bible. The knowledge that the same Bible is quoted by Christian pacifists and nonpacifists, by defenders and attackers of infant baptism, and by proponents of different views of the Atonement should lead us to realize that we see through a glass darkly. And when our vision is so limited, we should not be quick to claim that we know that certain people ought to be killed.

"What was Kierkegaard's view of Atonement?" the reader may be wondering. I quoted in chapter 7 a journal entry in which he says that Christ was crucified because he refused to conform to the ways of the world. We "pretend as if Christ himself and God's providence ordained it this way" because we don't want to honestly acknowledge the evil in our world and in our hearts (JP, 1: 305 [1847]). This seems to be a direct denial of the view which sees the crucifixion in precisely those terms, as something ordained and required by God for the satisfaction of justice. But this journal passage is in tension with other passages in Kierkegaard's authorship in which he dwells comfortably within the language of the penal substitution tradition. In his discourse on "The High Priest," for example, he says:

> If he, if the Redeemer's suffering and death is the satisfaction for your sin and guilt—if it is the satisfaction, then he does indeed step into your place for you, or he, the one who makes satisfaction, steps into your place, suffering in your place the punishment of sin so that you might be saved, suffering in your place death so that you might live—did he not and does he not then put himself completely in your place? . . .
>
> Thus when punitive justice here in the world or in judgment in the next seeks the place where I, a sinner, stand with all my guilt, with my many sins— it does not find me. I no longer stand in that place; I have left it and someone else stands in my place, someone who puts himself completely in my place. (WA, 123)

It is difficult to imagine a clearer and more concise restatement of the substitutionary motif than this. The prayer at the beginning of the second part of *Judge for Yourself!* reiterates this idea:

---

14. George Lindbeck, "Atonement and the Hermeneutics of Social Embodiment," *Pro Ecclesia* 5 (1996): 160.

O Redeemer, by your holy suffering and death you have made satisfaction for everyone and everything; no eternal salvation either can or shall be earned—it has been earned. Yet you left your footprints, you, the holy prototype for the human race and for every individual, so that by your Atonement the saved might at every moment find the confidence and boldness to want to strive to follow you. (JFY, 147)

We see here Kierkegaard's affirmation of the Lutheran stress on salvation by grace alone, along with his concern that this doctrine not lead to spiritual and ethical laxity. In other words, Christ's death ought not to make Christians forget Christ's life and the divine call to live as he did to the best of one's abilities. (For other passages along similar lines as those just quoted, see CD, 298–299; JFY, 209; SUD, 100; WA, 64–65, 158–159.)

Volume IV/1 of Karl Barth's *Church Dogmatics* contains a treatment of the doctrine of Atonement which is well known in theological circles. Barth continues to develop the satisfaction theory along the trajectory seen in Kierkegaard's thought, under the subsection title "The Judge Judged in Our Place." Barth defines sin in this way:

All sin has its being and origin in the fact that man wants to be his own judge. And in wanting to be that, and thinking and acting accordingly, he and his whole world is in conflict with God. It is an unreconciled world, and therefore a suffering world, a world given up to destruction. (*Church Dogmatics* IV/1, 220)

The idea of "man wanting to be his own judge" is another way of expressing what I have described in this book. Human beings, as sinners, seek to withdraw themselves from the process of creation and deafen themselves to God's voice. This means being one's own judge in the sense of continually seeking to affirm one's own beliefs and actions so that one never has to change. Barth continues:

It is for this reason—the fault and evil are evidently great and deep enough to make it necessary—it is for this reason that God himself encounters man in the flesh and therefore face to face in the person of His Son, in order that He may pass on the one who feels and accepts himself as his own judge the real judgment which he has merited. This judgment sets him in the wrong as the one who maintains his own right against God instead of bowing to God's right. . . . Because it is a matter of the appearance and work of the true Judge amongst those who think they can and should judge and therefore exalt themselves, therefore the abasement of the Son to our status, the obedience which He rendered in humility as our brother, is the divine accusation against every man and the divine condemnation of every man. (IV/1, 220)

Barth seeks here to unpack the richness of meaning in the drama of the Cross as it is depicted in the Gospels. Christ prayed in Gethsemane, "Not my will but thine be done." What is the Father's will? It is that human beings be saved. It is that they be forgiven "for they know not what they do." Christ suffers in himself the unleashing of our sin and guilt and violence, so that we might see ourselves and God's mercy for the first time. Through his obedience to the Father's will, Christ made it impossible for us to script our own drama, to be our own judge. Now, the only way we can come to understand reality truly is by recognizing ourselves in the drama that God is directing:

> Jesus Christ as very man and very God has taken the place of every man. He has penetrated to that inner place where every man is in his inner being supremely by and for himself. This sanctuary belongs to Him and not to man. He has to do what has to be done there. What is man in relation to Him? One who is dispossessed, expelled, a displaced person. He has no more say even in this home of his, this place where the flesh is most intensively and happily and seriously flesh. His knowledge of good and evil is no longer of any value. He is no longer judge. Jesus Christ is Judge. (IV/1, 232)

The sentence passed on human beings is salvation:

> The suffering and death of Jesus Christ are the No of God in and with which He again takes up and asserts in man's space and time the Yes to man which He has determined and pronounced in eternity. Because Jesus Christ is the Yes of God spoken in world-history and itself become a part of world-history, there-fore and to that extent God is in Jesus Christ *pro nobis* [for us]. *Cur Deus Homo?* Because God, who became man in His Son, willed in this His Yes to do this work of His, but His human work, and therefore this work for the reconciliation of the world which is effective for us men. (IV/1, 257)

The essential outlines of the substitutionary theory are reaffirmed here in Barth, though he does not argue that the death of Christ appeased the Father's wrath, but that it expresses the Father's mercy, which acts to restore the right order of human existence which has been ruined by our sin. Barth states as clearly as pos-sible that "God does not need reconciliation with men, but men need reconcilia-tion with Him" (IV/1, 74).

The idea that Christ's death was required by the Father to appease him is one that strikes many people today as one that should be left behind, and I for one have no desire to revive it. Perhaps the most forceful recent blow to this idea is found in René Girard's sociological critique of "sacrifice" and divine violence. He has shown that most concepts of the wrath of God or the gods in human his-tory are a product of the existential disorder that generates the scapegoat mecha-nism. The idea that the heavens command the killing of sacrificial victims is a "primitive" idea, in the worst sense of the word, and to move forward into per-sonal and cultural sanity we need to become disciples of the God of truth, mercy, and love whom the Bible reveals in Christ. This Girardian idea is expressed well by Raymund Schwager:

> Redemption is thus necessary for humans to be freed and redeemed from their incapacity to will the good. God needs no reparation, but human beings must be extracted from their own prison if they are to be capable of accepting the pure gift of freely offered love. Paul pleads therefore with the congregation: "Be reconciled to God" (II Cor. 5:20). It is not God who must be appeased, but humans who must be delivered from their hatred. They should no longer offer stubborn resistance but surrender themselves to God's wooing love and let themselves be freed from their resentment.[15]

Girard's thought has raised powerful questions about the doctrine of Atonement, and in a few decades I believe that the preaching and teaching of Christianity will differ greatly from what they have been in centuries past.[16]

The kind of historical survey of concepts of the Atonement which we have just completed can lead us to a relativistic conclusion. Robert Jenson, after producing just such a summary, warns his readers against this temptation:

> Viewing the frustrated history we have just hastened through, much late-modern reflection has made a virtue of apparent necessity and retired to its any-way characteristic relativism. The atonement is said to be a mystery beyond statement; the various proposed doctrines are "pictures" or "metaphors," each of which provides a glimpse of one facet of the mystery. Thus we may rejoice in their multiplicity, and need take none with cognitive seriousness. But what this counsel amounts to is that we cannot say what God *in fact did* at the Crucifixion, and so cannot say that he actually did anything. It is a counsel of despair.[17]

Jenson's way out of this possibility is to question the need to think of the Atonement as a formula of cause and effect. It may be that arguing that the death of Christ had a certain *effect* on the Father or on us derives from a desire to see something going on behind the scenes. But this may signal a lack of attention to what is going on in the scene itself. In other words, the narrative account of the Crucifixion in the Gospels is itself God's atoning word to us. We do not need to weave an elaborate web of explanation around this account. For Jenson, the most im-

---

15. Raymund Schwager, *Must There Be Scapegoats?* trans. Maria L Assad (San Francisco: Harper & Row, 1987), 209.

16. See George Hunsinger's response to Girard, which discusses Hans Urs von Balthasar, T. F. Torrance, and Karl Barth. George Hunsinger, "The Politics of the Nonviolent God: Reflections on René Girard and Karl Barth," *Scottish Journal of Theology* 51 (1998): 61–85.

17. Robert W. Jenson, *Systematic Theology, vol. 1: The Triune God* (New York: Oxford University Press, 1997), 188.

portant thing we can do is to read the Gospel seriously, understanding that it shows us who God is and who we are:

> The Gospels tell a powerful and biblically integrated story of the Crucifix-
> ion; this story *is* just so the story of God's act to bring us back to himself at his
> own cost, and of our being brought back. There is no other story behind or
> beyond it that is the real story of what God does to reconcile us, no story of
> mythic battles or of a deal between God and his Son or of our being moved to
> live reconciled lives. The Gospel's passion narrative is the authentic and entire
> account of God's reconciling action and our reconciliation, as events in his life
> and ours. Therefore what is first and principally required as the Crucifixion's
> right interpretation is for us to tell this story to one another and to God as a
> story about him and about ourselves.[18]

The proper context for this telling is the liturgical life of the Church in the services during the weekend of Good Friday and Easter. The knowledge that the faithful gain from this participation ought to shape how they live their lives in the world during the rest of the year.

I end now with some personal reflections on what I see as the direction in which the doctrine of Atonement can develop. Of course, to do full justice to this topic would require a book in itself, while here I can only offer the sketchiest of comments in the hope of engendering further discussion.

My first point is that a deep and nuanced understanding of the psychology of violence is only now being articulated. This is significant because it means that efforts to present theories of the Atonement in the history of Christian thought have been built on a foundation of ignorance. One cannot clearly and convincingly explain the reconciliation of God and humanity if one does not understand humanity. Put differently, how can one claim to know the deepest mysteries of God's being and work if one doesn't even have a competent understanding of oneself and the society in which one lives? Calvin was entirely correct to stress that the knowledge of God and the knowledge of man are inextricably linked; but he and others were too confident in their assumed mastery of those poles of the dialectic. My effort in this book has been to articulate an understanding of humanity that is actually competent. My reader has every right to conclude that I have failed in this effort, but I believe that the point I am making here still remains. One cannot build a castle on a foundation of sand, which happens when one attempts to articulate the meaning of Atonement without giving due attention to the sinners being reconciled. I am not suggesting that theology needs to begin from below (with humanity) and move upward (to God). I am arguing, on the contrary, that we can only understand humanity by virtue of the divine

18. Ibid., 189.

revelation expressed in the Bible. But the task of interpreting the human condition ought not to be slighted or avoided by being satisfied with pat answers and clichés. We must continually press deeper and deeper into self-knowledge in the light of revelation.

Ironically, belief in a certain doctrine of the Atonement can become a comfortable nest that prevents one from actually hearing God's voice. In other words, the universal human tendency to seek shelter from the demands of spiritual growth can be aided and abetted by a Christian belief system. I agree with Dallas Willard's concern that in many churches Christianity has for the most part become simply a "gospel of sin management."[19] Belief in a particular theory of Atonement has become for many Christians their essential ticket into heaven. "Jesus died for my sins on the Cross. I have accepted him as my savior. That's all that is important." Notice the basic narcissism here. I am only concerned about number one; I am happy that God is my servant and makes everything turn out in my favor. The idea that Christ might have something (i.e., everything) to say about how we live our lives today is discomforting to this mindset. The kingdom of God is understood by some as a state of future bliss rather than as God's continual transforming presence in our sinful world. In other words, the whole tenor of Christ's life and ministry is ignored in favor of a particular interpretation of his death. As an alternative to this, I would like to suggest a vision of Christ as Doctor.

Our self-caused alienation from God and the event of creation produces spiritual deafness in us, analogously to the way various diseases or injuries can render us physically deaf. Christ's mission from the Father is to heal our spiritual deafness. He is, as the prologue of John says, the Word of God to us. But how are we going to hear this Word if we are deaf? Barth describes the difficulty:

> The Word of God whose revelation is attested in Scripture tells man that he is a rebel who has wantonly abandoned the fellowship between himself as creature and God as Creator and set himself in a place where this fellowship is impossible. It tells him that he wanted to be his own lord and therewith betrayed and delivered up himself to the sphere of God's wrath, the state of rejection by God, and therefore of being closed up against God. It tells him that contrary to its destiny by creation his existence is a contradiction against God, a contradiction which excludes listening to God. It thus tells him, strangely, that he cannot hear at all the Word of God which tells him this, and that he cannot hear it because he will not hear it, because his life-act is disobedience and therefore factually, in respect of the use he makes of his life, it is a refusal to listen to what God says to him. (*Church Dogmatics*, I/1, 407–408)

---

19. Dallas Willard, *The Divine Conspiracy: Rediscovering Our Hidden Life in God* (San Francisco: HarperCollins, 1998), 42–50

We can answer Anselm's question, *Cur Deus Homo?* by saying that the Incarnation is God the Father's action in sending the Son on a medical mission for the healing of humanity. This is where the doctrine of Atonement needs to begin: with Bethlehem, not only with Golgotha. Christ's work is to recover the lost, to cast out demons, to cause the lame to walk, to give the blind sight, to heal the broken-hearted, to forgive sinners. Why is it that this ministry provokes so much anger and rejection? Because the human race does not want to be healed. Christ knows this. He wants to give people back the true freedom and dignity that is theirs in being created in the image of God. But their whole strength is devoted precisely to resisting this offer. We, who are created to exist in loving communication with God and with our fellow human beings, prefer to live in separation, rancor, and despair. We, who are created to be part of a family, a community, exist instead in a radical isolation and deprivation, entering into social relations only for the purpose of reinforcing our deafness, alienation, and violence.

In Christ, the one true Doctor we need has come to us, loved us, and forgiven us. The medicine he employs is grace. Life-changing knowledge of his ministry reconciles us with God, takes away our spiritual deafness, and brings us back into our true family, the community of the creatures of God. Christ gives us the ability to hear once again the voice of creation and respond to it in faith. In him we can move forward to become the true human beings our heavenly Father intends us to be.

Christ is not naïve. He knows what he is up against. He is the Doctor who lets his patients kill him, knowing that they want to kill him precisely because they do not want to be healed. He lets them kill him knowing that this will make their healing possible by forcing them to see, in their rejection of that freedom, the freedom that energizes their being. Our true dignity as human beings will only be recovered through restoration of the relationship with our Creator which we have rejected in our fall into egocentric stasis. In praying for us from the Cross, Christ reveals that God is for us even when we are against ourselves. His grace, which always surrounds our evasion, restores us to "Our Father, who art in heaven . . ."

BIBLIOGRAPHY AND
KIERKEGAARD SIGLA

Alford, C. Fred. *What Evil Means to Us*. Ithaca, N.Y.: Cornell University Press, 1997.

Alison, James. *Raising Abel: The Recovery of the Eschatological Imagination*. New York: Crossroad, 1996.

Aquinas, St. Thomas. *On Law, Morality, and Politics*. Ed. William P. Baumgarth and Richard J. Regan. Indianapolis: Hackett, 1988.

Aulén, Gustav. *Christus Victor: An Historical Study of the Three Main Types of the Idea of Atonement*. Trans. A. G. Hebert. New York: Macmillan, 1969.

Bailie, Gil. *Violence Unveiled: Humanity at the Crossroads*. New York: Crossroad, 1995.

Barfield, Owen. *History, Guilt, and Habit*. Middletown: Wesleyan University Press, 1981.

Barth, Karl. *Christ and Adam: Man and Humanity in Romans 5*. Trans. T. A. Smail. New York: Macmillan, 1957.

———. *The Christian Life*. Trans. G. W. Bromiley. Grand Rapids: Eerdmans, 1981.

———. *Church Dogmatics*. Ed. G. W. Bromiley and T. F. Torrance. Edinburgh: T. & T. Clark, 1956–1969.

———. *The Epistle to the Romans*. Trans. Edwyn C. Hoskyns. London: Oxford University Press, 1968.

———. "Kierkegaard and the Theologians." *Canadian Journal of Theology* 13/1 (1967): 64–65.

———. "A Thank You and a Bow: Kierkegaard's Reveille." *Canadian Journal of Theology* 11/1 (1965): 3–7.

Bauman, Zygmunt. *Modernity and the Holocaust*. Ithaca: Cornell University Press, 1989.

Beabout, Gregory R. *Freedom and Its Misuses: Kierkegaard on Anxiety and Despair*. Milwaukee: Marquette University Press, 1996.

Becker, Ernest. *The Denial of Death*. New York: The Free Press, 1973.

———. *Escape from Evil*. New York: The Free Press, 1975.

Bellinger, Charles K. "'The Crowd is Untruth': A Comparison of Kierkegaard and Girard." *Contagion: A Journal of Violence, Mimesis, and Culture* 3 (1996): 103–119.

———. "Kierkegaard's *Either/Or* and the Parable of the Prodigal Son: Or, Three Rival Versions of Three Rival Versions." *International Kierkegaard Commentary: Either/Or*, part II. Ed. Robert L. Perkins. Macon: Mercer University Press, 1995. 59–82.

———. "Toward a Kierkegaardian Understanding of Hitler, Stalin, and the Cold War." *Foundations of Kierkegaard's Vision of Community: Religion, Ethics, and Politics in Kierkegaard*. Ed. George Connell and C. Stephen Evans. Atlantic Highlands: Humanities Press International, 1992. 218–230.

Berdyaev, Nikolai. *The Russian Revolution*. Ann Arbor: University of Michigan Press, 1961.

Berger, Peter L. *The Sacred Canopy: Elements of a Sociological Theory of Religion*. Garden City: Anchor Books, 1969.

Bonhoeffer, Dietrich. *Creation and Fall; Temptation: Two Biblical Studies*. Trans. John C. Fletcher and Kathleen Downham. New York: Macmillan, 1967.

Brunner, Emil. *Man in Revolt: A Christian Anthropology*. Trans. Olive Wyon. Philadelphia: Westminster Press, 1947.

Buber, Martin. *Between Man and Man*. Trans. Ronald Gregor Smith. New York: Macmillan, 1965.

———. *The Way of Man: According to the Teaching of Hasidism*. Secaucus: Citadel Press, 1966.

Caffara, Carlo. *Living in Christ: Fundamental Principles of Catholic Moral Teaching*. Trans. Christopher Ruff. San Francisco: Ignatius Press, 1987.

Calvin, John. *Institutes of the Christian Religion*. Philadelphia: Westminster Press, 1960.

Cauchy, Venant, ed. *Philosophy and Culture*, vol. 5. Montreal: Editions Montmorency, 1988.

Clive, Geoffrey. "The Sickness unto Death in the Underworld: A Study in Nihilism." *Harvard Theological Review* 51 (1958): 135–167.

Connell, George, and C. Stephen Evans, eds. *Foundations of Kierkegaard's Vision of Community: Religion, Ethics, and Politics in Kierkegaard*. Atlantic Highlands: Humanities Press International, 1992.

Conquest, Robert. *The Great Terror: A Reassessment*. New York: Oxford University Press, 1990.

Cotta, Sergio. *Why Violence: A Philosophical Interpretation*. Trans. Giovanni Gullace. Gainesville: University Presses of Florida, 1985.

Davis, Russell H. "Kierkegaard and Community." *Union Seminary Quarterly Review* 36/4 (1981): 205–222.

Deutscher, Isaac. *Stalin: A Political Biography*. 2nd ed. New York: Oxford University Press, 1966.

Dostoyevsky, Fyodor. *The Brothers Karamazov*. Trans. Constance Garnett. New York: Macmillan, 1928.

Dowley, Tim, ed. *Introduction to the History of Christianity*. Minneapolis: Fortress Press, 1995.

Dunning, Stephen N. *Kierkegaard's Dialectic of Inwardness: A Structural Analysis of the Theory of Stages*. Princeton: Princeton University Press, 1985.

Eller, Vernard. *Kierkegaard and Radical Discipleship: A New Perspective*. Princeton: Princeton University Press, 1968.

Ellul, Jacques. *The New Demons*. Trans. C. Edward Hopkin. New York: Seabury Press, 1975.

Elrod, John W. *Kierkegaard and Christendom*. Princeton: Princeton University Press, 1981.

———. "Kierkegaard on Self and Society." *Kierkegaardiana* 11 (1980): 178–196.

Evans, C. Stephen. "Human Persons as Substantial Achievers." *Philosophia Reformata* 58 (1993): 100–112.

———. *Søren Kierkegaard's Christian Psychology*. Grand Rapids: Zondervan, 1990.

Fairweather, Eugene R., ed. *A Scholastic Miscellany: Anselm to Ockham*. Philadelphia: Westminster Press, 1956.

Ferguson, Harvie. *Melancholy and the Critique of Modernity: Søren Kierkegaard's Religious Psychology*. London and New York: Routledge, 1995.

Ferreira, M. Jamie. "Religion's 'Foundation in Reason': The Common Sense of Hume's Natural History." *Canadian Journal of Philosophy* 24 (1994): 565–582.

———. *Transforming Vision: Imagination and Will in Kierkegaardian Faith*. Oxford: Oxford University Press, 1991.

Fjelde, Rolf. "Foreword" to Henrik Ibsen, *Peer Gynt*. Trans. Fjelde. Minneapolis: University of Minnesota Press, 1980.

Frei, Hans. *The Eclipse of Biblical Narrative: A Study in Eighteenth and Nineteenth Century Hermeneutics*. New Haven: Yale University Press, 1974.

Gilligan, James. *Violence: Reflections on a National Epidemic*. New York: Vintage Books, 1996.

Girard, René. *Deceit, Desire, and the Novel: Self and Other in Literary Structure*. Trans. Yvonne Freccero. Baltimore: The Johns Hopkins University Press, 1965.

———. "Dionysus versus the Crucified." *MLN* 99/4 (1984): 816–835.

———. *To Double Business Bound: Essays on Literature, Mimesis, and Anthropology*. Baltimore: Johns Hopkins University Press, 1978.

———. *The Girard Reader*. Ed. James G. Williams. New York: Crossroad, 1996.

———. *Job: The Victim of His People*. Trans. Yvonne Freccero. Stanford: Stanford University Press, 1987.

———. *Quand Ces Choses Commenceront: Entretiens avec Michel Treguer*. Paris: Arléa, 1994.

———. *Resurrection from the Underground: Feodor Dostoevsky*. Trans. James G. Williams. New York: Crossroad, 1997.

———. *The Scapegoat*. Trans. Yvonne Freccero. Baltimore: Johns Hopkins University Press, 1986.

———. "Superman in the Underground: Strategies of Madness—Nietzsche, Wagner, and Dostoevsky." *MLN* 91/6 (1976): 1161–1185.

———. *Things Hidden since the Foundation of the World*. Trans. Stephen Bann and Michael Metteer. Stanford: Stanford University Press, 1987.

———. *Violence and the Sacred*. Trans. Patrick Gregory. Baltimore: Johns Hopkins University Press, 1977.

————. Girand, René, Walter Burkert, and Jonathan Z. Smith. *Violent Origins: Ritual Killing and Cultural Formation*. Ed. Robert G. Hamerton-Kelly. Stanford: Stanford University Press, 1987.

Gouwens, David J. *Kierkegaard as Religious Thinker*. Cambridge: Cambridge University Press, 1996.

Gunton, Colin. *The Actuality of Atonement: A Study of Metaphor, Rationality, and the Christian Tradition*. Grand Rapids: Eerdmans, 1989.

Hamerton-Kelly, Robert G. *The Gospel and the Sacred: Poetics of Violence in Mark*. Minneapolis: Fortress Press, 1994.

————. *Sacred Violence: Paul's Hermeneutic of the Cross*. Minneapolis: Fortress Press, 1992.

Hume, David. *The Natural History of Religion*. Ed. H. E. Root. Stanford: Stanford University Press, 1957.

Hunsinger, George. "The Politics of the Nonviolent God: Reflections on René Girard and Karl Barth." *Scottish Journal of Theology* 51 (1998): 61–85.

Jenson, Robert W. *Systematic Theology Vol. 1: The Triune God*. New York: Oxford University Press, 1997.

Johnson, Howard A., and Niels Thulstrup, eds. *A Kierkegaard Critique*. Chicago: Henry Regnery, 1967.

Jones, L. Gregory. *Transformed Judgment: Toward a Trinitarian Account of the Moral Life*. Notre Dame: University of Notre Dame Press, 1990.

Jung, Carl. *Aion: Researches into the Phenomenology of the Self*. Trans. R. F. C. Hull. The Collected Works of Carl Jung 9, part 2. New York: Pantheon, 1959.

————. *Civilization in Transition*. Trans. R. F. C. Hull. The Collected Works of Carl Jung 10. New York: Pantheon Books, 1964.

Kee, Alistair. *Constantine versus Christ: The Triumph of Ideology*. London: SCM Press, 1982.

Keen, Sam, ed. *Voices and Visions*. New York: Harper & Row, 1974.

Khan, Abrahim H. "Kierkegaard's Conception of Evil." *Journal of Religion and Health* 14/1 (1975): 63–66.

Kierkegaard, Søren. [CA] *The Concept of Anxiety: A Simple Psychologically Orienting Deliberation on the Dogmatic Issue of Hereditary Sin*. Trans. Reidar Thomte in collaboration with Albert B. Anderson. Kierkegaard's writings, vol. 2. Princeton: Princeton University Press, 1980.

————. [CD] *Christian Discourses*. Trans. Howard V. Hong and Edna H. Hong. Kierkegaard's Writings, vol. 17. Princeton: Princeton University Press, 1997.

————. [COR] *The Corsair Affair*. Trans. Howard V. Hong and Edna H. Hong. Kierkegaard's Writings, vol. 13. Princeton: Princeton University Press, 1982.

————. [EUD] *Eighteen Upbuilding Discourses*. Trans. Howard V. Hong and Edna H. Hong. Kierkegaard's Writings, vol. 5. Princeton: Princeton University Press, 1990.

————.[EO] *Either/or.*Trans. Howard V. Hong and Edna H. Hong. Kierkegaard's Writings, vols. 3–4. Princeton: Princeton University Press, 1987.

————. [FSE and JFY] *For Self-Examination* and *Judge for Yourself!* Trans. Howard V. Hong and Edna H. Hong. Kierkegaard's Writings, vol. 21. Princeton: Princeton University Press, 1990.

———. [JP] *Søren Kierkegaard's Journals and Papers*, I-VII. Ed. and trans. Howard V. Hong and Edna H. Hong, assisted by Gregor Malantschuk. Bloomington: Indiana University Press, 1967–1978.

———. [LD] *Letters and Documents*. Trans. Henrik Rosenmeier. Kierkegaard's Writings, vol. 25. 1978; rpt. Princeton: Princeton University Press, 1999.

———. [PV] *The Point of View*. Trans. Howard V. Hong and Edna H. Hong. Kierkegaard's Writings, vol. 22. Princeton: Princeton University Press, 1998.

———. [PC] *Practice in Christianity*. Trans. Howard V. Hong and Edna H. Hong. Kierkegaard's Writings, vol. 20. Princeton: Princeton University Press, 1991.

———. *The Present Age and Two Minor Ethico-Religious Treatises*. Trans. Alexander Dru and Walter Lowrie. London: Oxford University Press, 1940.

———.[SLW] *Stages on Life's Way: Studies by Various Persons*. Trans. Howard V. Hong and Edna H. Hong. Kierkegaard's Writings, vol. 11. Princeton: Princeton University Press, 1998.

———. [SUD] *The Sickness unto Death: A Christian Psychological Exposition for Upbuilding and Awakening*. Trans. Howard V. Hong and Edna H. Hong. Kierkegaard's Writings, vol. 19. Princeton: Princeton University Press, 1983.

———. [TA] *Two Ages: A Literary Review*. Trans. Howard V. Hong and Edna H. Hong. Kierkegaard's Writings, vol. 14. Princeton: Princeton University Press, 1978.

———. [TM] *The Moment and Late Writings*. Trans. Howard V. Hong and Edna H. Hong. Kierkegaard's Writings, vol. 23. Princeton: Princeton University Press, 1998.

———. [UDVS] *Upbuilding Discourses in Various Spirits*. Trans. Howard V. Hong and Edna H. Hong. Kierkegaard's Writings, vol. 15. Princeton: Princeton University Press, 1993.

———. [WA] *Without Authority*. Trans. Howard V. Hong and Edna H. Hong. Kierkegaard's Writings, vol. 18. Princeton: Princeton University Press, 1997.

———. [WL] *Works of Love*. Trans. Howard V. Hong and Edna H. Hong. Kierkegaard's Writings, vol. 16. Princeton: Princeton University Press, 1995.

Kirmmse, Bruce H. *Kierkegaard in Golden Age Denmark*. Bloomington: Indiana University Press, 1990.

Kirmmse, Bruce H., ed. *Encounters with Kierkegaard: A Life as Seen by His Contemporaries*. Princeton: Princeton University Press, 1996.

Künkel, Fritz. *Creation Continues: A Psychological Interpretation of the First Gospel*. New York: Charles Scribner's Sons, 1947.

———. *How Character Develops*. New York: Charles Scribner's Sons, 1940.

———. *In Search of Maturity: An Inquiry into Psychology, Religion, and Self-Education*. New York: Charles Scribner's Sons, 1948.

Lenin, Vladimir I. *The Lenin Anthology*. Ed. Robert C. Tucker. New York: W. W. Norton, 1975.

Levenson, Jon D. *Creation and the Persistence of Evil: The Jewish Drama of Divine Omnipotence*. Princeton: Princeton University Press, 1988.

Lindbeck, George. "Atonement and the Hermeneutics of Social Embodiment." *Pro Ecclesia* 5 (1996): 144–160.

Lindström, Valter. "The First Article of the Creed in Kierkegaard's Writings." *Kierke-gaardiana* 12 (1982): 38–50.

Livingston, Paisley. *Models of Desire: René Girard and the Psychology of Mimesis*. Baltimore: Johns Hopkins University Press, 1992.

Luther, Martin. *Sermons on the Gospel of St. John, Chapters 1–4*. Ed. Jaroslav Pelikan. Luther's Works XXII. St. Louis: Concordia, 1957.

MacIntyre, Alasdair. *After Virtue*. Notre Dame: University of Notre Dame Press, 1984.

Mackey, Louis. *Kierkegaard: A Kind of Poet*. Philadelphia: University of Pennsylvania Press, 1971.

Maidenbaum, Aryeh, and Stephen A. Martin, eds. *Lingering Shadows: Jungians, Freudians, and Anti-Semitism*. Boston and London: Shambala, 1991.

Malantschuk, Gregor. *The Controversial Kierkegaard*. Trans. Howard V. Hong and Edna H. Hong. Waterloo: Wilfrid Laurier University Press, 1980.

———. "Kierkegaard and the Totalitarians." *American-Scandanavian Review* 34/3 (1946): 246–248.

———. *Kierkegaard's Thought*. Trans. Howard V. Hong and Edna H. Hong. Princeton: Princeton University Press, 1971.

———. *Kierkegaard's Way to the Truth*. Trans. Mary Michelsen. Minneapolis: Augsburg, 1963.

Marsden, George M. *The Outrageous Idea of Christian Scholarship*. New York: Oxford University Press, 1997.

Marx, Karl. *The Marx-Engels Reader*. 2nd ed. Ed. Robert C. Tucker. New York: W. W. Norton, 1978.

McCarthy, Vincent A. "'Psychological Fragments': Kierkegaard's Religious Psychology." *Kierkegaard's Truth: The Disclosure of the Self*. Ed. Joseph H. Smith. Psychiatry and the Humanities 5. New Haven: Yale University Press, 1981. 235–265.

McCracken, David. "Scandal and Imitation in Matthew, Kierkegaard, and Girard." *Contagion* 4 (1997): 146–162.

———. *The Scandal of the Gospels: Jesus, Story, and Offense*. New York: Oxford University Press, 1994.

McManners, John, ed. *The Oxford Illustrated History of Christianity*. Oxford: Oxford University Press, 1990.

Merton, Thomas. "Introduction" to Mahatma Gandhi, *Gandhi on Non-Violence*. Ed. Merton. New York: New Directions, 1965.

Milbank, John. *Theology and Social Theory: Beyond Secular Reason*. Cambridge: Basil Blackwell, 1991.

———. *The Word Made Strange: Theology, Language, Culture*. Cambridge: Blackwell, 1997.

Miller, Alice. *For Your Own Good: Hidden Cruelty in Child-Rearing and the Roots of Violence*. Trans. Hildegarde Hannum and Hunter Hannum. New York: Farrar, Straus, Giroux, 1984.

Miller, Libuse Lukas. *In Search of the Self: The Individual in the Thought of Kierkegaard*. Philadelphia: Muhlenberg Press, 1962.

Moore, Sebastian. *The Crucified Jesus Is No Stranger*. Minneapolis: Seabury Press, 1977.

Moore, Stanley R. "Religion as the True Humanism: Reflections on Kierkegaard's Social Philosophy." *Journal of the American Academy of Religion* 37 (1969): 15–25.

Mosse, George L., ed. *Nazi Culture: Intellectual, Cultural, and Social Life in the Third Reich*. New York: Grosset & Dunlap, 1966.

Murphy, Nancey, and George F. R. Ellis. *On the Moral Nature of the Universe: Theology, Cosmology, and Ethics*. Minneapolis: Fortress Press, 1996.

Neumann, Erich. *Depth Psychology and a New Ethic*. Trans. Eugene Rolfe. New York: Harper & Row, 1973.

Nicolaevsky, Boris. *Power and the Soviet Elite*. Ed. Janet D. Zagoria. Ann Arbor: University of Michigan Press, 1975.

Niebuhr, Reinhold. *The Nature and Destiny of Man*. Vol. 1. New York: Charles Scribner's Sons, 1941.

Nietzsche, Friedrich. *On the Genealogy of Morals* and *Ecce Homo*. Trans. Walter Kaufmann and R. J. Hollingdale. New York: Vintage Books, 1989.

———. *Thus Spake Zarathustra*. Trans. Walter Kaufmann. New York: Viking, 1966.

Nordentoft, Kresten. *Kierkegaard's Psychology*. Trans. Bruce H. Kirmmse. Pittsburgh: Duquesne University Press, 1978.

Palaver, Wolfgang. "Hobbes and the *Katéchon*: The Secularization of Sacrificial Christianity." *Contagion* 2 (1995): 57–74.

Pattison, George. *Kierkegaard: The Aesthetic and the Religious*. London: Macmillan, 1992.

Peck, M. Scott. *People of the Lie: The Hope for Healing Human Evil*. New York: Simon & Schuster, 1983.

———. *The Road Less Traveled: A New Psychology of Love, Traditional Values, and Spiritual Growth*. New York: Simon & Schuster, 1978.

Perkins, Frances. *The Roosevelt I Knew*. New York: Viking, 1946.

Perkins, Robert L., ed. *The Concept of Anxiety*. International Kierkegaard Commentary 8. Macon: Mercer University Press, 1985.

———. *The Corsair Affair*. International Kierkegaard Commentary 13. Macon: Mercer University Press, 1990.

———. *Either/Or*. International Kierkegaard Commentary 3, 4. Macon: Mercer University Press, 1995.

———. *The Sickness unto Death*. International Kierkegaard Commentary 19. Macon: Mercer University Press, 1987.

———. *Two Ages*. International Kierkegaard Commentary 14. Macon: Mercer University Press, 1984.

Peters, Ted. *God—The World's Future: Systematic Theology for a Postmodern Era*. Minneapolis: Fortress Press, 1992.

———. *Sin: Radical Evil in Soul and Society*. Grand Rapids: Eerdmans, 1994.

Picard, Max. *The Flight from God*. Trans. Marianne Kuschnitzky and J. M. Cameron. Washington: Regnery Gateway, 1989.

———. *Hitler in Our Selves*. Trans. Heinrich Hauser. Hinsdale: Henry Regnery, 1947.

Plekon, Michael. "'Anthropological Contemplation': Kierkegaard and Modern Social Theory." *Thought* 55 (1980): 346–369.

——. "'Introducing Christianity into Christendom': Reinterpreting the Late Kierkegaard." *Anglican Theological Review* 64/3 (1982): 327–352.

——. "Kierkegaard the Theologian: The Roots of His Theology in *Works of Love*." *Foundations of Kierkegaard's Vision of Community: Religion, Ethics, and Politics in Kierkegaard.* Ed. George Connell and C. Stephen Evans. Atlantic Highlands: Humanities Press International, 1992. 2–17.

——. "Moral Accounting: Kierkegaard's Social Theory and Criticism." *Kierkegaardiana* 12 (1982): 69–80.

——. "'Other Kierkegaards': New Views and Reinterpretations in Scholarship." *Thought* 55 (1980): 370–375.

——. "Prophetic Criticism, Incarnational Optimism: On Recovering the Late Kierkegaard." *Religion* 13 (1983): 137–153.

——. "Protest and Affirmation: The Late Kierkegaard on Christ, the Church, and Society." *Quarterly Review* 2/3 (1982): 43–62.

Porter, J. M., ed. *Luther: Selected Political Writings.* Philadelphia: Fortress Press, 1974.

Roberts, Robert C. *Taking the Word to Heart: Self and Other in an Age of Therapies.* Grand Rapids: Eerdmans, 1993.

Rose, Eugene. *Nihilism: The Root of the Revolution of the Modern Age.* Forestville: Fr. Seraphim Rose Foundation, 1994.

Rosenbaum, Ron. "Explaining Hitler." *The New Yorker*, May 1, 1995, 50–70.

——. *Explaining Hitler: The Search for the Origins of His Evil.* New York: Random House, 1998.

Sartre, Jean-Paul. *Anti-Semite and Jew.* Trans. George J. Becker. New York: Schocken, 1948.

Sayers, Dorothy L. *The Mind of the Maker.* San Francisco: Harper & Row, 1987.

Schmemann, Alexander. *For the Life of the World.* Crestwood: St. Vladimir's Seminary Press, 1973.

Schwager, Raymund. *Must There Be Scapegoats? Violence and Redemption in the Bible.* Trans. Maria L. Assad. San Francisco: Harper & Row, 1987.

Sobosan, Jeffrey G. "Kierkegaard and Jung on the Self." *Journal of Psychology and Theology* 3 (1975): 31–35.

Staub, Ervin. *The Roots of Evil: The Origins of Genocide and Other Group Violence.* Cambridge: Cambridge University Press, 1989.

Steiner, George. *In Bluebeard's Castle: Some Notes towards the Redefinition of Culture.* New Haven: Yale University Press, 1971.

Suchocki, Marjorie Hewitt. *The Fall to Violence: Original Sin in Relational Theology.* New York: Continuum, 1994.

Thiele, Leslie Paul. *Friedrich Nietzsche and the Politics of the Soul: A Study of Heroic Individualism.* Princeton: Princeton University Press, 1990.

Thompson, Josiah, ed. *Kierkegaard: A Collection of Critical Essays.* Garden City: Anchor Books, 1972.

Tinder, Glenn. "Can We Be Good Without God?" *Atlantic Monthly*, Dec. 1989, 69–85.

——. *The Political Meaning of Christianity: An Interpretation.* Baton Rouge: Louisiana State University Press, 1989.

Tolstoy, Leo. *The Law of Love and the Law of Violence.* Trans. Mary Koutouzow Tolstoy. New York: Holt, Rinehart and Winston, 1970.

Tucker, Robert C. "Foreword" to *Stalin's Letters to Molotov 1925–1936*. Ed. Lars Lih, Oleg V. Naumov, and Oleg V. Khlevniuk. New Haven: Yale University Press, 1995.

Veith, Gene Edward. *Modern Fascism: Liquidating the Judeo-Christian Worldview*. St. Louis: Concordia, 1993.

Viallaneix, Nelly. *Ecoute, Kierkegaard: Essai sur la Communication de la Parole*. Paris: Cerf, 1979.

Voegelin, Eric. *Autobiographical Reflections*. Ed. Ellis Sandoz. Baton Rouge: Louisiana State University Press, 1989.

———. "The Eclipse of Reality." In *Phenomenology and Social Reality*. Ed. Maurice Natanson. The Hague: Martinus Nijhoff, 1970. 185–194.

———. *The Ecumenic Age*. Order and History 4. Baton Rouge: Louisiana State University Press, 1974.

———. *The New Science of Politics*. Chicago: University of Chicago Press, 1952.

———. *Political Religions*. Trans. T. J. DiNapoli and E. S. Easterly. Lewiston: Edwin Mellen Press, 1986.

———. *Published Essays 1966–1985*. Ed. Ellis Sandoz. The Collected Works of Eric Voegelin 12. Baton Rouge: Louisiana State University Press, 1990.

———. *Science, Politics, and Gnosticism*. Washington: Regnery Gateway, 1968.

Walsh, David. *The Growth of the Liberal Soul*. Columbia: University of Missouri Press, 1997.

Ward, Keith. *Religion and Creation*. Oxford: Oxford University Press, 1996.

Webb, Eugene. "Mimesis, Evolution, and Differentiation of Consciousness." *Paragrana* 4 (1995): 151–165.

———. *Philosophers of Consciousness: Polanyi, Lonergan, Voegelin, Ricoeur, Girard, Kierkegaard*. Seattle: University of Washington Press, 1988.

———. *The Self Between: From Freud to the New Social Psychology of France*. Seattle: University of Washington Press, 1993.

Westermann, Claus. *Creation*. Trans. John J. Scullion. Philadelphia: Fortress Press, 1974.

Westphal, Merold. *Kierkegaard's Critique of Reason and Society*. Macon: Mercer University Press, 1987.

Wilken, Robert L. *Remembering the Christian Past*. Grand Rapids: Eerdmans, 1995.

Willard, Dallas. *The Divine Conspiracy: Rediscovering Our Hidden Life in God*. San Francisco: HarperCollins, 1998.

Williams, George Hunston, ed. *Spiritual and Anabaptist Writers*. Philadelphia: Westminster Press, 1957.

Williams, James G. *The Bible, Violence, and the Sacred: Liberation from the Myth of Sanctioned Violence*. San Francisco: HarperCollins, 1991.

Windass, Stanley. *Christianity versus Violence: A Social and Historical Study of War and Christianity*. London: Sheed and Ward, 1964.

Winter, Michael. *The Atonement*. Collegeville, Minn.: Liturgical Press, 1995.

Yoder, John Howard. *The Original Revolution: Essays on Christian Pacifism*. Scottdale: Herald Press, 1971.

———. *The Politics of Jesus: Vicit Agnus Noster*. Grand Rapids: Eerdmans, 1972.

———. "*The Scapegoat* by René Girard." *Religion and Literature* 19.3 (1987): 89–92.

INDEX